British

British Civilization provides a comprehensive introduction to a wide range of aspects of contemporary Britain, including its country and people, politics and government, education, the economy, the media, arts and religion. The fifth edition of this highly praised textbook has been comprehensively updated and revised. It includes:

- a concise chronology of the most significant events in British history
- fully revised illustrations to portray contemporary British life.
- exercises and questions to stimulate classroom discussion
- updated coverage of British politics to include the 2001 general election and Blair's second term
- new material on devolution and on Wales, Scotland and Ireland more generally
- insights into the attitudes of British people today towards important issues
- updated guide to further reading, including key web site addresses to assist research

John Oakland is Senior Lecturer in English at the Norwegian University of Science and Technology. He is author of *Contemporary Britain: A Survey with Texts* (Routledge, 2001), *A Dictionary of British Institutions* (Routledge, 1993) and, with David Mauk, of *American Civilization* (3rd edition, Routledge, 2002).

British Civilization

An introduction

FIFTH EDITION

■ John Oakland

Routledge
Taylor & Francis Group

LONDON AND NEW YORK

First published in 1989

Second edition 1991
Third edition 1995
Fourth edition 1998

Fifth edition published in 2002
by Routledge
2 Park Square, Milton Park, Abingdon, Oxon, OX14 4RN

Simultaneously published in the USA and Canada
by Routledge
270 Madison Ave, New York, NY 100016

Reprinted 2004

Routledge is an imprint of the Taylor & Francis Group

© 1989, 1991, 1995, 1998, 2002 John Oakland

Typeset in Sabon and Futura
by Florence Production Ltd.
Printed and bound in Great Britain
by TJ International Ltd, Padstow, Cornwall

British Library Cataloguing in Publication Data
A catalogue record for this book is available from the British Library

Library of Congress Cataloging in Publication Data
has been applied for

ISBN 0–415–26149–X (hbk)
ISBN 0–415–26150–3 (pbk)

Contents

Plates

Figures

Tables

Preface and acknowledgements

This book examines some central features of British society and places them within a historical context. Current debates, developments and attitudes on many issues are also evaluated.

The book is necessarily indebted to many sources for its facts, ideas and statistics, to which acknowledgement is gratefully made (see Further reading). Particular thanks are due to *Britain: An Official Handbook* (annual) and the *Annual Abstract of Statistics* (both published by the Sationery Office, London); *British Social Attitudes*; and *Market and Opinion Research International* (MORI).

The websites included in this book are mainly those of public institutions. Although these may present official and standard views, they are often more permanent, up-to-date and informative than many independent websites, which can quickly change their addresses and content or simply disappear.

The term 'billion' in this book means 'thousand million'.

Chronology of significant dates in British history

Early history

Prehistory	British-Irish islands once part of European land mass: warmer conditions alternated with Ice Ages
500,000 BC	earliest human bones found in southern England
250,000 BC	nomadic Old Stone Age (Palaeolithic) peoples
50,000 BC	warmer climate encouraged the arrival of distant ancestors of the modern populations
10,000 BC	end of Ice Ages. Population consisted of hunter-gatherers and fishers
5000 BC	contemporary islands gradually separated from continental Europe
3000 BC	New Stone Age (Neolithic) peoples populated the western parts of the islands. Farming introduced
2400 BC	Beaker Folk (Bronze Age) settled in southeast and eastern England
ca 600 BC	settlement of the Celts (Iron Age) began
55–54 BC	Julius Caesar's exploratory expeditions
AD 43	Roman conquest of England, Wales and (temporarily) lowland Scotland by Claudius. Christian influences
200–400	the Scots from Ireland colonized western Scotland
122–38	Hadrian's Wall built between Scotland and England
409	Roman army withdrew from Britain
410	Germanic (Anglo-Saxon) invasions began; Anglo-Saxon kingdoms created from the 450s in England. Mainly Celtic peoples in Wales, Ireland, parts of Scotland and Cornwall
430	Existing Christianity in Ireland later spread by St Patrick and others in Ireland and Scotland
597	St Augustine converted Anglo-Saxons to Christianity

664	Synod of Whitby chose Roman Catholic church model
789–95	Scandinavian (Viking) raids began
820	the Anglo-Saxon kingdoms dominated by Wessex
832–60	union of the Celts (Scots and Picts) in Scotland to form most of the eventual kingdom of Scotland
878	Vikings defeated in England by King Alfred of Wessex
954	the Kingdom of England formed
1014	Vikings defeated in Ireland

The early Middle Ages

1066	William the Conqueror defeated King Harold at Hastings and ascended the English throne. Feudalism introduced
1086	*Domesday Book* (tax records) compiled in England
1169	Henry II invaded the east coast of Ireland
1215	King John signed Magna Carta, which protected English feudal (aristocratic) rights against royal abuse
c. 1220	first Oxford and Cambridge colleges created
1258 and 1264	first English parliamentary structures
1275	the Model Parliament (first regular English Parliament)
1282	much of Wales controlled by England under Edward I
1296	the Scots defeated by Edward I
1297	first Irish Parliament
1314	battle of Bannockburn regained Scottish independence
1326	first Scottish Parliament

The late Middle Ages

1337	Hundred Years War between England and France began
1348–49	Black Death (bubonic plague) destroyed a third of the islands' population
1362	English replaced French as the official language
1381	Peasants' Revolt in England
ca 1387– ca 1394	Geoffrey Chaucer wrote *The Canterbury Tales*
1400–10	Failed Welsh revolt by Owain Glyndwr against English
1407	the House of Commons became responsible for taxation
1411	the first university in Scotland founded (St Andrews)
1415	the Battle of Agincourt; England defeated France
1455–87	Wars of the Roses between Yorkists and Lancastrians
1477	first book printed in England, by William Caxton

Towards the nation state (Britain)

1509	accession of Henry VIII
1534–40	English Reformation; Henry VIII broke with Papacy and became Head of the English Church (Roman Catholic)
1536–42	Acts of Union integrated England and Wales
1547–53	Protestantism became official religion in England under Edward VI
1553–58	Catholic reaction under Mary I
1558–1603	Elizabeth I. Protestant ascendancy
1558	Calais, England's last possession in France, lost
1560	creation of Protestant Church of Scotland by John Knox
1584	first English colony (Virginia) in North America
1587	Mary Stuart, Queen of Scots, executed in London
1588	defeat of Spanish Armada
ca 1590– ca 1613	plays of William Shakespeare written
1600	East India (trading) Company founded
1603	union of the two crowns under James VI of Scotland (James I of England)
1607	Plantation of Ulster with Scottish and English settlers
1611	the Authorized (King James) Version of the Bible issued
1642–48	Civil Wars between King and Parliament
1649	execution of Charles I, monarchy abolished
1653–58	Oliver Cromwell ruled as Lord Protector
1660	monarchy restored under Charles II
1665	the Great Plague in England
1666	the Great Fire of London
1679	Habeus Corpus Act passed. Party political system grew
1688	The Glorious Revolution: accession of William III and Mary II to the throne
1689	the Declaration of Rights
1690	Irish defeated by William III at the Battle of the Boyne

The eighteenth century

1707	Acts of Union joined England/Wales and Scotland (Great Britain)
1715	Scottish Jacobite rebellions crushed
1721	Walpole became Britain's first prime minister
1739	War with Spain
1742	War with France
1745	Failed Scottish rebellion under Bonnie Prince Charlie
1760s–1830s	Industrial Revolutions

1761	opening of the Bridgewater Canal began the Canal Age
1769	the steam engine and the spinning machine invented
1775–83	American War for Independence; loss of 13 Colonies
1793–1815	Revolutionary and Napoleonic Wars

The nineteenth century

1801	Act of Union joined Great Britain and Ireland (United Kingdom)
1805	Battle of Trafalgar. Nelson defeated the French navy
1807	abolition of the slave trade in the British Empire
1815	Napoleon defeated by Wellington at Waterloo
1825	opening of the Stockton and Darlington Railway, the world's first passenger railway
1829	Catholic emancipation (freedom of religious worship)
1832	First Reform Act extended the male franchise (vote)
1838	the People's Charter and the beginning of trade unions
1839	The Durham Report on dominion status for some colonies
1845	disastrous harvest failure in Ireland
1851	first trade unions appeared
1853–56	The Crimean War
1868	Trades Union Congress (TUC) established
1870	elementary state school education introduced
1871	legal recognition of trade unions
1899	The Boer War (South Africa)

The twentieth century

1901	death of Queen Victoria (born 1837)
1911	political power of the House of Lords restricted
1914–18	First World War
1916	Easter Rising against Britain in Dublin
1918	all men over twenty-one receive the vote
1921–22	Irish Free State established; Northern Ireland remained part of the United Kingdom
1924	the first Labour government
1926	the General Strike
1928	votes for all women over twenty-one
1931	the Commonwealth officially formed
1939–45	Second World War (W. Churchill, Prime Minister 1940)
1944	the Butler Education Act: compulsory secondary school education
1945	United Nations formed
1947	Independence for India and Pakistan

1948	National Health Service created
1949	Irish Free State became Republic of Eire. NATO created
1952	accession of Elizabeth II
1956	the Suez Canal Crisis
1965	death penalty abolished
1965–69	oil and gas discoveries in the North Sea
1968	protest and violence erupted in Northern Ireland
1972	direct rule from Westminster in Northern Ireland
1973	Britain entered European Economic Community (now EU)
1975	referendum on Britain's continued membership of EEC
1979	Margaret Thatcher: Britain's first woman Prime Minister
1982	the Falklands War with Argentina
1994	the Channel Tunnel between France and Britain opened
1997	referendums on devolution for Scotland and Wales
1999–2000	devolution structures in Scotland (a Parliament) and Wales and Northern Ireland (Assemblies)

Introduction

THE FOLLOWING CHAPTERS EXAMINE Britain's physical geography, the British people and the historical evolution of structural features in the society. The latter currently take many different forms and sizes; operate on both national and local levels; embrace a range of attitudes and values; and help to promote and condition cultural identities.

The major formal features, such as Parliament, monarchy, law and government, are concerned with state or public business and initiate policies in top-down and hierarchical form. But there are many other structures on both public and private levels of social activity, such as sports, families, leisure activities, neighbourhoods, popular culture and habitual ways of life which have their own value-systems. They frequently have a bottom-up form and may illustrate more localized, informal and individualistic characteristics.

The 'British way of life' and British identities are partly determined by how people function within and react to national and local structures, whether positively or negatively. These are not remote abstractions but directly influence individuals in their daily lives. For example, government policies affect citizens and families; commercial organizations influence choices in music, clothes and fashion; the media try to shape news values and agendas; sponsorship and advertising may determine sports activities; and local government partly conditions community life. These features cover a range of practices on both high and popular cultural levels. Their number and variety mean that there are many different 'ways of life' in Britain and all contribute to the diversity and pluralistic identities of contemporary society.

Social structures must adapt to new situations if they are to survive and their present roles may be very different from their original functions.

In earlier centuries, England, Scotland, Wales and Ireland experienced very varied events and conflicts in their historical growth. But, since 1707 when England and Wales were united with Scotland as Great Britain and since 1801 when the United Kingdom (England, Scotland, Wales and Ireland) was formed, British state structures and a resulting social life have generally evolved slowly, unevenly and pragmatically, rather than by violent change.

These characteristics have often been attributed to the allegedly insular and conservative mentalities of island peoples, with their supposed preference for traditional habits and institutions. Some influences have come from abroad. But the absence of any successful external military invasion of the islands since the Norman Conquest of AD 1066 has allowed England, Scotland, Wales and Ireland to develop internally in distinctive ways, despite wars and disputes between them. The resulting social principles, such as parliamentary democracy and religion, have often been imitated by other countries, or exported overseas through the creation of an empire and a commercial need to establish world markets for British goods.

The development of the British state and its empire historically was aided by increasing military and economic strength so that by the nineteenth century Britain had become a dominant world power. But the country has experienced substantial changes since the earlier imperial period and from the mid-twentieth century. Today it is a complex society in which diversity has created problems as well as advantages.

Britain today may give an impression of homogeneous or uniform behaviour. But there are differences in the society, such as the cultural distinctiveness and separate identities of Wales, Scotland and Northern Ireland (leading to the devolution of some political power in 1999–2000); subsequent demands for local autonomy in some English regions (such as the north-east); disparities between affluent and economically depressed areas throughout the country (including the decay and social deprivation of many inner-city locations); alleged cultural gaps between North and South; political variety (reflected in support for different political parties in different parts of Britain); debates on the positions of women, minority groups and ethnic communities (with tensions between national identity and ethnicity); campaigns for individual and collective rights (with the conflict between rights and responsibilities); a gulf between rich and poor (with a growing underclass of disadvantaged, alienated people); and generational differences between young and old.

Such features illustrate the present divisions in British society. They suggest a decline in the traditional deference to authority, consensus views and national institutions. The people are now more Nonconformist, multi-ethnic and individualistic than in the past. Opinion polls suggest that the

British feel that they have become more aggressive, more selfish, less tolerant, less kind, less moral, less honest and less polite. Their society is sometimes portrayed as one riddled with mistrust, coarseness and cynicism in which materialism, relativistic values, celebrity worship and a sensationalist tabloid media constitute the new standards.

Arguably, such developments have led to an increase in anti-social behaviour, yobbishness, public scruffiness, serious alchohol and drug abuse, disputes between neighbours, street crime and public disorder. The tolerant civic image of individual liberty and sense of community, which foreigners and the British often have of the country, has suffered. Critics and politicians want a return to social responsibility, consensus or inclusive politics and a caring society in which individuals feel that they have a place.

Many Britons are worried about the quality and services of their society. An opinion poll prior to the 2001 general election found which issues were important for them in deciding which party to vote for (Table 0.1). Such issues are of concern to and affect British people on a personal level in their daily lives.

Pressures are consequently placed on social structures and politicians to reflect and respond more adequately to current worries. The performances of British national and local institutions are vigorously debated and many are found wanting. Questions are asked as to whether the existing structures can cope with the needs and demands of contemporary life, and whether (and how) they might be reformed in order to operate more efficiently and responsively. Such questioning is also linked to debates about how the country should be organized socially, politically and economically.

This domestic situation has been influenced by external pressures. Since the Second World War (1939–45), Britain has had to adjust with difficulty to the results of a withdrawal from empire; a reduction in world status; global economic recessions; increased foreign competition; and changes in the geo-political world order. Britain has been forced into a reluctant search for a new identity and direction. While maintaining many of its traditional worldwide commercial and cultural links, it has moved from empire and the Commonwealth towards an economic and political commitment to Europe, mainly through membership of the European Union (EU).

In recent centuries, Britain rarely saw itself as part of mainland Europe. It sheltered behind the barrier of the English Channel and its outlook was westwards and worldwide. Today the psychological and physical isolation from Europe is changing, as illustrated by increased co-operation between Britain and other European countries and by the opening (1994) of a Channel rail tunnel between England and France. But the relationship between Britain and Europe continues to be problematic,

TABLE 0.1 Top issues facing British society, 2001

	Per cent
Health care	73
Education	62
Law and order	50
Pensions	40
Taxation	37
Public transport	31
Managing the economy	31
Unemployment	30
Asylum seekers/immigration	27
Europe	26
Protecting the natural environment	26
Housing	21
Animal welfare	11
Defence	11
The constitution and devolution	8
Northern Ireland	7
Trade unions	6

Source: *MORI* June 2001

and new associations have been forced by events and circumstances, rather than wholeheartedly sought.

Despite such developments and more internal social diversity, there is still a conservatism in British life which regards change with suspicion. The 'forces of conservatism' (in Tony Blair's words) may lead to tension between the often enforced need for reform and a nostalgia for an assumed ideal past. They can cause difficulties for progress and the evolution of social structures. Historical fact demonstrates that the past in Britain was not as idyllic as is sometimes imagined. But the myth and traditional patterns of behaviour still hold considerable attraction for many people.

Fundamental change does not come easily to old cultures such as Britain, and social structures (or the human beings who operate them) are often resistant to major alteration. It is argued that Britain since the 1950s has been unwilling to face large-scale reassessment in its social, political, economic and institutional structures. A relative economic decline since the late nineteenth century was joined to a political system and national mentality which could not cope with the reality or needs of the post-industrial and culturally diverse society that Britain had become. Much of this decline was supposedly due to long-term and global events which were not reversible. But it is argued that the country still suffers from structural defects, which need radical rethinking. Pragmatic evolution and a complacent attachment to past habits are, in this view, no longer sufficient.

Britain does have its problems. There is continuing social instability, such as the tension between tradition and modernization; a gap between rich and poor; industrial and technological change; inadequacies in social institutions (such as education and health); alleged lack of governmental competence and vision; social fragmentation; and an apparent decline in cohesion and identity.

But, despite the often lurid picture of social decay painted by some commentators, the essential fabric of British society is not falling apart. Biased ideological views and a British capacity for self-denigration and complaint can encourage unbalanced, sensational views, and events may be exaggerated beyond their national importance or representative value. Most British people now enjoy greater prosperity and opportunities, although the economy suffered a globally influenced downturn in some sectors from 2001. But continuing structural and social problems warn against undue complacency.

Assumptions about British life have in fact been strongly questioned in recent decades. Conservative governments under Margaret Thatcher (1979–90) tried to reform social structures and promote new attitudes. They attempted to reduce the state's role in public affairs and replace it by 'market forces'. The focus was upon economic growth; competition; privatization (state concerns transferred to the private sector); the creation of choice and standards in public services such as education and health; and the reform of bodies such as the trade unions, some professions and local government. People were encouraged to be more responsible for their own affairs without reliance on the state for support (the 'dependency culture') and to adopt more individual competitiveness and efficiency (the 'enterprise culture').

Such policies were partially successful on the economic level, but there was resistance to the alleged accompanying selfishness and social divisiveness. While some people applauded the freedoms of an enterprise culture, others strongly wished for more intervention and funding in public social services. This suggests that it is difficult to change Britons' attitudes and that many people still look to the state for support in areas such as health, education and Social Security. Nevertheless, market programmes continued under the Conservative Prime Minister John Major (1990–97).

Meanwhile, the Labour Party modernized its policies and moved to the political centre. Since gaining power in 1997, the Labour government under Tony Blair has not deviated from the Conservative economic approach, while pursuing cautious policies. It has also attempted (not without opposition) to modernize Britain by creating a 'new, young and inclusive' society. It is addressing social and economic realities, emphasizes personal initiative and responsibility and stresses that hard choices must be made. But the government will have to deliver on its 2001 election promises to improve public services. It has spent large amounts of money on education, health and transport in order to prevent their collapse, raising fears of personal income tax rises.

Opposition to some government programmes (such as the local government property tax under Thatcher or fuel prices and rural policy under Blair) and acceptance of others demonstrate that social change can occur in various, often interconnected, ways. Some social structures wither away because they are no longer used. Others are reformed internally as new situations arise. Additional forces for change are opposition political parties with their alternative programmes; interest or pressure groups exerting influence upon decision-makers; grassroots movements protesting at some action or lack of action; campaigns by the media to promote reform or uncover scandals; and the weight of public opinion for or against official plans. However, government initiatives are the single most important factor in determining structural change as politicians implement policies or respond to events.

The British allow their governments a great deal of power in the running of the country. But there is a limit to their tolerance and their disquiet may be shown in public opinion polls, demonstrations and general election results. Most politicians are sensitive to the views of the people, since their hold upon political power is dependent upon the electorate. Governments usually govern with at least one eye on public opinion and generally attempt to gain acceptance for their policies. They have to move cautiously (even with big majorities in the House of Commons like the Labour government) and may suffer setbacks in some of their programmes.

The British assume, rightly or wrongly, that they have an individual independence and liberty within the framework of social institutions and are quick to voice disapproval if their interests are threatened. Protest is a natural and traditional reaction, as well as being a safety valve against more serious social and political disruption. But dissension may be neutralized by the promise of reform, or ignored by government. Adequate responses may not come from the authorities and there is always the danger of more serious conflict and public alienation. However, peaceful evolution characterizes most of British life and gradualist changes reflect the diverse nature of the society and its attitudes.

But the British are healthily cynical, irreverent, critical and increasingly apathetic about their state institutions and political leaders. *British Social Attitudes: 1988–9* (pp. 121–2) suggested that 'The [British] public's trust in the pillars of the British establishment is at best highly qualified ... [They] seem intuitively to have discovered that the surest protection against disillusionment with their public figures and powerful institutions is to avoid developing illusions about them in the first place.'

The British today are confronting cultural and economic realities different from those of the past. They do not enjoy the benefits of earlier industrial revolutions, such as cheap raw materials, cheap labour and an uncompetitive world market. The society has seen a decline in traditional certainties and become more diverse, mobile, stressful, conflict-ridden and individualistic. Old pragmatic methods of innovation, which illustrate the British tendency to muddle through difficulties without long-term planning or fundamental reform, are no longer sufficient for an era in which special-ized education and training, high-technology competence and a need to respond to international competition are the main determinants.

But a *British Council/MORI* poll in November 1999 showed that many overseas countries see Britain as tradition-ridden, backward-looking and conventional, with images of monarchy, kilts, castles and aristocracy predominating. It is argued that Britain must change this image and reduce the gap between such foreign perceptions and the country's contemporary reality, while preserving its traditional strengths.

On the other hand, a survey by *Encyclopaedia Britannica* in November 2001 found that most recent school-leavers in Britain were igno-rant of some of the key events in British history and a quarter had no interest in bygone days. Historical knowledge was also sorely lacking among adults.

Exercises

Explain and examine the following terms:

insular	grassroots	pragmatic	sponsorship
deference	conservatism	inner-city	diversity
consensus	kilts	pluralism	ethnic
nostalgia	autonomy	post-industrial	modernization
myth	dependency	nonconformist	evolution
enterprise	Thatcher	yobbishness	community
hierarchies	homogeneous	inclusive	apathetic

Write short essays on the following topics:

1   Examine the view that Britain is a quaint, old-fashioned museum piece, backward-looking and conventional.
2   What are some of the characteristics that you would associate with the British people and their society?

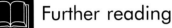 **Further reading**

Abercrombie, Nicholas and Warde, Alan (2000) *Contemporary British Society* Oxford: Blackwell Publishers

Blair, Tony (1996) *New Britain: My Vision of a Young Country* London: Fourth Estate

English, Richard and Kenny, Michael (eds) (1999) *Rethinking British Decline* London: Macmillan

Halsey, A.H. and Webb, J. (2000) *Twentieth-Century British Social Trends* London: Palgrave/Macmillan

Marwick, Arthur (2000) *A History of the Modern British Isles 1914–1999* Oxford: Blackwell Publishers

Obelkevich, James and Catterall, Peter (eds) (1994) *Understanding Post-War British Society* London: Routledge

Savage, S.P. and Atkinson R. (2001) *Public Policy Under Blair* London: Palgrave/Macmillan

 Websites

Central Office of Information: www.coi.gov.uk

Prime Minister's Office: www.number-10.gov.uk

British Tourist Authority: www.visitbritain.com

British Council: http://www.mori.com/polls/1999/britcoun.shtml

The *MORI Organization*: www.mori.com

The country

chapter 1

A MORI POLL IN JUNE 2001 (before later terrorist attacks on the USA) reported that Britons' greatest global concerns (ahead of world war and poverty) were the environment and global warming. Such attitudes are also reflected in how the British respond to their own physical geography and its industries and led the Labour government to create a new Department for the Environment, Food and Rural Affairs (DEFRA) in 2001. A knowledge of Britain's geography serves both to contextualize these worries and to indicate the role it plays in partly forming British identities.

Geographical identities

Most British people identify themselves at one level with the larger political and geographical areas in which they live. The country's title for constitutional and political purposes is the United Kingdom of Great Britain and Northern Ireland, with the short forms 'UK' and 'Britain' being used for convenience. It is part of those islands, known geographically as the British Isles (but more correctly as the British-Irish Islands), which lie off the north-west coast of continental Europe. The mainlands of England, Scotland and Wales form the largest island with the political title of Great Britain. Northern Ireland shares the second-largest island with the Republic of Ireland (Ireland or Eire), which has been independent of Britain since 1921–22. Smaller islands, such as Anglesey, the Isle of Wight, the Orkneys, Shetlands, Hebrides and Scillies, are also part of the British political union.

But the Isle of Man in the Irish Sea and the Channel Islands off the French west coast are not part of the United Kingdom. They are self-governing Crown Dependencies which have a historical relationship with the British Crown and possess their own independent legal systems, legislatures and administrative structures. However, the British government is responsible for their defence and foreign relations and can intervene if good administration is not maintained.

On a smaller level of geographical identification, Britain is often divided up into 'regions'. These are not the same as local government structures (see Chapter 3). They can be politico-economic structures for British and EU purposes; assistance and development areas; or service locations for supplies of gas, water and electricity. They are often based, as in figure 1.3, on former economic planning regions. In 1999, Regional Development Agencies (RDAs) were created in England which cover the same areas.

'Regionalism' and 'localism', as cultural factors, are significant in British life, but opinions differ on how strong they actually are. They can illustrate a sense of belonging, which becomes more evident with increasing distance from London and the UK government. They may reflect a determination by regional or local populations to assert their individual identities. These have increased in Scotland, Wales and (arguably) Northern Ireland with the devolution of political power from London and the establishment (1999–2000) of a Parliament in Edinburgh and Assemblies in Cardiff and Belfast. But smaller local government areas in these countries may well react to centralized power in the capital cities. Devolution has also provoked demands for greater autonomy in some English regions such as the north-east, and the RDAs may serve as future sites for devolved regional government in England.

Identification with even smaller local areas was arguably more significant when the British were a rural people living in villages and were less mobile. But today, this identity may still be strongly focused on cities (such as Manchester, Liverpool, Glasgow, Belfast, London and Cardiff) or on English and Welsh counties rather than the larger regional areas.

Physical features and climate

Historically, Britain's physical features have influenced human settlement, population movements, military conquest and political union. They have also conditioned the location and exploitation of industry, transport systems, agriculture, fisheries, woodlands and energy supplies. Today they continue to influence such activities and are tied to public concerns about pollution, weather change, the state of the natural environment and the quality of food products. Some have been affected by government policies (such as privatization) and European Union directives on agriculture and fisheries.

In recent years, the countryside has become a fierce political issue. Many rural inhabitants, groups such as The Countryside Alliance and farmers feel neglected by the UK central government. They and others object to the alleged destruction of the physical environment and the lack of understanding of country life. In Britain, there has historically been a tension between urban and rural cultures but many people (even in the cities) feel a traditional (if romanticized) nostalgia and identity for the countryside.

Britain's geographical position is marked by latitude 50°N in southern England and by latitude 60°N across the Shetlands. It thus lies within only 10° of latitude and has a small and compact size when compared with some European countries. Yet it also possesses a great diversity of physical features, which surprises those visitors who expect a mainly urban and industrialized country. The many beauty spots and recreation areas, such as the ten National Parks in England and Wales and areas of natural beauty in Scotland and Northern Ireland, may be easily reached without much expenditure of time or effort.

Britain's physical area covers 93,025 square miles (242,842 square kilometres). Most is land and the rest comprises inland water such as lakes and rivers. England has 50,052 square miles (129,634 sq km), Wales has 7,968 (20,637), Scotland has 29,799 (77,179) and Northern Ireland has 5,206 (13,438). England is significantly larger than the other countries and also has (2000) the biggest population (49,753,000) in a UK total of 59,501,000. These factors partly explain the English dominance in British history and the mixed attitudes of Scotland, Ireland and Wales towards their large neighbour.

The distance from the south coast of England to the most northerly tip of the Scottish mainland is 600 miles (955 km), and the English east coast and the Welsh west coast are 300 miles (483 km) apart. These relatively small distances have aided the development of political union and communications and contributed to social, economic and institutional norms throughout Britain. But, prior to the eighteenth century, there were considerable obstacles to this progress, such as difficult terrain and inadequate transportation.

Britain's varied physical characteristics are a source of identification for many people, such as the Giant's Causeway in Northern Ireland, the cliffs of Dover in southern England, the Highlands of Scotland and the Welsh mountains. These result from a long geological and climatic history. Earth movements forced mountains to rise from the sea-bed to form the oldest parts of Britain. Warmer, sub-tropical periods then created large swamp forests covering lowland zones. These, in turn, were buried by sand, soil and mud, and the forests' fossil remains became coal deposits. Later, the climate alternated between warmth and Arctic temperatures. During the latter Ice Age periods, glaciers moved southwards over the islands, with only southern England free from their effects.

Highland areas were slowly worn away by weathering agents such as wind, ice and water. This process rounded off the mountain peaks and moved waste materials into lowland zones, where they were pressed into new rocks and where the scenery became softer and less folded.

FIGURE 1.1   The British-Irish Isles

The geological and weathering changes shaped valleys and plains and dictated the siting of Britain's major rivers, such as the Clyde in Scotland; the Tyne, Trent, Severn and Thames in England and Wales; and the Bann and Lagan in Northern Ireland.

Natural forces have also affected the coastlines as the seas have moved backwards and forwards over time. Parts of the coastal area have either sunk under the sea or risen above it. These processes continue today, particularly on the English coasts. Geological tilting, rising sea levels and sea erosion have resulted in the loss of land, houses and farms, while the sea's retreat in some places has created either chalk and limestone uplands or sand beaches along the coasts.

Britain was originally part of the European mainland. But the melting of the glaciers in the last Ice Age caused the sea level to rise. The country was separated from the continent by the North Sea at its widest, and by the English Channel at its narrowest, points. The shortest stretch of water between the two land masses is now the Strait of Dover between Dover in southern England and Calais in France (24 miles, 38 km).

There are many bays, inlets, peninsulas and estuaries along the coasts, and most places in Britain are less than 75 miles (120 km) from some kind of tidal water. Tides on the coasts and in inland rivers (in addition to heavy rainfall) can cause flooding in many parts of the country. Substantial finance is needed by local authorities to construct defences against this threat. For example, a London flood barrier was completed in 1984 across the River Thames. Flooding seriously affected many low-lying inland areas of Britain in 2000–01, with people suffering property and financial loss.

The coastal seas are not deep and are often less than 300 feet (90 metres) because they lie on the Continental Shelf, or raised sea-bed adjacent to the mainland. The warm North Atlantic Current (Gulf Stream) heats the sea and air as it travels from the Atlantic Ocean across the Shelf. This gives the country a more temperate climate than would otherwise be the case, when one considers its northerly position. It also influences the coastal fish breeding grounds, on which the national fishing industry is considerably dependent.

Britain's physical relief can be divided into highland and lowland Britain (see figure 1.2). The highest ground is mainly in the north and west. Most of the lowland zones, except for the Scottish Lowlands and central areas of Northern Ireland, are in the south and east of the country, where only a few points reach 1,000 feet (305 metres) above sea level.

The north and west consist of older, harder rocks created by ancient earth movements, which are generally unsuitable for cultivation. The south and east comprise younger, softer materials formed by weathering processes, which have produced fertile soils and good agricultural conditions. Much of the lowland area, except for urban and industrial regions,

1 North-West
  Highlands
2 Central
  Highlands
  (Grampians)

3 Southern
  Uplands
4 Sperrin
  Mountains

5 Antrim
  Mountains
6 Mourne
  Mountains
7 Cumbrian
  Mountains

8 Pennines
9 Peak District
10 Welsh Massif
  (Cambrians)

FIGURE 1.2   Highland and lowland Britain

is cultivated and farmed. It largely comprises fields, which are divided by fences or hedges. Animal grazing land in upland zones is separated either by moorland or stone walls.

England

England (population 49,753,000) consists mainly of undulating or flat lowland countryside, with highland areas in the north and south-west. Eastern England has the low-lying flat lands of the Norfolk Broads, the Cambridgeshire and Lincolnshire Fens and the Suffolk Marshes. Low hill ranges stretch over much of the country, such as the North Yorkshire Moors, the Cotswolds, the Kent and Sussex Downs and the Chiltern Hills.

Highland zones are marked by the Cheviot Hills (between England and Scotland); the north-western mountain region of the Lake District and the Cumbrian mountains; the northern plateau belt of the Pennines forming a backbone across north-west England; the Peak District at the southern reaches of the Pennines; and the south-western plateau of Devon and Cornwall.

The heaviest population concentrations centre on the largest towns and cities, such as London and in south-east England generally; the West Midlands region around Birmingham; the Yorkshire cities of Leeds, Bradford and Sheffield; the north-western industrial area around Liverpool and Manchester; and the north-east region comprising Newcastle and Sunderland.

Wales

Wales (population 2,937,000) is a highland country, with moorland plateau, hills and mountains, which are often broken by deep river valleys. This upland mass contains the Cambrian mountains and descends eastwards into England. The highest mountains are in Snowdonia in the north-west, where the dominant peak is that of Snowdon (3,560 feet, 1,085 metres).

The lowland zones are restricted to the narrow coastal belts and to the lower parts of the river valleys in south Wales, where two-thirds of the Welsh population live. The chief urban concentrations of people and industry are around the bigger southern cities, such as the capital Cardiff, Swansea and Newport. In the past, the highland nature of Wales hindered conquest, agriculture and the settlement of people.

Scotland

Scotland (population 5,119,000) may be divided into three main areas. The first is the North-West and Central Highlands (Grampians), together with

PLATE 1.1   Welsh countryside (*Brenda Prince/Format*)

a number of islands off the west and north-east coasts. These areas are thinly populated, but comprise half the country's land mass. The second is the Central Lowlands, which contain one-fifth of the land area but three-quarters of the Scottish population, most of the industrial and commercial centres and much of the cultivated land. The third is the Southern Uplands, which cover a number of hill ranges stretching towards the border with England.

The Highlands, with their lochs and fiord coastlines, and the Southern Uplands are now smooth, rounded areas since the original jagged mountains have been worn down. The highest point in the Central Highlands is Ben Nevis (4,406 feet, 1,343 metres), which is also the highest place in Britain.

The main population concentrations are around the administrative centre and capital of Edinburgh; the commercial and industrial area of Glasgow; and the regional centres of Aberdeen (an oil industry city) and Dundee. The climate, isolation and harsh physical conditions in much of Scotland have made conquest, settlement and agriculture difficult.

Northern Ireland

Northern Ireland (population 1,692,000) has a north-east tip which is only 13 miles (21 km) from the Scottish coast, a fact that has encouraged both Irish and Scottish migration. Since 1921–22, Northern Ireland has had a 303-mile (488-km) border in the south and west with the Republic of Ireland. It has a rocky northern coastline, a south-central fertile plain and mountainous areas in the west, north-east and south-east. The south-eastern Mourne Mountains include the highest peak, Slieve Donard, which is 2,796 feet high (853 metres). Lough Neagh (153 square miles, 396 sq km) is Britain's largest freshwater lake and lies at the centre of the country.

Most of the large towns, such as the capital Belfast, are situated in valleys which lead from the Lough. Belfast lies at the mouth of the river Lagan and has the biggest population concentration. But Northern Ireland generally has a sparse and scattered population and is a largely rural country.

Climate

The relative smallness of the country and the influences of a warm sea and westerly winds mean that there are no extreme contrasts in temperature throughout Britain. The climate is mainly temperate, but with variations between coolness and mildness. Altitude modifies temperatures, so that much of Scotland and highland areas of Wales and England are cool in summer and cold in winter compared with most of England. In general, temperatures are lower in the north than the south and national average temperatures rarely reach 32°C (90°F) in the summer or fall below −10°C (14°F) in the winter.

The main factors affecting rainfall in Britain are depressions (low-pressure areas) which travel eastwards across the Atlantic Ocean; prevailing south-westerly winds throughout much of the year; exposure of western coasts to the Atlantic Ocean; and the fact that most high ground lies in the west.

The heaviest annual rainfalls are in the west and north (60 inches, 1,600 millimetres), with an autumn or winter maximum. The high ground in the west protects the lowlands of the south and east, so that annual rainfall here is moderate (30 inches, 800 mm). March to June tend to be the driest months; September to January the wettest; and drought conditions are infrequent, although they do occur and can cause problems for farmers, water companies and consumers.

Low-pressure systems normally pass over northern areas and can produce windy, wet and unstable conditions. In recent years, Britain has had more frequent storms, heavier rainfall and flooding, with suggestions that weather changes are linked to controversial theories on global warming. But high-pressure systems, which occur throughout the year, are stable and slow-moving, resulting in light winds and settled weather. They can give fine and dry effects, in both winter and summer.

Sunshine in Britain decreases from south to north; inland from the coastal belts; and with altitude. In summer, average daily sunshine varies from five hours in northern Scotland to eight hours on the Isle of Wight. In winter, it averages one hour in northern Scotland and two hours on the English south coast.

These statistics show that Britain is not a particularly sunny country, although there are periods of relief from the general greyness. The frequent cloud-cover over the islands means that even on a hot summer's day there may be little sunshine breaking through the clouds, giving humid, sticky conditions. Sunshine can frequently mix with pollutants to give poor air quality in both cities and rural areas.

Such climatic features give the British weather its changeability and what some regard as its stimulating variety. Discrepancies between weather forecasts and actual results often occur and words such as 'changeable' and 'unsettled' are generously employed. The weather is virtually a national institution, a topic of daily conversation and for some a conditioning factor in the national character. Britons tend to think that they live in a more temperate climate than is the case. But many escape abroad in summer and smaller numbers in the winter.

Agriculture, fisheries and forestry

Agriculture

Soils vary in quality from the thin, poor ones of highland Britain to the rich, fertile land of low-lying areas in eastern and southern England. The climate usually allows a long, productive growing season without extremes. But farmers can sometimes have problems with droughts or when there is too much rain and too little sunshine at ripening time.

Britain's long agricultural history includes a series of farming revolutions from Neolithic times. Today, there are 239,000 farm units, ranging from small farms to huge business concerns, and many are owner-occupied. They use 76 per cent of the land area, although there is concern that farmland is being increasingly used for building and recreational purposes. Some 600,000 people (2.1 per cent of the workforce) are engaged in farming. But agriculture provides two-thirds of Britain's food needs and its exports are important.

Many farms in Scotland, Northern Ireland, Wales and northern and south-western England specialize in dairy farming, beef cattle and sheep

PLATE 1.2 Barley fields in Devon, England (*Ken Lambert/Barnaby*)

herds. Some farms in eastern and northern England and Northern Ireland concentrate on pig production. Poultry meat and egg industries are widespread, with intensive 'factory farming'. Most of the other farms in southern and eastern England and in eastern Scotland grow arable crops such as wheat, barley, oats, potatoes, oilseed rape, and sugar beet. Horticultural products such as apples, berries and flowers are also widely grown.

Agriculture is still a significant industry and organized interest group. It is productive, intensive, mechanized and specialized. But, after a profitable period in the early 1990s, farming is now in crisis owing to the high value of the pound, a fall in farm prices and a series of disasters such as BSE (Bovine Spongiform Encephalopathy) in cows (1996), its link to CJD (Creutzfeldt-Jakob disease) in humans, swine fever and foot and mouth disease (2001). Animals have been lost, farming income has been seriously reduced and many farmers have left the industry or turned to non-farming activities.

The Common Agricultural Policy (CAP) of the European Union (EU), which accounts for 48 per cent of the EU's budget, has also affected British farmers. Its original protectionist aims were to increase productivity and efficiency; stabilize the market; ensure regular supplies of food; give farmers reasonable rewards by providing them with subsidies; set minimum guaranteed prices for food products through price support; and standardize the quality and size of produce.

British governments argue that CAP is unwieldy, costly for consumers, bureaucratic, restrictive for producers, open to fraud and leads to surplus food. They maintain that supply and demand should reflect the needs of the market and meet consumers' demands. The Labour government is now evaluating the future of British farming with more emphasis on consumer wishes, better land management and reduction of subsidies. Foreign countries (such as the USA) have also objected to EU restrictions (now liberalized), and the future entry of Eastern European nations to the EU has led to calls for CAP reform.

Fisheries

Britain is one of Europe's leading fishing nations and operates in the North Sea, the Irish Sea and the Atlantic. The fishing industry is important to the national economy and is centred on a number of ports around the coasts. The most important fish catches are cod, haddock, whiting, herring, mackerel, plaice and sole, which are caught by the 7,448 registered vessels of the fishing fleet. The fish-farming industry (salmon, trout and shellfish) is a large and expanding business, particularly in Scotland.

But employment in and income from fishing have declined substantially in recent years. This is partly due to changes in fish breeding patterns and a reduction in fish stocks because of overfishing. Many fishermen have become unemployed and fishing towns on the English and Scottish coasts have suffered. But the industry still accounts for 40 per cent of Britain's fish consumption. Fishermen number 15,961, with some three jobs in associated occupations for every one fisherman.

The industry has also been affected by the EU's Common Fisheries Policy (CFP) and government policies, which have affected the fishermen's old freedom of operation. The need to conserve fish resources and prevent overfishing is stressed. Zones have been created in which fishermen may operate and quota systems operate inside and beyond the zones to restrict fish catches. Measures to limit the time fishing vessels spend at sea and to decommission (take out of operation) fishing boats have further restricted employment and the fishing fleet. Fishermen are angry with British government and EU policies and their loss of livelihood. But without fish conservation, there will be reduced supplies in future.

Forestry

Woodlands cover an estimated 6.6 million acres (2.7 million hectares) of Britain and comprise 8 per cent of England, 17 per cent of Scotland, 14 per cent of Wales and 6 per cent of Northern Ireland. These figures amount to some 10 per cent of total land area, which is considerably below the European average. Some 35 per cent of productive national forests are managed by the state Forestry Commission or government departments and the rest by private owners. About 35,000 people are employed in the state and private forestry industries and 10,000 are engaged in timber processing.

However, these activities contribute only 15 per cent to the national consumption of wood and associated timber products, which means that the country is heavily dependent upon wood imports. The government has encouraged tree planting programmes in Scotland, Wales and the English Midlands, and allowed the sale of state woodlands to private owners in order to reduce public expenditure and to increase productivity. New plantings, controlled felling, expansion of timber industries and a profitable private sector may reduce Britain's present dependence upon imports and benefit the environment.

Forestry policy is supposed to take conservation factors into account in the development of timber facilities. But such aims are not always achieved and there is disquiet about some government programmes. Environmentalists campaign against the destruction of woodlands for road building, advocate increased tree planting to combat global warming and pollution and try to preserve the quality of the existing woodlands. These in recent years have been badly affected by disease, unreasonable felling and substantial storm damage in 1987 and 1990.

Energy resources

Primary energy sources are oil (45 per cent), gas (30), nuclear/hydro power (5) and coal (20). The most important secondary source is electricity. 200,000 people work in energy production, and three of Britain's largest companies (Shell, BP and British Gas) are in this sector. But there are problems with energy sources and concerns about pollution and environmental damage. Most energy industries have now been privatized, but there is criticism about their services and regulation.

Since 1980, Britain has produced an increased amount of its own energy needs. This is due to the growth in offshore oil and gas supplies, which make a crucial contribution to the economy. Multinational companies operate under government licence and extract these fuels from the North Sea and newly discovered West Atlantic fields.

PLATE 1.3   The Tate Modern art gallery from the north side of the Thames, converted from a disused power station (© *Popperfoto/Reuters*)

But, because governments encourage high extraction rates, large supplies of oil and gas will continue only into the early twenty-first century. Even now, there is some dependence on imported gas and oil. Development of existing resources and the search for alternative forms of energy are crucial for Britain and its economy. The positions of coal and nuclear power have to be debated, and further research is needed into renewable energy such as solar, wind, wave and tidal power.

Coal is an important natural energy resource, but there are objections to its use on pollution and cost grounds. After a reduction in the work-force and the closure of uneconomic pits in the 1980s, the coal industry was privatized and Britain produces most of its own coal needs. But coal is expensive and there is a lack of demand from big consumers, such as electricity generating stations, which have moved to gas, oil and cheap coal imports. More pit closures have occurred, and the future of the coal industry is uncertain.

Electricity is mainly provided by coal-, gas- and oil-fired power stations, and a small amount of hydro-electricity: 26 per cent of electricity is produced by fifteen nuclear power stations. But expansion of nuclear power (partially privatized in 1996) to satisfy energy needs is uncertain. Some advocates argue very strongly that replacement of ageing reactors and more nuclear stations is essential, while a slight majority of public opinion favours nuclear power.

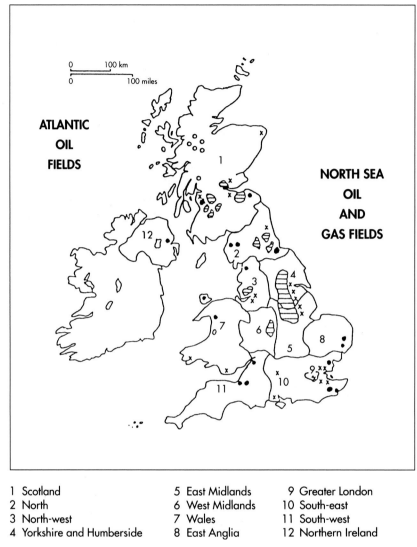

1 Scotland
2 North
3 North-west
4 Yorkshire and Humberside

5 East Midlands
6 West Midlands
7 Wales
8 East Anglia

9 Greater London
10 South-east
11 South-west
12 Northern Ireland

• Nuclear power stations
x Coal-, gas- or oil-fired
  power stations

⌂ Active coalfields
○ Hydro-electric power
  stations

FIGURE 1.3 The British regions and energy sources

Alternative forms of renewable energy are becoming more important. Electricity generation by wind power is already operative, although there is opposition to wind farms in the countryside. The use of tidal and wave power is being implemented on some coasts and estuaries and solar energy is already provided, with plans for more research. These, and other, forms of renewable energy are important for Britain's future energy needs, particularly as environmental concerns grow. But their capacity is limited at present to 3 per cent of all electricity production, although the Labour government wishes to increase this amount to 10 per cent by 2010.

Critics argue that insufficient work and research money is being devoted to potential alternative supplies; that the advantages of nuclear power have not been sufficiently investigated; that oil and gas have been wasted rather than extracted more slowly; and that not enough consideration has been given to a cleaner coal industry. British domestic and industrial energy users are still extravagant when compared to other European countries. Consequently, the provision of cheap and environmentally suitable energy for both domestic and industrial use will be a problem for Britain in the future.

Transport and communications

Transport and communications are divided between the public and private sectors of the economy, although many state businesses have now been privatized. Roads, railways, shipping and civil aviation provide the country's transport system. British Telecom, competing telecommunications companies and the Post Office supply most communications needs.

Transport

Central and local government agencies are responsible for different roads in the *road network*. Motorways and trunk roads are the largest elements and carry most of the passenger traffic and heavy goods vehicles. But some roads are in bad condition and unable to handle the number of vehicles on them, leading to traffic congestion. Expansion, modernization and repair of roads are environmentally damaging and may also be inadequate to meet the estimated future number of vehicles. While the Labour government has cancelled some controversial road-building programmes in an attempt to cut the demand for road space and to persuade drivers to adopt alternative methods of transport, new road building is still planned.

There are 25 million licensed vehicles, of which 21 million are private cars and the rest are mainly commercial vehicles. Car transport is most popular and accounts for 86 per cent of passenger mileage, while buses and

PLATE 1.4 A London bus (© *Joanne O'Brien/Format*)

coaches take 6 per cent. Britain has one of the highest densities of road traffic in the world, but also a relatively good safety record in which road accidents continue to decrease.

Private road haulage has a dominant position in the movement of inland freight. Lorries have become larger and account for 80 per cent of this market. Critics campaign to transfer road haulage to the railways and the publicly owned inland waterways (canals). But the waterways are used for only a small amount of freight transportation because of expense, although they are popular for recreational purposes. Rail freight, however, is increasing for bulk commodities.

Public bus services have declined (particularly in rural areas) because of increased private car usage and cost. Conservative governments deregulated bus operations and most local bus companies have now been privatized, although some services are still operated by local government authorities. There has been a considerable expansion in private long-distance express coach services, which are cheaper than the railways. But bus services generally in Britain are underfunded and inadequate for potential demand.

The world's first public passenger steam *railway* opened in 1825 between Stockton and Darlington in north-east England. After a hundred years of private operation, the railways became state-owned in 1947. But they were privatized in 1997. A company (Railtrack) owned the railway lines and stations; the trains are owned and operated by regional

PLATE 1.5   Waterloo International railway terminal, London
(© *Maggie Murray/Format*)

companies; and rail accounts for 5 per cent of passenger mileage. But, following dismal performances by Railtrack, the government took control of the company in 2001 and its future structure is uncertain.

Rail passenger services consist of a fast inter-city network, linking all the main British centres; local trains which supply regional needs; and commuter services in and around the large areas of population, particularly London and south-east England. Increased electrification of lines and the introduction of diesel trains such as the Inter-City 125s travelling at a maximum speed of 125 m.p.h (201 km/h) have improved rail journeys considerably. But such speeds and facilities are still inferior to those in other countries.

Many railway lines and trains are old and need replacing. Privatization has not solved the problems of underfunding and lack of adequate services. A series of fatal crashes in recent years and the resulting repair of large sections of rail track caused chaos in the railway network and drew attention to the shortcomings of Railtrack. The situation is slowly returning to normal but passenger totals are still depressed. There is much criticism, particularly in south-east England, about the performances of the privatized rail companies, fare increases, overcrowding, cancellations, delays, staffing and poor services. Similar complaints are also made about the London Underground system (the Tube), which covers 254 miles (408 km) of railway line in the capital, and which will be partly (and controversially) privatized. It is argued that the inadequate state of Britain's railways is due largely to underfunding, with expenditure being below European averages.

The *Channel Tunnel*, privately run by a French/British company (Eurotunnel), opened for commercial use in 1994 under the English Channel with the two terminals, Folkestone and Coquelles, being 31 miles (50 km) apart. It was meant to improve passenger and freight rail travel between Britain and mainland Europe and has succeeded in taking business from sea/ferry services. It provides a drive-on, drive-off service (Le Shuttle) for cars, coaches and freight vehicles, as well as passenger trains (Eurostar) from Waterloo Station in London. But a new high-speed rail connection between Folkestone and London is still uncompleted.

Although there are over 300 *ports* in Britain, most are small concerns. The bigger ports, such as Clyde, Dover, Hull, Grimsby, Southampton, Felixstowe and Cardiff, service most of the trade and travel requirements. But work and labour have declined since the great days of the ports in the past.

The British shipping fleet has greatly decreased from its peak year in 1975. The cargo market is now dominated by a small number of large private sector groups. But 77 per cent of Britain's overseas trade is still carried by sea, although passenger mileage has been much reduced. Both may decline further because of competition with the Channel Tunnel.

Britain's *civil aviation* system accounts for 1 per cent of passenger mileage and is in the private sector following the privatization of the former state airline, British Airways, in 1987. There are other carriers, such as British Midland International, Britannia Airways and Virgin Atlantic, which run scheduled and charter passenger services on domestic and international routes, as well as air freight services. All are controlled by the Civil Aviation Authority (CAA), an independent body which regulates the industry and air traffic control. The latter's partial privatization has been heavily criticized on safety and economic grounds.

There are 142 licensed civil aerodromes in Britain, varying considerably in size. Heathrow and Gatwick Airports outside London are the largest. These airports, together with Stansted in south-east England and Glasgow, Edinburgh and Aberdeen in Scotland, are owned by the private sector BAA. They handle 73 per cent of air passengers and 84 per cent of air cargo. Most of the other larger regional airports, such as Manchester, Birmingham, Luton, Belfast, Newcastle and East Midlands, are controlled by local authorities and cater for the country's remaining passenger and cargo needs.

Expansion of existing airports (particularly regional facilities) and the provision of new ones will be necessary if Britain is to cope with increased consumer demand and competition from Europe. But such projects are very expensive and controversial because of environmental problems, such as construction work, noise, pollution and traffic. There is also disquiet about plane congestion in the skies over Britain.

It is argued that the inadequacy of British transport systems stem from the lack of an integrated infrastructure of roads, railways and airports catering for both passengers and freight. This would arguably ease road congestion, satisfy demand and improve the environment. But such developments involve considerable expenses and Britain invests less in transport than any other European country. Governments are reluctant to spend more public money, although the Labour government hopes to persuade the private sector to invest in the transport infrastructure in partnership with the state.

Communications

Communications systems in Britain are also divided between the public and private sectors. The main suppliers are private telecommunications companies and the public Post Office.

Telecommunications is one of the most competitive and rapidly expanding sectors of the economy. *British Telecom (BT)* was privatized in 1984 and provides domestic and international telephone and telecommunications systems, with 20 million domestic and 8.5 million business subscribers. There was much criticism of BT's performance after privatization. Although some service problems were solved, and it became an influential world force, it has again experienced problems with its funding and expansion programmes.

The private companies, Vodafone and Cable and Wireless, compete fiercely with British Telecom. Other competitors, such as cable networks, are growing rapidly and have been licensed to provide telecommunications facilities and the development of broadband services.

The strongest and most competitive growth in recent years has been in mobile telephones and services provided over the Internet. By 2000, the number of mobile phone users had risen to over 33 million and access to the Internet and e-mail covered 25 per cent of households. However, Internet access and usage is much greater in companies, libraries and schools.

The *Post Office*, established in 1635, is a government-owned body (Consignia) and is responsible for collecting, handling and delivering some 80 million letters and parcels every day. It has sorting offices throughout the country with sophisticated handling equipment, based on the postcodes which every address in Britain has. Local post offices throughout the country (although controversially reduced in rural and some urban areas) provide postal and other services, as well as paying out pensions and benefits, and a very large Parcelforce Worldwide operates domestically and overseas. The Post Office's international connections and customers are expanding, and the growth of electronic communications has had only a limited effect on its markets. The Post Office does not have a monopoly on the collection and delivery of letters. But licensed competition by private sector couriers and express operators is limited at present, although consumer groups would like to see it increased.

Attitudes to the environment

There is considerable public concern about pollution, traffic congestion, the quality of the natural habitat, the use of energy sources and the safety of agricultural products.

Agricultural, forest and other greenfield land is increasingly used for building and recreational purposes; there has been an increase in suburban sprawl as house building encroaches into rural areas; new towns are proposed to cater for an estimated need of 4.4 million new homes; and giant supermarkets or shopping centres are being located in the countryside. A *Research Survey of Great Britain* (1997) found that 80 per cent of people were worried about the future of the countryside and 69 per cent wanted to stop housing and road schemes which damaged the environment.

Government directives now force planning authorities to allow homes to be built on empty land within towns before granting permission to develop greenfield sites.

A 1997 *MORI* poll reported that 60 per cent of respondents felt that environmental problems damaged their health. A majority stated that environmental protection should rate higher than economic growth; environmental problems should be tackled; and they were prepared to make sacrifices to clean up the environment and conserve wildlife. But such views do not always lead to sensitive behaviour and there is widespread vandalism and dirtiness in both rural and urban areas.

Awareness of environmental issues coincided with the rise of the Green movement in the 1980s and all political parties conveniently adopted 'green' policies. An Environment Agency was created; Environmental Protection Acts were supposed to safeguard the environment, reduce pollution and penalize polluters; and EU legislation makes very stringent demands.

But it is argued that such action is insufficient and ineffective. Controls and protection lack force; polluters evade regulations or suffer only minor fines; little pressure is put on companies to modernize their facilities; and there are disputes over protection costs between local and central government priorities. Polls in *The Ecologist* magazine in 2001 found that 65 per cent of respondents said that the Labour government had not improved the environment since coming to power in 1997 and was spending too little on it.

Air pollution in Britain is caused by factories and power stations discharging pollutants into the air and by emissions from cars, buses and lorries. It seriously affects both urban and rural areas, is a threat to people's health (particularly asthmatics) and was linked for the first time in 1997 to heart attacks. Although pollution was reduced by Clean Air Acts in the 1950s and 1960s, it still reaches harmful levels, particularly in summer when pollutants mix with sunshine and still humid conditions to produce high ozone levels.

Although Britain has reduced carbon dioxide emissions and the Labour government is concerned to improve its record, pollution will worsen as the deterioration in public transport encourages more people to use private vehicles. Britons are overly dependent on the car, and alternatives have been neglected. The car is now seen as the greatest transport problem, and the Labour government intends to curb its unnecessary use, ration road space in favour of buses, increase taxes or charges on car usage in cities and give funding to local schemes which improve public transport.

But governments have not provided an integrated transport system (roads, rail and air) which would relieve environmental pressures. The problem arises because of the varied geography of Britain's cities and the devolution of control to local authorities. It is thus difficult to implement one overall plan and to agree on who will pay the costs. But a 2001 poll in *The Ecologist* showed that 61 per cent of respondents did not want more roads and preferred money to be spent on alternatives. A large majority in a 2001 *MORI* poll wanted to see more goods carried by rail and heavy lorries restricted.

Increased freight and private car transport has resulted in traffic congestion, noise and damage to roads and property. The Channel Tunnel and its rail links have also attracted opposition from environmentalists, although landscaping and noise suppression have alleviated some damage. Fears have been raised about safety in the Tunnel, and outbreaks of fire in 1996 and 1997 forced the cancellation of services.

Polls consistently show that a majority of respondents wish for better public transport, cuts in traffic pollution, reduction of congestion and removal of freight from the roads. But they are less keen on keeping cars out of towns and cities or banning cars completely, although they seem to accept car taxes, charges or tolls as a reasonable alternative.

There are other forms of environmental damage. Sea and beach pollution is partly caused by untreated sewage and toxic industrial waste being pumped into the sea by commercial companies, particularly the North Sea. Britain is committed to reducing discharge levels but, although 90 per cent of beaches meet European quality standards, pollution levels on some beaches still exceed safety levels. Some rivers are polluted by industrial waste, toxic fertilizers, pesticides and farm silage. This has caused public concern about the safety of drinking water from reservoirs, and the water companies (the worst business polluters in 2001) have been pressurized to raise the quality of their services. Many polluted rivers, lakes and estuaries have now been cleaned up and more stringent controls of the oil and shipping industries in the North Sea have reduced pollution levels.

Problems have been experienced with the exploitation of energy resources, such as expense, capacity and availability, and there are environmental concerns about the burning of fossil fuels (coal, oil and gas), global warming and the damage to the countryside caused by new developments. Nuclear expansion has been halted because of some public opposition to nuclear facilities, the danger of radioactive leaks, the reprocessing of nuclear waste at the Thorp and Sellafield plants in north-west England and the dumping of radioactive waste. But according to *The Ecologist* in 2001, 50 per cent of respondents wanted to keep nuclear power, while 35 per cent were opposed.

Considerable public worry surrounds the agricultural industry because of its widespread use of fertilizers and pesticides, its methods of animal feeding and the effects of intensive farming on the environment. Much hedgerow, which is important for many forms of animal and

PLATE 1.6   Sellafield nuclear reprocessing plant, Windscale (*P. Wolmuth/The Hutchison Library*)

vegetable life, has been lost in recent years as fields have become bigger and farming more mechanized. The quality and standards of food products, particularly those concerned with intensive farming techniques, are of concern. Cases of food poisoning have risen sharply and there are worries about standards of hygiene in the food and farming businesses. The BSE scare seriously affected the consumption of beef and other meats and led to a drop in demand for traditional foods. The foot and mouth outbreak in 2000–01 also raised questions about the quality of British food and intensive methods of farming.

Yet there is public disquiet about the experimental use of genetically modified (GM) crops, and the success of organic farming in Britain has been small, largely because of the cost of such goods and confusion about their actual benefit. But an *NOP* poll in 2001 reported that 82 per cent of respondents favoured a return to traditional farming methods, even if this meant paying more for food. A *Good Housekeeping* magazine poll in August 2001 found that only one person in six trusts the supermarkets to sell safe food; three in four were more concerned than ever before about the safety of the food they buy; and, although 97 per cent of respondents buy most of their food from supermarkets, their faith in them has suffered.

Exercises

Explain and examine the following terms:

Britain	Heathrow	Intercity 125	Post Office
weathering	Highland Britain	Lough Neagh	Ben Nevis
arable	Channel Islands	horticulture	BT
CAP	earth movements	the Tube	drought
Eire	British Telecom	postcodes	GM crops
BSE	global warming	CFP	tidal
CAP	organic food	'regionalism'	RDAs

Write short essays on the following topics:

1 Does Britain have an energy crisis? If so, why?
2 Examine the impact of Britain's membership of the European Union upon its agricultural and fisheries industries.
3 What are the reasons for environmental concerns in Britain?

 Further reading

Barnett, A. and Scruton, R. (1999) *Town and Country* London: Vintage

Champion, A.G. and Townsend, A.R. (1990) *Contemporary Britain: A Geographical Perspective* London: Edward Arnold

Clapp, B.W. (1994) *An Environmental History of Britain since the Industrial Revolution* London: Longman

Connelly, J. and Smith, G (1999) *Politics and the Environment: From Theory to Practice* London: Routledge

Gray, T. (1995) *UK Environmental Policy in the 1990s* London: Macmillan

Harvey, G. (1998) *The Killing of the Countryside* London: Vintage

Regional Trends, Office for National Statistics, London: The Stationery Office

Websites

National Statistics: www.statistics.gov.uk

Environment, Food and Rural Affairs: www.defra.gov.uk

Transport, Local Government and the Regions: www.dtir.gov.uk

Office of the Rail Regulator: www.rail-reg.gov.uk

Office of Telecommunications: www.oftel.gov.uk

Office of Water Services: www.open.gov.uk/ofwat

Office of Gas and Electricity Markets: www.ofgem.gov.uk

Scottish Executive: www.scotland.gov.uk

Northern Ireland Executive: www.nio.gov.uk

Wales Office: www.wales.gov.uk

Countryside Commission: www.countryside.gov.uk

The Green Party: http://www.greenparty.org.uk

The people

THE BRITISH-IRISH ISLES HAVE ATTRACTED settlers, invaders and immigrants throughout their history. The contemporary British are consequently composed of people from worldwide origins and are divided into what became the English, Scots, Welsh and Northern Irish. But these groups often have mixed roots derived from varied settlement, internal migration and assimilation. Such descent patterns are important elements in considering the ethnicities of the British peoples today.

For example, an individual may have an ethnic family background consisting of intermarriage between English, Irish, Scottish or Welsh. A *Guinness* survey in March 2001 reported that 42 per cent of people aged 18–34 in England, Scotland and Wales believed that they had Irish roots. Other polls show that one in four adult Britons claims Irish blood, although experts argue that the true figure is probably one in ten.

There are also immigrant minorities with their own identities who have come to Britain over the centuries and who have sometimes inter-married with the existing populations. Even the English language, which binds most of these people together linguistically, is a blend of Germanic, Romance and other world languages. This historical development has created a contemporary society with multinational and multi-ethnic characteristics. But it also raises controversial questions about the meaning of 'Britishness' and national identities.

Early settlement to AD 1066

There is no accurate picture of what the early settlement of the British-Irish Isles was actually like, and there were long periods when the islands were uninhabited. Historians and archaeologists constantly revise traditional theories about the gradual growth of the country as new evidence comes to light.

The earliest human bones found (1994) in Britain are 500,000 years old. The first people were probably Palaeolithic (Old Stone Age) nomads from mainland Europe, who were characterized by their use of rudimentary stone implements. They travelled to Britain by land and sea, especially at those times when the country was joined to the European land mass.

Later settlers in the Mesolithic and Neolithic (Middle and New Stone Age) periods between 8300 and 2000 BC had more advanced skills in stone carving. Some came from central Europe and settled in eastern Britain. Others arrived by sea from Iberian (Spanish-Portugese) areas and populated Cornwall, Ireland, Wales, the Isle of Man and western Scotland. Their descendants live today in the same western parts. Neolithic groups built large wood, soil and stone monuments, such as Stonehenge, and later arrivals (the Beaker Folk) introduced a Bronze Age culture.

Between ca 600 BC and AD 43 there was a movement of Celtic tribes into the islands from mainland Europe, bringing an Iron Age civilization with them. But the Celts possessed at least two main languages and were divided into many different tribes with conflicts between them. Celtic civilization dominated the British-Irish Isles until it was overcome by Belgic tribes (also of Celtic origin) around 200 BC.

The Belgic tribes were then subjected to a series of Roman expeditions from 55 BC. The Roman military occupation of the islands (except for Ireland and most of Scotland) lasted from AD 43 until 409. The term 'Britain' derives from the Greek and Latin names given to England and Wales by the Romans, although it may stem from Celtic originals. It is argued that the Romans did not mix with the existing population and that their lasting influence was slight. But some Christian practices spread throughout the islands and there is still physical evidence of the Roman presence.

After Roman withdrawal, Germanic tribes such as Angles (from which 'England' is derived), Saxons and Jutes from north-western Europe invaded the country. They either mixed with the existing population or pushed it westwards. The country was divided into separate and often warring Anglo-Saxon kingdoms in England (except for Cornwall), with Celtic areas in Wales, Scotland and Ireland.

Many of these regions suffered from Scandinavian (Viking) military invasions in the eighth and ninth centuries, until the Scandinavians were defeated in England, Scotland and Ireland in the tenth and eleventh centuries. The Scandinavian presence, after initial fleeting raids, was reflected in some permanent settlement, assimilation, farming and political institutions.

Early English history was completed when the Anglo-Saxons were defeated by French-Norman invaders at the Battle of Hastings in 1066 and England was subjected to their rule. The Norman Conquest was an important watershed in English history and marked the last successful external military invasion of the country. It influenced the English people and their language (since French was the language of the nobility for the next three hundred years) and initiated many of the social, legal and institutional frameworks, such as a feudal system (hierarchical structure from top to bottom of society), which were to characterize future British society.

But Celtic civilizations continued in what are now Wales, Scotland and Ireland. Roman rule did not extend to Scotland, which was inhabited (except for Angles in the south) by the original Picts and the later Scots from Ireland who colonized western Scotland (200–400), giving their name to present-day Scotland. In the tenth and eleventh centuries Ireland and its tribal kingdoms were influenced by Scandinavians.

Different peoples had entered the British-Irish Isles from the south-west, the east and the north by 1066. But settlement was often hindered by climatic and geographical obstacles, particularly in the north and west. Many newcomers tended to concentrate initially in southern England, and settlement patterns were not uniform over all of Britain at the same time. Despite some intermixture between the various settlers, there were ethnic differences between the English and the people of Ireland, Wales and Scotland, as well as varying identities between groups in all regions. It is this mixture, increased by later immigration, which has produced the present ethnic and national diversity in Britain.

The early settlement and invasion movements substantially affected the developing fabric of British life and formed the first foundations of the modern state. The newcomers often imposed their cultures on the existing society, as well as adopting some of the native characteristics. Today there are few British towns which lack any physical evidence of the successive changes. They also profoundly influenced social, legal, economic, political, agricultural and administrative institutions and contributed to the evolving language.

There are no realistic population figures for the early British-Irish Isles. The nomadic lifestyle of groups of up to twenty people gradually ceased and was replaced by more permanent settlements of a few hundred inhabitants. It is estimated that the English population during the Roman occupation was one million. By the Norman period, the eleventh-century

TABLE 2.1 Early settlement to AD 1066

500,000–8300 BC	Palaeolithic (Old Stone Age)
8300 BC	Mesolithic (Middle Stone Age)
4000 BC	Neolithic (New Stone Age)
2000 BC	Beaker Folk (Bronze Age)
ca 600 BC	Celts (Iron Age)
200 BC	Belgic tribes
AD 43	The Romans
AD 410	Germanic tribes (Anglo-Saxons)
8th to 11th centuries	The Scandinavians
AD 1066	The Norman Conquest

Domesday Book showed an increase to 2 million. The *Domesday Book* was the first systematic attempt to evaluate England's wealth and population, mainly for taxation purposes.

Growth and immigration to the twentieth century

England, Scotland, Wales and Ireland had more clearly (if not completely) defined identities and geographical areas by the twelfth century. The British state then gradually developed through colonization and political unification. This process was accompanied by fierce and bloody conflicts between the nations, often resulting in lasting tensions and bitterness.

Political and military attempts were made by England to unite Wales, Scotland and Ireland under the English Crown. English monarchs tried to conquer or ally themselves with these other countries as a protection against threats from within the islands and from continental Europe, as well as for increased power and possessions.

Ireland was invaded by Henry II in 1169. Much of the country was then controlled by Anglo-Norman nobles but little direct authority was initially exercised from England. The later colonization of Ireland by the English and the Scots became a source of conflict between the countries. But it also led to Irish settlements in Scotland, London and west-coast ports such as Liverpool. Ireland later became part of the United Kingdom in 1801 but, after a period of violence and political unrest, was divided in 1921–22 into the independent Republic of Ireland and Northern Ireland (which is part of the UK).

Wales, after Roman rule, remained a Celtic country, although influenced by Anglo-Norman England. Between 1282 and 1285 Edward I's military campaign brought Wales under English rule, and he built castles and deployed garrisons there. Apart from a period of freedom in 1402–07, Wales was integrated legally and administratively with England by Acts of Union 1536–42.

The English also tried to conquer Scotland by military force, but were repulsed at the Battle of Bannockburn in 1314. Scotland was then to remain independent until the political union between the two countries in 1707, when the creation of Great Britain (England/Wales and Scotland) took place. But Scotland and England had shared a common monarch since 1603 when James VI of Scotland became James I of England.

England, Wales and Scotland had meanwhile become predominantly Protestant in religion as a result of the European Reformation. But Ireland remained Catholic and tried to distance itself from England, thus adding religion to colonialism as a foundation for future problems.

Britain therefore is not a single, ethnically homogeneous country, but rather a recent and potentially unstable union of four old nations. Great Britain is only slightly older than the USA, and the United Kingdom (1801) is younger. Nor did the political unions appreciably alter the relationships between the four nations. The English often treated their Celtic neighbours as colonial subjects rather than equal partners, and Englishness became a dominant strand in concepts of Britishness, because of the role that the English have played in the formation of Britain.

However, despite the tensions and bitterness between the four nations, there was a steady internal migration between them. This mainly involved movements of Irish, Welsh and Scottish people into England. Relatively few English emigrated to Wales and Scotland, although there was English and Scottish settlement in Ireland over the centuries.

Immigration from abroad also continued over the centuries owing to factors such as religious and political persecution, trade, business and employment. Immigrants have had a significant impact on British society. They have contributed to financial institutions, commerce, industry and agriculture, and influenced artistic, cultural and political developments. But immigrant activity and success have resulted in jealousy, discrimination and violence from the native population.

In addition to political integration, Britain's growth was also conditioned first by a series of agricultural changes and second by a number of later industrial revolutions. Agriculture started with Neolithic settlers and continued with the Saxons in England who cleared the forests, cultivated crops and introduced inventions and equipment which remained in use for centuries. Their open-field system of farming (with strips of land being worked by local people) was later replaced by widespread sheep-herding and wool production.

Britain expanded agriculturally and commercially from the eleventh century, and also developed manufacturing industries. Immigration was often characterized by financial and agricultural skills. Jewish money-lenders entered England with the Norman Conquest, to be followed later by Lombard bankers from northern Italy. This commercial expertise helped to create greater wealth and was influenced by the merchants of the German Hansa League, who set up their trading posts in London and on the east coast of England. Around 1330, Dutch and Flemish weavers arrived, who by the end of the fifteenth century had helped to transform England into a major nation of sheep farmers, cloth producers and textile exporters. Fourteenth-century immigration also introduced specialized knowledge in a variety of manufacturing trades.

Some immigrants stayed only for short periods. Others remained and adapted themselves to British society, while preserving their own cultural and ethnic identities. Newcomers were often encouraged to settle in Britain, and the policy of using immigrant expertise continued in later centuries. But foreign workers had no legal rights, and early immigrants, such as Jews and the Hansa merchants, could be summarily expelled.

Agricultural and commercial developments were reflected in changing population concentrations. From Saxon times to around 1800, Britain had an agriculturally based economy and some 80 per cent of the people lived in villages in the countryside. Settlement was mainly concentrated in the south and east of England, where the rich agricultural regions of East Anglia and Lincolnshire had the greatest population densities. During the fourteenth century, however, the steady increase of people was halted by a series of plagues, and numbers did not start to increase again for another hundred years.

As agricultural production moved into sheep farming and clothing manufactures, larger numbers of people settled around woollen ports, such as Bristol in the west and coastal towns in East Anglia. Others moved to cloth-producing areas in the West Country (south-western parts of England) and the Cotswolds and initiated the growth of market towns. The south midland and eastern English counties had the greatest densities of people, and the population at the end of the seventeenth century is estimated at 5.5 million for England and Wales and 1 million for Scotland.

Other newcomers continued to arrive from overseas, including gypsies, blacks (associated with the slave trade) and a further wave of Jews, who in 1655 created the first permanent Jewish community. In the sixteenth and seventeenth centuries, the country attracted a large number of refugees, such as Dutch Protestants and French Huguenots, who were driven from Europe by warfare, political and religious persecution and employment needs. This talented and urbanized immigration contributed considerably to the national economy and added a new dimension to a largely agricultural population. But, from around 1700, there was to be no more large immigration into the country for the next two hundred years. Britain was exporting more people than it received, mainly to North America and the expanding colonies worldwide.

A second central development in British history was a number of industrial revolutions in the eighteenth and nineteenth centuries. These transformed Britain from an agricultural economy into an industrial and manufacturing country. Processes based on coal-generated steam power were discovered and exploited. Factories and factory towns were needed to mass-produce new manufactured goods. Villages in the coalfields and industrial areas grew rapidly into manufacturing centres. A drift of population away from the countryside began in the late eighteenth century, as people sought work in urban factories to escape rural poverty and unemployment. They moved, for example, to textile mills in Lancashire and Yorkshire and to heavy industries and pottery factories in the West Midlands.

The earlier agricultural population changed radically in the nineteenth century into an industrialized workforce. The 1801 census (the first modern measurement of population) gave figures of over 8 million for England, Wales half a million, 1.5 million for Scotland and over 5 million for Ireland. But, between 1801 and 1901, the population of England and Wales trebled to 30 million. The numbers in Scotland increased less rapidly, owing to emigration, but in Ireland the population was reduced from 8 to 4 million because of famine, deaths and emigration. The greatest concentrations of people were now in London and industrial areas of the Midlands, south Lancashire, Merseyside, Clydeside, Tyneside, Yorkshire and south Wales.

The industrial revolution reached its height during the early nineteenth century. It did not require foreign labour because there were enough skilled British workers and a ready supply of unskilled labourers from Wales, Scotland, Ireland and the English countryside. Welshmen from north Wales went to the Lancashire textile mills; Highland Scots travelled to the Lowland Clydeside industries; and Irishmen flocked to England and Scotland to work in the manual trades of the industrial infrastructure constructing roads, railways and canals. These migratory movements promoted conflicts but also assimilation.

Industrialization expanded commercial markets, which attracted new immigrants who had the business and financial skills to exploit the industrial wealth. Some newcomers joined City of London financial institutions and the import/export trades, to which they contributed their international

PLATE 2.1 Women at work in a McVitie's food factory (© *Karen Robinson/Format*)

connections. Other settlers were involved in a wide range of occupations and trades. Immigration to Britain might have been greater in the nineteenth century had it not been for the attraction of North America, which was receiving large numbers of newcomers from all over the world, including Britain.

By the end of the nineteenth century, Britain was the world's leading industrial nation and one of the richest. But it gradually lost its world lead in manufacturing industry, most of which was in native British hands. However, its position in international finance, some of which was under immigrant control, was retained into the twentieth century.

Immigration from 1900

Immigrants historically had relatively free access to Britain. But they could be easily expelled; had no legal rights to protect them; and restrictions were increasingly imposed upon them. But the 1871 census showed that the number of people in Britain born outside the British Empire was only 157,000 out of a population of some 31.5 million.

Despite these low figures, immigration and asylum seekers caused public and political concern, which continued through the twentieth century. In the early years of the century, Jews and Poles escaped persecution in Eastern Europe and settled in the East End of London, which has always been an area of immigrant concentration. Demands for immigration control grew and an anti-foreigner feeling spread, fuelled by the nationalism and spy mania caused by the First World War (1914–18). But laws (such as the Aliens Act of 1905), which were designed to curtail foreign entry, proved ineffective. By 1911 the number of people in Britain born outside the empire was 428,000 or 1 per cent of the population.

Despite legal controls, and partly as a result of the 1930s world recession and the Second World War, refugees from Nazi-occupied Europe and immigrants entered Britain. After the war, Poles, Latvians, Ukrainians and other nationalities chose to stay in Britain. Later in the twentieth century, political refugees arrived, such as Hungarians, Czechs, Chileans, Libyans, East African Asians, Iranians, Vietnamese and other Eastern Europeans, in addition to Italian, French, German, Irish, Turkish, Cypriot, Chinese and Spanish economic immigrants. These groups today form sizeable ethnic minorities and are found throughout the country. Such newcomers have often suffered from discrimination, some more than others, since racism is not a new phenomenon in Britain.

But public and political concern then turned to the issues of race and colour, which were to dominate the immigration debate and focused on non-white Commonwealth immigration. Before the Second World War, most Commonwealth immigrants to Britain came from the largely white Old Commonwealth countries of Canada, Australia and New Zealand, and from South Africa. All Commonwealth citizens were allowed free access and were not treated as aliens.

But from the late 1940s, people from the non-white New Commonwealth nations of India, Pakistan and the West Indies came to Britain (sometimes at the invitation of government agencies) to fill the vacant manual and lower-paid jobs of an expanding economy. West Indians worked in public transport, catering, the Health Service and manual trades in London, Birmingham and other large cities. Indians and Pakistanis later arrived to work in the textile and iron industries of Leeds, Bradford and Leicester (which may be the first British city to have a non-white majority population). By the 1970s, non-white people became a familiar sight in other British towns such as Glasgow, Sheffield, Bristol, Huddersfield, Manchester, Liverpool, Coventry and Nottingham. There was a considerable dispersal of such immigrants throughout Britain, although many tended to settle in the central areas of industrial cities.

These non-white communities have now increased and work in a broad range of occupations. Some, particularly Indian Asians and black Africans, have been successful in economic and professional terms. Others have experienced considerable problems such as low-paid jobs, unemployment, educational disadvantage, decaying housing in the inner cities and racial discrimination. It is argued that Britain possesses a deep-rooted (or institutional) racism based on the legacy of empire and notions of racial superiority, which continues to manifest itself and has hindered the integration of the non-white population into the larger society. Many young non-whites who have been born in Britain feel particularly bitter at their experiences and at their relative lack of educational and employment possibilities and advancement.

So many New Commonwealth immigrants were coming to Britain that from 1962 governments treated most Commonwealth newcomers as aliens and followed a two-strand policy on immigration. This consisted, first, of Immigration Acts to restrict the number of immigrants entering the country and, second, of Race Relations Acts to protect the rights of those immigrants already settled in Britain.

Race Relations Acts make it unlawful to discriminate against persons on grounds of racial, ethnic or national origin in areas such as education, housing, employment, services and advertising. Those who suffer alleged discrimination can appeal to Race Relations Tribunals, and anti-discrimination bodies have also been established, culminating with the Commission for Racial Equality in 1976. This body, which is not without its critics, works for the elimination of discrimination and the promotion of equality of opportunity.

There is still criticism of the immigration laws and race-relations organizations. Some people argue that one cannot legislate satisfactorily against discrimination, and others would like stricter controls. The concerns of some white people are made worse by racialist speeches; the growth of extreme nationalist parties such as the National Front and the British National Party; and racially inspired violence. Non-white citizens, on the other hand, often feel that they too easily and unfairly became scapegoats for any problems that arise. Some become alienated from British society and reject institutions such as the police, legal system and political structures. Government policies since the 1940s have not always helped to lessen either white or non-white anxieties.

Immigration and race remain problematic. They are complex matters; are exploited for political purposes from both the right and the left; and can be over-dramatized. Many non-white immigrants and their British-born children have slowly adapted to the larger society, whilst retaining their ethnic identities. Britain does have a relatively stable diversity of cultures and the highest rate of intermarriage and mixed-race relationships in Europe, with one in eight children under five having parents from different ethnic backgrounds. But outbreaks of racial tension, violence and harassment do occur, and there are accusations that the police and the courts ignore or underplay race crimes. A central concern for some people is that race problems are not being openly and fairly debated.

In 1999–2000, 93.3 per cent of Britons were classified as white and 6.7 per cent belonged to non-white groups of whom 46 per cent were born in Britain. Non-whites therefore constitute a relatively small proportion of the total British population and 49 per cent of them live in London (as opposed to 10 per cent of the white population) (Table 2.2).

TABLE 2.2   Non-white ethnic minorities in Britain, 1999–2000

Indian	942,000
Pakistani	671,000
Black Caribbean	504,000
Black African	374,000
Bangladeshi	257,000
Black mixed	184,000
Black other (non-mixed)	124,000
Chinese	133,000
Other Asian (non-mixed)	217,000
Others	427,000
Total non-white ethnic minorities	3,832,000

Source: Labour Force Survey/Office for National Statistics, 2001

The non-white population was earlier largely composed of immigrant families or single people. But this structure has changed as more dependants join settled immigrants, as British-born non-whites develop their own family organizations and as more people intermarry. The term 'immigrant' has now lost some of its earlier significance and the emphasis has switched to debates about what constitutes a 'multi-ethnic society'.

Apart from a few categories of people who have a right of abode in Britain and are not subject to immigration control, all others require either entry clearance or permission to enter and remain. Generally speaking, such newcomers (apart from short-term visitors) need a work permit and a guaranteed job if they hope to stay in the country for longer periods of time. But dependants of immigrants already settled in Britain may be granted the right of entry and permanent settlement.

There are also many other ethnic minority communities in Britain, which are usually classified as white. Immigration from the Republic of Ireland continues; the Irish have historically been a large immigrant group; and there are some 800,000 people of primary Irish descent. Movement from the Old Commonwealth countries (such as Australia, Canada and South Africa) has increased slightly, while that of other Commonwealth citizens has dropped following entry restrictions. There has been an increase in immigrants from European Union countries (such as Germany, Spain, Italy and France), who have the right to seek work and reside in Britain, with sizeable numbers from the USA and Middle East.

There are legal distinctions between immigration (a controlled entry system often based on economic factors) into Britain and political asylum (fleeing from persecution). In 2000, 125,000 immigrants were accepted for permanent settlement (more than in previous years). They came from Africa, the Indian subcontinent, the rest of Asia and non-EU Europe, with many being dependants of settled immigrants. This suggests that a significant immigration continues, despite restrictive legislation.

But the Labour government is evaluating the rules for the admission of asylum seekers following public concern and controversy about the increasing numbers entering Britain and suspicions that many are economic migrants rather than being genuinely in humanitarian need. In 2001, the top six countries from which registered asylum seekers came to Britain were Afghanistan, Iraq, Somalia, Sri Lanka, Turkey and Iran. However, it is estimated that there may be one million illegal asylum seekers and immigrants in Britain. On the other hand, the country's economy is dependent upon immigrant labour to compensate for a declining birth rate and it is argued that immigration and asylum regulations need to be realistically reformed.

Opinion polls for some years had suggested that race relations, immigration and asylum were of less concern for British people than they were from the 1940s to the 1980s. A *MORI* poll in 1995 found that 78 per cent of respondents said that they were not at all prejudiced against people of other races. But a *Guardian* newspaper poll in 2001 said that 70 per cent of its readers thought that race relations were not getting better in Britain. A *MORI* poll in June 2001 reported that actual worries about immigration and race relations have increased from 3 per cent in 1996 to 19 per cent in 2001.

Acceptance for settlement does not mean automatic citizenship. Naturalization occurs only when certain requirements have been fulfilled, together with a period of residence. New conditions for naturalization and redefinitions of British citizenship are contained in the Nationality Act of 1981. This Act has been criticized by some as providing further restrictions on immigration procedures.

However, it is important that emigration from Britain is considered if the immigration/race debate is to be kept in perspective. Historically, there has usually been a balance of migration, with emigration cancelling out immigration in real terms. But there have been periods of high emigration. Groups left England and Scotland in the sixteenth and seventeenth centuries to become settlers and colonists in Ireland and North America. Millions in the nineteenth and twentieth centuries emigrated to New Zealand, Australia, South Africa, Canada, other colonies and the USA. But in 1998, there was a net gain of 181,000 to the population as more people entered the country than left. More entrants were from the Old Commonwealth and the EU than in previous years.

Population movements from 1900

Industrial areas with heavy population densities developed in the nineteenth century. But considerable population shifts occurred in the twentieth century, which were mainly due to economic and employment changes.

There was a drift of people away from industrial Tyneside and South Wales during the 1920s and 1930s trade depressions as coal production, steel manufacture and other heavy industries were badly affected. Since the 1950s there has been little increase in population in industrial areas of the Central Lowlands of Scotland, Tyneside, Merseyside, West Yorkshire, south Wales and Northern Ireland, which have seen a run-down in traditional industries and rises in unemployment. Instead, people moved away from these regions, first to the English Midlands with their diversified industries and then to London and south-east England where employment opportunities (despite fluctuations) and affluence were greater.

The reduction of the rural population and the expansion of urban centres continued into the twentieth century. But, by the middle of the century, there was a movement of people away from the centres of big cities such as London, Manchester, Liverpool, Birmingham and Leeds. This was due to bomb damage during the Second World War, slum clearance and the need to use inner-city land for shops, offices, warehouses and transport utilities. So-called New Towns in rural areas and council housing estates outside the inner cities were specifically created to accommodate the displanted population. Road systems were built with motorways and bypasses to avoid congested areas, and rural locations around some cities were designated as Green Belts, in which no building was permitted.

Many people choose to live some distance from their workplaces, often in a city's suburbs, neighbouring towns (commuter towns) or rural areas. This has contributed to the decline of inner-city populations, and one British person in five now lives in the countryside with the rest in towns and cities. Densities are highest in Greater London and in south-east England and lowest in rural regions of northern Scotland, the Lake District, Wales and Northern Ireland. The latest figures suggest an increasing movement of people to rural areas. This has been accompanied by population losses in and company relocations from large cities, particularly London.

In 1999–2001 the population of the United Kingdom was 59,501,000, which consisted of England with 49,753,000, Wales with 2,937,000, Scotland with 5,119,000 and Northern Ireland with 1,692,000. These figures give a population density for the United Kingdom of some 600 persons per square mile (242 per sq km), well above the European Union average. England has an average density of some 940 persons per sqare mile (381 per sq km) and this average does not reveal the even higher densities in some areas of the country, such as London, the West Midlands, West Yorkshire, Greater Manchester, Merseyside, Tyne and Wear, Edinburgh and Cardiff. Within Europe, only the Netherlands has a higher population density than England.

The British population grew by only 0.3 per cent between 1971 and 1978, which gave it one of the lowest increases in Western Europe. A similarly low growth rate is forecast in the twenty-first century, with the population expected to be 60.4 million by 2011 and 61.8 million by 2021. But the non-white ethnic minorities are growing fifteen times faster than

TABLE 2.3   Populations of major British cities (estimated 2000)

Greater London	7,187,000	Liverpool	461,000
Birmingham	1,013,000	Edinburgh	450,000
Leeds	727,000	Manchester	422,000
Glasgow	619,000	Bristol	402,000
Sheffield	531,000	Cardiff	320,000
Bradford	483,000	Belfast	279,000

the white population and are also much younger. It is estimated that the counties of southern and central England will have the highest population growth up to 2011 and that the heaviest population losses will occur on Tyneside and Merseyside.

Attitudes to national, regional and local identities

Immigration to Britain has often been seen as a threat to British moral, social and cultural values. Yet the British-Irish Isles have always been culturally and ethnically diverse. There are many differences between England, Wales, Scotland and Northern Ireland and distinctive ways of life and identities within each nation at national, regional and local levels. The meaning of contemporary 'Britishness' consequently becomes problematic.

The history of the British-Irish Isles before the eighteenth century is not about a single British identity or political entity. It is about four different nations and their peoples, who have often been hostile towards one another. 'Britishness' since the 1707 union between England/Wales and Scotland has been largely identified with representative and centralized state institutions, such as monarchy, Parliament, law and Protestant churches, and their values. Concepts of Britishness were more widely used in the nineteenth century and tied to the Victorian monarchy and Britain's imperial, industrial and military position in the world. These elements have since weakened relative to Britain's decline.

Terms such as 'British' and 'Britain' can seem artificial to many people in the contemporary UK population, who have retained different cultural and national identities. Foreigners often call all British people 'English' and have difficulties in appreciating the distinctions, or the irritation of the non-English population at such labelling. The Scots, Welsh and Northern Irish are regarded largely as Celtic peoples (with admixtures over centuries), while the English are considered to be mainly Anglo-Saxon in origin. It is argued that the 'British' today do not have a strong sense of a 'British' identity. In this view, there needs to be a rethinking of what it means to be British in the contexts of a multinational, multi-ethnic UK and a changing Europe.

There has obviously been ethnic and cultural assimilation in Britain over the centuries, which resulted from adaptation by immigrant groups and internal migration between the four nations. Social, political and institutional standardization and a British awareness were established. However, the British identification is often equated with English norms because of England's historical role: political unification occurred under the English Crown, UK state power is still mainly concentrated in London, and the English dominate numerically.

English nationalism has historically been the most potent of the four nationalisms, and the English had no real problem with the dual national role. But some now seem to be unsure about their identity in a devolved Britain. The Scots and Welsh are more aware of the difference between their nationalism and Britishness; resent the English dominance; see themselves as different from the English; and regard their cultural feelings as crucial. Their sense of identity is conditioned by the tension between their distinctive histories and a history of centralized government from London.

National identity in the four nations was until recently largely cultural and the British political union was generally accepted, except for some people in the minority Catholic population of Northern Ireland. But political nationalism increased in the 1960s and 1970s in Scotland and Wales. Today, following devolution in 1999–2000, calls for full independence in these two nations are not strong, except from the Scottish National Party (SNP) and (arguably) the Welsh National Party (Plaid Cymru). It has been suggested that Scottish and Welsh devolution may spark a resurgence in English nationalism.

The Welsh, English and Scottish seem increasingly to be defining themselves more in terms of their individual nationalities, rather than as British. A *Sunday Times* poll in 2000 found that schoolchildren clearly saw themselves as English (66 per cent), Scottish (82) or Welsh (79). Some 84 per cent of English children regarded England as their home (rather than Britain) and 75 per cent felt that their nationality was important to them. But there was little interest in the creation of regional English assemblies and little desire for a break-up of the United Kingdom.

However, there are also differences on regional and local levels within the four nations themselves. Some English regions such as the north-east and north-west react against London influences and demand decentralized political autonomy. Since the English are a relatively mixed people, their customs, accents and behaviour vary considerably and some regional identifications are still strong. The Cornish, for example, see themselves as a distinctive cultural element in English society and have an affinity with Celtic and similar ethnic groups in Britain and Europe. The northern English have often regarded themselves as superior to the southern English, and vice versa. On a smaller level, English county and local loyalties (often centred on cities such as Manchester, Liverpool, Newcastle, Birmingham or London) are still maintained and may be shown in sports, politics, food habits, competitions, cultural activities or a specific way of life.

In Wales, there are cultural and political differences between the industrial south (which supports the Labour Party) and the rest of the mainly rural country; between Welsh-speaking Wales in the north-west and centre (which supports Plaid Cymru) and English-influenced Wales in the

PLATE 2.2   A Scottish fling (*The Hutchison Library*)

east and south-west (where the Conservative Party has some support); and between the cities of Cardiff and Swansea.

Yet Welsh people generally are very conscious of their differences from the English, despite the fact that many Welsh people have mixed English-Welsh ancestry. Their national and cultural identity is grounded in their history; literature; the Welsh language (actively spoken by 19 per cent of the population); sport (such as rugby football); and festivals such as the National Eisteddfod (with its Welsh poetry competitions, dancing and music). It is also echoed in close-knit industrial and agricultural communities and in a tradition of social, political and religious dissent from English norms. Today, many Welsh people feel that they are struggling for their national identity against political power in London and the erosion of their culture and language by English institutions. A limited form of devolution has helped to alleviate these feelings and increase Welsh identity.

Similarly, Scots generally unite in defence of their national identity and distinctiveness because of historical reactions to the English. They are conscious of their traditions, which are reflected in cultural festivals and different legal, religious and educational systems. There has been resentment against the centralization of political power in London and alleged economic neglect of Scotland (although the UK government provides greater economic subsidies per head of population to Scotland, Wales and Northern Ireland than to England). Devolved government in Edinburgh has removed some of these objections and focused on Scottish identity.

But Scots are divided by three languages (Gaelic, Scots and English, the first of these being spoken by 1.5 per cent of the Scottish population or 70,000 people), different religions, prejudices and regionalisms. Cultural differences separate Lowlanders and Highlanders and deep rivalries exist between the two major cities of Edinburgh and Glasgow.

In Northern Ireland, the social, cultural and political differences between Roman Catholics and Protestants have long been evident and today are often reflected in geographical ghettos. Groups in both communities feel frustration with the English and hostility towards the British government in London. But the Protestant Unionists are loyal to the Crown; regard themselves as British; and wish to continue the union with Britain. Many Catholic Nationalists feel Irish and would prefer to be united with the Republic of Ireland. Devolution in Northern Ireland has not succeeded in eradicating deep-seated differences between the two communities.

These features suggest that the contemporary British are a very diverse people with varying identities. It is as difficult to find an English, Welsh, Scottish or Irish person who conforms to all or even some of their assumed national stereotypes as it is to find a typical Briton. Within Britain, ethnic minorities (both white and non-white) may use dual or multiple identities

PLATE 2.3   Notting Hill Carnival, a popular annual event in London
(© *Jenny Matthews/Format*)

and embrace different loyalties. Many call themselves British or more specifically English, Welsh, Irish or Scottish, while still identifying with their countries of origin or descent. Sometimes they employ their ethnic ties to define themselves as Afro-Caribbean, Black British or British Asians. They may also embrace identities which relate to their religion, for example British Muslims or Hindus and British Jews. But a *Sunday Times* survey in November 2001 suggested that 68 per cent of Muslims considered that being Muslim was more important than being British (14 per cent thought the opposite).

Foreigners often have either specific notions of what they think the British are like or, in desperation, seek a unified picture of national character, based sometimes upon stereotypes, quaint traditions or tourist views of Britain. The emphasis in this search should perhaps be more upon an examination of ethnic diversity or pluralism in British life. A *British Council/MORI* poll in 1999 found that overseas respondents felt that Britain is a multicultural society though opinion was divided as to whether or not it is also racially tolerant. It found that the countries that are least willing to believe that UK society is racially tolerant are those that are least aware of its multicultural composition.

But 'multiculturalism' is a strongly debated issue in Britain. Some critics favour the separate development of cultural groups and the preservation of their ethnic identities. Others argue for assimilation. The latter implies an acceptance of basic common values, including those represented by civic social and political structures, which have primacy over individual cultural identities.

These concerns are central to attempts to define 'Britishness'. Surveys (such as the Springpoint *I? UK – Voices of Our Times*, 1999) suggest there is a popular movement away from the allegedly negative, imperial and English-dominated historical implications of Britishness to a more positive, value-based, inclusive image with which the four nations and their populations can feel comfortable. A Britishness which encompasses opportunity, respect, tolerance, supportiveness, progress and decency is supposed to be attractive to the Celtic nations and ethnic minorities. But these values have to be realized within defining institutional structures.

 Exercises

Explain and examine the following terms:

nomads	bypass	Anglo-Saxon	industrialization
Neolithic	East End	Hansa	National Front
density	Celtic	devolution	Hastings
Merseyside	*Domesday Book*	immigrant	naturalization
racism	Britishness	Iberian	discrimination
census	emigration	Huguenots	Green Belt

Write short essays on the following topics:

1   Describe in outline the history of settlement and immigration in Britain.
2   Examine the changing patterns of population distribution in Britain.
3   Is it correct to describe contemporary Britain as a 'multi-ethnic' and 'multinational' society? If so, why?

 Further reading

Alibhai-Brown, Y. (2001) *Who Do We Think We Are? Imagining the New Britain* London: Allen Lane

Davies, N. (2000) *The Isles: A History* London: Macmillan

Donnell, A. (2001) *Companion to Contemporary Black British Culture* London: Routledge

Grant, A. and Stringer, K.J. (eds) (1995) *Uniting the Kingdom? – The Making of British History* London: Routledge

Harvie, C. (1998) *Scotland and Nationalism: Scottish Society and Politics, 1707 to the Present* London: Routledge

McKay, S. (2000) *Northern Protestants: An Unsettled People* Belfast: Blackstaff Press

Nairn, T. (2000) *After Britain* London: Granta Books

O'Connor, F. (1993) *In Search of a State: Catholics in Northern Ireland* Belfast: Blackstaff Press

Owusa, K. (1999) *Black British Culture and Society* London: Routledge

Paxman, J. (2000) *The English: A Portrait of a People* London: Penguin Books

Phillips, M. and Phillips, T. (1999) *Windrush: The Irresistible Rise of Multi-racial Britain* London: HarperCollins

Solomos, J. (2001) *Race and Racism in Britain* London: Macmillan

Storry, M. and Childs, P. (eds) (1997) *British Cultural Identities* London: Routledge

Websites

Campaign for the English Regions: http://www.cfer.org.uk

Devolution: http://www.britishcouncil.org/devolution/index.htm

Looking into England: www.britishcouncil.org/studies/english

British Studies Now: www.britishcouncil.org/studies/bsn.htm

Scotland Office: www.scottishsecretary.gov.uk

Wales Office: www.wales.gov.uk

Northern Ireland Office: www.nio.gov.uk

Chapter 3

Politics and government

POLITICAL HISTORY IN THE BRITISH-IRISH Isles over the past eight hundred years illustrates the developing identity of the British state and evolutionary changes in its composition. The slow weakening of non-democratic monarchical and aristocratic power led to political and legislative authority being transferred to UK parliamentary structures, a central UK government and a powerful Prime Minister. Changing social conditions resulted in a growth of political parties, the extension of the vote to all adults, the development of local government, and a twentieth-century devolution (transfer) of some political power to Wales, Scotland and Northern Ireland. These historical processes have been accompanied by political, social and religious conflicts and constitutional compromise.

Political structures are still vigorously debated. The UK government in London is accused of being too secretive, too centralized and insufficiently responsive to the needs of the diverse peoples of the United Kingdom. It is argued that the UK Parliament has lost control over the UK government; that political power has shifted to a presidential Prime Minister and unelected bodies and advisers; that there are serious weaknesses at devolved and local levels; and that the British political system must be reformed in order to make it more efficient, accountable and adaptable to modern requirements.

However, a 1999 *British Council/MORI* poll of overseas countries reported that 65 per cent of respondents felt that Britain is a good model of democratic government. But younger people had confused and uncertain views. Respect for long traditions was mixed with more negative images such as the monarchy, judges in wigs and lords in ermine, which they felt were out of keeping with a modern democracy.

Political history

Early political history in the British-Irish Isles is the story of four geographical areas (now England, Wales, Scotland and Ireland) and their turbulent struggles for independent nationhood. But an English political and military expansionism over the centuries conditioned the development of the other three nations. Ireland was controlled by England from the twelfth century;

England and Wales were united by the 1536–42 Acts of Union; the thrones of England and Scotland were dynastically amalgamated in 1603; England/Wales and Scotland were united by the 1707 Acts of Union; and the 1801 Act of Union joined Great Britain and Ireland as the United Kingdom. In this process, English governmental systems were adopted in the modern period for all of Britain. Scotland, the Republic of Ireland, Wales and Northern Ireland regained some of their former political identities only in the twentieth century.

Decline of monarchy and the rise of Parliament

Early monarchs or political leaders in the four nations had considerable power, but generally accepted advice and feudal limitations on their authority. However, later English kings, such as King John (1199–1216), ignored these restraints and powerful French-Norman barons opposed John's dictatorial rule by forcing him to sign Magna Carta in 1215. This document protected the aristocracy rather than the ordinary citizen. It was later regarded as a cornerstone of British (not merely English) liberties; restricted the monarch's powers; forced him to take advice; increased aristocratic influence; and stipulated that citizens should have fair trials.

Such inroads into royal power encouraged embryonic parliamentary structures. An English Council was formed in 1258 by disaffected nobles under Simon de Montfort, who in 1264 summoned a broader Parliament. These aristocratic, elected and part-time initiatives were followed in 1275 by the Model Parliament of Edward I (1272–1307), which was the first representative English Parliament. Its two Houses (as now) consisted of the Lords/Bishops and the Commons (male commoners). An independent Scottish Parliament was first created in 1326 and Ireland had a similarly old Parliament, dating from medieval times.

However, the English Parliament was too large to rule the country effectively. A small Privy Council (royal government outside Parliament), comprising the monarch and court advisers, developed. It continued as a powerful influence until it lost authority to increasingly strong parliamentary structures in the late eighteenth and early nineteenth centuries.

But, although the English Parliament had limited powers against the monarch, there was a return to royal dominance in Tudor England (1485–1603). The nobility had been weakened by wars and internal conflicts (such as the Wars of the Roses between Yorkists and Lancastrians). Monarchs controlled Parliament and summoned it only when they needed to raise money. Tudor monarchs (of Welsh ancestry) united England and Wales administratively, politically and legally in the sixteenth century. They also intervened forcefully in Ireland, with frequent campaigns against Irish insurgents.

Following the Tudors, James VI of Scotland become James I of England in 1603, formed a Stuart dynasty and considered himself to be king of Great Britain. But the two countries were not closely joined politically or culturally. However, the English Parliament now showed more resistance to royal rule by using its weapon of financial control. It refused royal requests for money and later forced the Stuart Charles I to sign the Petition of Rights in 1628, which prevented him from raising taxes without Parliament's consent. Charles ignored these political developments and then failed in his attempt to arrest parliamentary leaders in the House of Commons. The monarch was in future banned from the Commons.

Charles's rejection of parliamentary ideals and belief in his right to rule without opposition provoked anger against the Crown, and a Civil War broke out in 1642. The Protestant Parliamentarians under Oliver Cromwell won the military struggle against the Catholic Royalists. Charles was beheaded in 1649; the monarchy was abolished; Britain was ruled as a Protectorate by Cromwell and his son Richard (1653–60); and Parliament comprised only the House of Commons. Cromwell also asserted the Protestant and parliamentary cause in Scotland and Ireland, which provoked lasting hatred in these countries.

Cromwell's Protectorate was unpopular and most people wanted the restoration of the monarchy. The two Houses of Parliament were re-established and in 1660 they restored the Stuart Charles II to the throne. Initially Charles co-operated with Parliament, but his financial needs, belief in royal authority and support of Catholicism lost him popular and parliamentary backing. Parliament ended his expensive wars and imposed further reforms.

The growth of political parties and constitutional structures

The growing power of the English Parliament against the monarch in the seventeenth century saw the development of more organized political parties in Parliament. These derived partly from the religious and ideological conflicts of the Civil War. Two groups (Whigs and Tories) became dominant. This is a characteristic feature of British two-party politics, in which political power generally shifts between two main parties. The Whigs were mainly Cromwellian Protestants and gentry, who did not accept the Catholic James II as successor to Charles II and wanted religious freedom for all Protestants. The Tories generally supported royalist beliefs, and helped Charles II to secure James's right to succeed him.

But James's attempt to rule without Parliament and his ignoring of its laws caused a further reduction in royal influence. His manipulations forced the Tories to join the Whigs in inviting the Dutch Protestant William of Orange to intervene. William arrived in England in 1688, James fled to

France and William succeeded to the throne as England's first constitutional monarch. Since no force was involved, this event is called the Bloodless or Glorious Revolution. Royal powers were further restricted under the Declaration of Rights (1689), which strengthened Parliament. Future monarchs could not reign or act without Parliament's consent and the Act of Settlement (1701) gave religious freedom to all Protestants.

The Glorious Revolution affected the constitution and politics. It created a division of powers between an executive branch (the monarch and Privy Council); a parliamentary legislative branch (the House of Commons, the House of Lords and the monarch); and the judiciary (judges independent of monarch and Parliament). Acts of Union joining England/ Wales and Scotland followed in 1707, Scotland lost its Parliament and power was now centralized in the London Parliament.

Parliamentary influence grew in the early eighteenth century, because the Hanoverian George I lacked interest in British politics. He distrusted the Tories with their Catholic sympathies and appointed Whigs such as Robert Walpole to his Privy Council. Walpole became Chief Minister in 1721 and led the Whig majority in the House of Commons, which comprised land and property owners. Walpole increased the parliamentary role and he has been called Britain's first Prime Minister.

But parliamentary authority was not absolute and later monarchs tried to restore royal power. However, George III lost much of his standing after the loss of the American colonies (1775–83). He was obliged to appoint William Pitt the Younger as his Tory Chief Minister and it was under Pitt that the office of Prime Minister really developed. Meanwhile, Ireland's Parliament achieved legislative independence in 1782. But it represented only the privileged Anglo-Irish minority and the Roman Catholic majority was excluded.

The expansion of voting rights

Although parliamentary control continued to grow in the late eighteenth and early nineteenth centuries, there was still no widespread democracy in Britain. Political authority was in the hands of landowners, merchants and aristocrats in Parliament, and most people did not possess the vote. Bribery and corruption were common, with the buying of those votes which did exist and the giving away or sale of public offices.

The Tories were against electoral reform, as were the Whigs initially. But the country was rapidly increasing its population and developing industrially and economically. Pressures for political reform became irresistible. The Whigs extended voting rights to the expanding middle class in the First Reform Act of 1832 and later the franchise was given to men with property and a certain income. However, the majority of the working class had no votes and were unrepresented in Parliament. All males over twenty-one received the vote only in 1918.

Women over twenty-one had to wait until 1928 for the franchise to be fully established in Britain. Previously, only women over thirty had achieved some political rights and for centuries wives and their property had been the legal possessions of their husbands. The traditional role of women of all classes had been confined to that of mother in the home, although some found employment in home industries and factories or as domestic servants, teachers and governesses.

Women's social and political position became marginally better towards the end of the nineteenth century. Elementary education was established and a few institutions of higher education began to admit women in restricted numbers. Some women's organizations had been founded in the mid nineteenth century to press for greater political, employment and social rights. But the most famous suffragette movement was that of the Pankhursts in 1903. Their Women's Social and Political Union campaigned for the women's vote and an increased female role in society. However, it is argued that a substantial change in women's status in the mid twentieth century occurred largely because of a recognition of the essential work that they performed during two World Wars.

The growth of governmental structures

In 1801, Ireland was united with Great Britain by the Act of Union to form the UK. The Irish Parliament was abolished and Irish members sat in both Houses of the London Parliament.

The elements of modern British government developed somewhat haphazardly in the eighteenth and nineteenth centuries. Government ministers were generally members of the House of Commons; became responsible to the Commons rather than the monarch; shared a collective responsibility for the policies and acts of government; and had an individual responsibility to Parliament for their own ministries. The prime ministership developed from the monarch's Chief Minister to 'first among equals' and finally the leadership of all ministers. The central force of government became the parliamentary Cabinet of senior ministers, which grew out of the Privy Council. The government was formed from the majority party in the House of Commons. The largest minority party became the Official Opposition, which attempted through its policies to become the next government chosen by the people.

Historically, the elected House of Commons gained political power from the unelected monarch and House of Lords and become the main element in Parliament. Subsequent reforms of the Lords (the Parliament Acts of 1911 and 1949) removed their political authority. Later Acts created non-hereditary titles (life peers), in addition to the existing hereditary peerages. The House lost most of its hereditary members in 2000, has only delaying and amending power over parliamentary legislation and cannot interfere with financial bills.

The nineteenth century also saw the growth of more organized political parties. These were conditioned by changing social and economic factors and reflected the modern struggle between opposing ideologies. The Tories became known as the Conservatives around 1830. They believed in established values and the preservation of traditions; supported business and commerce; had strong links with the Church of England and the professions; and were opposed to radical ideas.

The Whigs, however, were becoming a progressive force and wanted social reform and economic freedom without government restrictions. They developed into the Liberal Party, which promoted enlightened policies in the late nineteenth and early twentieth centuries. But the party declined after 1918. Following an alliance with the now-defunct Social Democratic Party in the 1980s, it merged and became the Liberal Democrats. It is the third-largest party in UK politics but lacks substantial representation in the House of Commons.

The Labour Party, created in its present form in 1906, became the main opposition party to the Conservatives and continued the traditional two-party system in British politics. It was supported by the trade unions, the working class and some middle-class voters. The first Labour government was formed in 1924 under Ramsey MacDonald. But it achieved majority power only in 1945 under Clement Attlee, when it embarked on radical programmes of social and economic reform, which laid the foundations for a welfare state.

The political framework

Contemporary politics operate on UK, devolved and local government levels (see figure 3.1). The UK Parliament and government in London organize the UK as a whole. A Parliament in Scotland, Assemblies in Wales and Northern Ireland and a London Authority have varying degrees of devolved self-government. Local government throughout Britain organizes society at local level.

Local government

Britain has had a local government system in one form or another for centuries. It began with the Anglo-Saxon division of England into large counties and small parishes, which were organized by the monarch's local representatives.

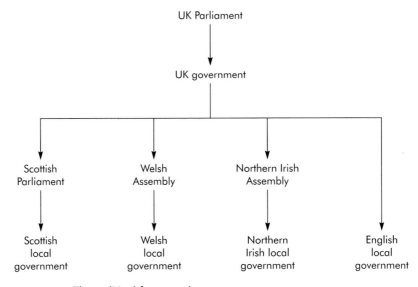

FIGURE 3.1 The political framework

Local government has grown through the centuries, particularly in the nineteenth century. It now provides local services throughout the UK, such as education, health, fire services, transport, social services, sanitation and housing, through elected councils. In England, it is administered through an elected non-professional two-tier system of county and district councils, with some single-tier (unitary) authorities, as well as by professional staff. Scotland and Wales have 29 and 22 unitary authorities respectively, while Northern Ireland has 26 district councils.

But although people count on the services of local government, the system at present is languishing, is subjected to centralized control and funding and no longer provides the full range of traditional local services. Interest in local government is low and a *MORI* poll in August 2000 suggested that dissatisfaction with local councils has increased.

Since July 2000 London has been run by a Greater London Authority with its elected Mayor and Assembly. It was hoped that similar mayors would be elected in other British cities, in an attempt to increase devolved powers.

Devolution

Devolution (self-government or transfer of some powers from the Westminster Parliament) was first adapted in Ireland. Growing nationalist feelings in the nineteenth century led to calls for Home Rule for Ireland with its own Parliament in Dublin. But early attempts failed. Hostilities

PLATE 3.1   Ken Livingstone, Mayor of London (© *Popperfoto/Reuters*)

continued in the twentieth century until Ireland was partitioned in 1921–22 into the Irish Free State (later the Republic of Ireland), with its own Parliament, and Northern Ireland. The latter had a devolved Parliament (1921–72), but remained part of the UK.

Political nationalism also grew in Wales and Scotland from the 1960s. After failed attempts to give them devolved political power, the Labour government created in 1999–2000 (after referendums) an elected Parliament with legislative and tax-varying powers in Scotland and an elected non-legislative, non-tax-raising elected Assembly in Wales. Northern Ireland achieved an elected Assembly in 2000, which has legislative and executive authority, except for reserved UK powers over policing, security matters, prisons and criminal justice.

Devolution provides a tier of decentralized government. It allows these countries (with their Executives and First Ministers) to decide more of their own affairs, such as education, health, transport, environment, home affairs and local government. The Westminster Parliament still has reserved powers over UK matters such as defence, foreign affairs, Social Security, taxation, broad economic policy and immigration. Roles and procedures (except sometimes for elections) in local and devolved structures are generally similar to those at the UK level.

The Welsh Assembly in practice lacks extensive powers, the London Parliament provides its primary legislation and it had initial political problems. The Northern Irish Assembly was suspended in 2000 and 2001 because of the failure of the IRA to disarm, although partial disarmament

PLATE 3.2   The Scottish Parliament, Edinburgh (© *Popperfoto/Reuters*)

has now been achieved (2001) and the Assembly is functioning. The Scottish Parliament initially attracted criticism, being seen as parochial, ineffective and controlled by London, although it is now becoming more independent. Devolution has had a shaky start. It still needs to settle down and justify its existence. Some critics argue that the devolved structures are inadequate and that the Labour government has not thought through the implications of its devolution policies, particularly in terms of the anomalous position of England.

England has no intermediate tier. It has a network of Regional Development Agencies (RDAs) which implement UK government politico-economic programmes in the regions. But these areas do not provide devolved government, although they may form the basis for a future regional devolution of power from Westminster, analogous to the devolved structures in Scotland, Wales and Northern Ireland. Alternatively, England could have its own Parliament.

Devolution does not mean independence for Scotland, Wales and Northern Ireland nor a British federal system, although it is argued that a form of 'quasi-federalism' has been created. The Labour government says that devolution will strengthen the UK and that legal sovereignty still rests with the UK Parliament at Westminster. In this sense, Britain has a unitary political system and remains a union of the United Kingdom (England, Scotland, Wales and Northern Ireland).

Some fear that devolution may lead to independence for Scotland and Wales. A *National Opinion Poll* in 1997 found that 43 per cent of respondents believed that devolution would lead to the break-up of the UK.

But *British Social Attitudes* (2000–01) reported that, while some English thought of themselves as strongly British, many have become more aware of being English rather than British in response to devolution. However, devolution is not viewed as a threat to the Union and the English have adapted to the new *status quo*.

Constitution and monarchy

The constitution

The constitutional system has experienced relatively few upheavals since 1688, despite devolution. Rather, existing principles have been pragmatically adapted to new conditions.

Britain is described either as a constitutional monarchy (with the monarch as head of state) or as a parliamentary system, which is divided into legislative, executive and judicial branches. The Westminster Parliament possesses supreme legislative power in UK matters. The executive UK government governs by passing its policies (many of which are applicable to most of Britain) through Parliament as Acts of Parliament and operates through ministries or departments headed by Ministers or Secretaries of State. The judiciary is independent of the legislative and executive branches of government. The judges of the higher courts determine the law and interpret Acts of Parliament and European Union law.

These branches of the governmental system, although distinguishable from each other, are not entirely separate. For example, the monarch is formally head of the executive, the legislature and the judiciary. A Member of Parliament (MP) in the House of Commons and a peer of the House of Lords may both be in the government of the day. A Law Lord in the House of Lords also serves that House as the highest appeal court.

Britain has no written constitution contained in any one document. Instead, the constitution consists of statute law (Acts of Parliament); common law or judge-made law; conventions (principles and practices of government which are not legally binding but have the force of law): some ancient documents such as Magna Carta; and the new addition of European Union law.

These constitutional elements are said to be flexible enough to respond quickly to new conditions. UK law and institutions can be created or changed by the Westminster Parliament through Acts of Parliament. The common or judge-made law can be extended by the judiciary and conventions can be altered, formed or abolished by general agreement.

In constitutional theory, the British people, although subjects of the Crown, have political sovereignty to choose the UK government, while

Parliament, consisting partly of elected representatives in the Commons, has legal supremacy to make laws and is the focus of UK sovereignty.

But challenges to traditional notions of parliamentary sovereignty have arisen, and the Westminster Parliament is no longer the sole legislative body in Britain. British membership of the European Union (1973) means that EU law is now superior to British national law in certain areas and British courts must give it precedence in cases of conflict between the two systems. EU law coexists with Acts of Parliament as part of the British constitution.

Since devolution, Parliament can still legislate for the UK as a whole and for any parts of it separately. But it has undertaken not to legislate on devolved matters without the agreement of the devolved Parliament and Assemblies. The Scottish Parliament has power to legislate for devolved matters in Scotland in which Westminster has no say. Any conflicts between the two Parliaments will be resolved by the Judicial Committee of the Privy Council. The Welsh Assembly has no primary legislative powers, although the Northern Irish Assembly can legislate in devolved matters. Ultimately, however, the UK Parliament still has the legal right to abolish the Scottish Parliament, the Welsh and Northern Irish Assemblies and to withdraw from the EU.

Criticisms of the constitutional system

The British system has been admired in the past. It combined stability and adaptability with a balance of authority and toleration. But it has often been criticized. UK governments have become more radical in their policies and are able to implement them because of big majorities in the Commons. This means that there are few effective parliamentary restraints upon a strong government. There has also been concern at the absence of constitutional safeguards for citizens against state power, since historically there have been few legal definitions of civil liberties in Britain.

These features are seen as potentially dangerous, particularly when UK governments and administrative bodies are arguably too centralized and secretive. It is argued that Britain is ruled by small (often unelected) groups at the heart of government. There have been campaigns for more open government and more effective protection of individual liberties in the forms of a written constitution (to define and limit the powers of Parliament and government); greater judicial scrutiny of parliamentary legislation; a Freedom of Information Act (to allow the public to examine official documents held by Whitehall departments, local councils, the National Health Service and schools and universities); and the incorporation of the European Convention on Human Rights into domestic law (allowing British citizens to pursue cases in Britain rather than having to go through the European Court of Human Rights).

The Labour government created a Freedom of Information Act in 2000 (which is criticized as lacking teeth) and has incorporated the European Convention into British law by the creation of a Human Rights Act, 1998. Both developments could improve the civil and constitutional rights of British people.

The Human Rights Act is already having a controversial effect on many levels. It allows the courts to rule in cases of alleged breaches of fundamental human rights which are brought to them. While they cannot directly overrule an Act of Parliament they can declare that such an Act is in breach of the Human Rights legislation. In effect, this could force a government to change its legislation and is seen as an encroachment upon parliamentary sovereignty. The implications of the Human Rights Act have yet to be fully worked out.

A *MORI* poll in 1997 revealed that 50 per cent of respondents thought that the British governmental system is out of date and 79 per cent said that a written constitution was needed. A *MORI* poll in 2000 reported that only 45 per cent of respondents were satisfied with the British constitution. Critics claim that the UK political system no longer works satisfactorily. They maintain that it is still too centralized and its traditional bases are inadequate for the organization of a complex society. It is felt that political policies have become too conditioned by party politics at the expense of consensus; that government is too removed from popular and regional concerns and does not reflect contemporary diversity; and that national programmes lack a democratic and representative basis. However, changes have been made to the apparatus, such as devolution and the Human Rights Act, indicating that evolutionary principles may be successfully adapted to new demands and conditions.

The monarchy

The constitutional title of the UK Parliament is the 'Queen-in-Parliament'. This means that state and government business is carried out in the name of the monarch by the politicians and officials of the system. But the Crown is only sovereign by the will of Parliament and acceptance by the people.

The monarchy is the oldest secular institution in Britain and there is hereditary succession to the throne, but only for Protestants. The eldest son of a monarch currently has priority over older daughters. The monarchy's continuity has been interrupted only by Cromwellian rule (1653–60), although there have been different lines of descent such as the Tudors, Stuarts and Hanoverians.

Royal executive power has disappeared. But the monarch still has formal constitutional roles and is head of state, head of the executive, judiciary and legislature, 'supreme governor' of the Church of England and commander-in-chief of the armed forces. Government ministers and officials are the monarch's servants, and many public office-holders swear allegiance to the Crown. The monarchy is thus a permanent fixture in the British system, unlike temporary politicians. It still has a practical and constitutional role to play in the operation of government.

The monarch is expected to be politically neutral; is supposed to reign but not rule; and cannot make laws, impose taxes, spend public money or act unilaterally. The monarch acts only on the advice of political ministers, which cannot be ignored, and contemporary Britain is therefore governed by Her Majesty's Government in the name of the Queen.

The monarch performs important duties such as the opening and dissolving of Parliament; giving the Royal Assent (or signature) to bills which have been passed by both Houses of Parliament; appointing government ministers and public figures; granting honours; leading proceedings of the Privy Council; and fulfilling international duties as head of state.

A central power still possessed by the monarch is the choice and appointment of the UK Prime Minister. By convention, this person is normally the leader of the political party which has a majority in the Commons. However, if there is no clear majority or if the political situation is unclear, the monarch could in theory make a free choice. In practice, advice is given by royal advisers and leading politicians in order to present an acceptable candidate.

The monarch has a right to be informed of all aspects of national life by receiving government documents and meeting regularly with the Prime Minister. The monarch also has the right to encourage, warn and advise ministers. The impact of royal advice on formal and informal levels could be significant and raises questions about whether such influence should be held by an unelected figure who could potentially either support or undermine political leaders.

Much of the cost of the royal family's official duties is met from the Civil List (public funds which are approved by Parliament). Following concern over expense, the Civil List has now been reduced to a few members of the immediate royal family. Other costs incurred by the monarch as a private individual or as sovereign come either from the Privy Purse (finance received from the revenues of some royal estates) or from the Crown's own investments, which are very considerable and on which the monarch now pays income tax.

Critics of the monarchy argue that it lacks adaptability, is out-of-date, non-democratic, expensive, associated with aristocratic privilege and establishment thinking and reflects an English rather than a British identity. It is argued that the monarchy's distance from ordinary life sustains class divisions and hierarchy in society. It is also suggested that, if the monarch's functions today are merely ceremonial and lack power, it would be more rational to abolish the office and replace it with a cheaper non-executive presidency.

Critics who favour the monarchy argue that it is popular, has adapted to modern requirements and is a symbol of national unity. It is a personification of the state; shows stability and continuity; has more prestige than politicians; is not subject to political manipulations; plays a worthwhile role in national institutions; is neutral; performs ambassadorial functions; and promotes the interests of Britain abroad.

But the monarchy in recent years has attracted much criticism. However, while an *ICM* poll in August 1997 showed that its support had fallen to 48 per cent, a *MORI* poll in April 2001 reported that 70 per cent of respondents favoured Britain remaining a monarchy, with 19 per cent preferring a republic. 65 per cent thought that the monarchy should be modernized to reflect changes in British life.

Traditionalists fear that a modernized monarchy would lose that aura of detachment which is described as its main strength. It would then be associated with change rather than the preservation of existing values. At present, it balances uncomfortably between tradition and modernizing trends.

The Privy Council

The ancient Privy Council is still constitutionally tied to the monarchy. Historically, it developed from a small group of royal advisers into the executive branch of the monarch's government. But its powerful position declined in the eighteenth and nineteenth centuries as its functions were transferred to a parliamentary Cabinet and new ministries. Today, its members (such as cabinet ministers) advise the monarch on government business which does not need to pass through Parliament and may serve on influential committees.

There are about four hundred Privy Councillors, but the body works mostly through small groups. A full council is summoned only on the death of a monarch and the accession of a new one or when there are constitutional issues at stake. Should the monarch be indisposed, counsellors of state or a regent would work through the Privy Council.

Apart from its practical duties and its role as a constitutional forum, the most important tasks of the Privy Council today are performed by its Judicial Committee. This is the final court of appeal from some Commonwealth countries and dependencies. It may be used by some bodies in Britain and overseas and its rulings can be influential. It also rules on any conflicts between Westminster and the Scottish Parliament.

UK Parliament: role, legislation and elections

Role

The UK Parliament is housed in the Palace of Westminster in London. It comprises the non-elected House of Lords, the elected House of Commons and the monarch. The two Houses contain members from England, Wales, Scotland and Northern Ireland and represent people with varied backgrounds and traditions. Parliament gathers as a unified body only on ceremonial occasions, such as the State Opening of Parliament by the monarch in the House of Lords. Here it listens to the monarch's speech from the throne, which outlines the UK government's forthcoming legislative programme.

In constitutional theory, Parliament has legal sovereignty in all matters and can create, abolish or amend laws and institutions for all or any part(s) of Britain. In practice, this means the implementation of the government's policies. All three parts of Parliament must normally pass a bill before it can become an Act of Parliament and law. Parliament also votes money to government; examines government policies and administration; scrutinizes European Union legislation; and debates political issues.

Parliament is supposed to legislate according to the rule of law, precedent and tradition. Politicians are generally sensitive to these conventions and to public opinion. Formal and informal checks and balances, such as party discipline, the Official Opposition, public reaction and pressure groups, normally ensure that Parliament legislates according to its legal responsibility. While critics argue that Parliament's programmes may not reflect the will of the people, a *MORI* poll in 2000 showed that satisfaction with the way Parliament works had (perhaps surprisingly) increased to 43 per cent with dissatisfaction at 29 per cent.

A Parliament has a maximum duration of five years, except in emergency situations. But it is often dissolved earlier and a general election called. A dissolution of Parliament and the issue of writs for the election are ordered by the monarch on the advice of the Prime Minister. If an MP dies, resigns or is given a peerage, a by-election is called only for that member's seat, and Parliament as a whole is not dissolved.

The *House of Lords* consists of Lords Temporal and Lords Spiritual. Lords Spiritual are the Archbishops of York and Canterbury and 24 senior bishops of the Church of England. Lords Temporal comprise (1) some 92 peers and peeresses with hereditary titles elected by their fellows; (2) about 577 life peers and peeresses, who have been selected by political parties and an independent Appointments Commission; and (3) the Lords of Appeal (Law Lords). The latter serve the House of Lords as the ultimate

PLATE 3.3
Houses of Parliament
(*Maggie Murray/
Format*)

court of appeal for many purposes from most parts of Britain. This court does not consist of the whole House, but only of nine Law Lords who have held senior judicial office under the chairmanship of the Lord Chancellor.

Daily attendance varies from a handful to a few hundred. Peers receive no salary for parliamentary work, but may claim attendance and travelling expenses. The House collectively controls its own procedure, but is often guided by the Lord Chancellor, who is a political appointee of the government and who sits on the Woolsack (or stuffed woollen sofa).

There have long been demands that the unrepresentative, unelected House of Lords should be replaced. The problem lies in deciding on an alternative model. A wholly elected second chamber could threaten the powers of the House of Commons and result in conflict between the two. An appointed House could consist of unelected members chosen by political parties or an independent Appointments Commission. As a first step, the Labour government abolished the sitting and voting rights of hereditary peers, except for 92 of them. The life peers continue to be in

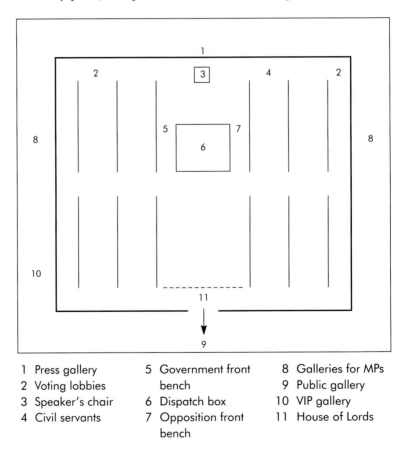

1	Press gallery	5	Government front bench	8	Galleries for MPs
2	Voting lobbies	6	Dispatch box	9	Public gallery
3	Speaker's chair	7	Opposition front bench	10	VIP gallery
4	Civil servants			11	House of Lords

FIGURE 3.2   The House of Commons

actual practice appointed by the present independent Appointments Commission. It is likely that a future House of 750 members will be mainly appointed together with a small number (120) of elected members, no hereditary peers and a reduction (to 16) of Lords Spiritual.

The House of Lords does its job well as an experienced and less partisan forum than the House of Commons and also takes on a legislative and administrative burden. It has an amending function, which may be used to delay government legislation for up to one year (three months in future) or to persuade governments to have a second look at bills. It is a safeguard against over-hasty legislation by the Commons and is an antidote to powerful governments. This is possible because the Lords are more independently minded than MPs in the Commons and do not suffer rigid party discipline. The House is now more evenly divided in terms of party affilliation. But it has a number of crossbenchers (or Independents sitting across the back of the chamber) who do not belong to any political party. A *MORI* poll in 2000 showed that opinions about the Lords have hardly changed, with 32 per cent of respondents being satisfied and 29 per cent dissatisfied.

The *House of Commons* comprises 659 Members of Parliament (MPs). They are elected by voters (from age eighteen) and represent citizens in Parliament. In 2001, 118 of them were women. But women face problems in being selected as parliamentary candidates and winning seats in the Commons. There are 529 parliamentary seats for England, 40 for Wales, 72 for Scotland and 18 for Northern Ireland. MPs are paid expenses and a salary, which is relatively low for comparable jobs.

Legislation and procedure

Parliamentary procedure in both Houses of Parliament is based on custom, convention, precedent and detailed rules (standing orders). The House of Commons meets most weekday afternoons (outside lengthy vacations), although business can continue beyond midnight. Many MPs then spend the weekend in their constituencies attending to business. They may also follow their professions (such as lawyers) on a part-time basis. The organization and procedures of the Commons have been criticized. It is felt that the number of hours spent in the House should be reduced and that pay and resources should be improved. Women MPs feel that it should become a more women-friendly place instead of the traditional male club.

The Speaker is the chief officer of the House of Commons; is chosen by MPs; interprets the rules of the House; and is assisted by three deputy speakers. The Speaker is an elected MP who, on election to the Speaker's chair, ceases to be a political representative and becomes a neutral official.

The Speaker protects the House against any abuse of procedure by controlling debates and votes. Where there is a tied result, the Speaker has the casting vote, but must exercise this choice so that it reflects established conventions. The Speaker is important for the orderly running of the House. MPs can be very combative and often unruly, so that the Speaker is sometimes forced to dismiss or suspend a member from the House.

Debates in both Houses of Parliament usually begin with a motion (or proposal) which is then debated. The matter is decided by a simple majority vote at the end of discussion. In the Commons, MPs enter either the 'Yes' or 'No' lobbies (corridors running alongside the Commons chamber) to record their vote, but they may also abstain from voting.

The proceedings of both Houses are open to the public and may be viewed from the public and visitors' galleries. The transactions are published daily in *Hansard* (the parliamentary 'newspaper'); debates are televised; and radio broadcasts may be in live or recorded form. This exposure to public scrutiny has increased interest in the parliamentary process, although negative comments are made about low attendance in both Houses and the behaviour of MPs in the Commons.

Before the creation of new UK law (which may take a few days or many months) and changes to existing law a government will usually issue certain documents before the parliamentary law-making process commences. A Green Paper is a consultative document which allows interested parties to state their case before a bill is introduced into Parliament. A White Paper is not normally consultative, but is a preliminary document which details prospective legislation.

A draft law takes the form of a bill. Most bills are 'public' because they involve state business and are introduced in either House of Parliament by the government. Other bills may be 'private' because they relate to matters such as local government, while some are 'private members' bills' introduced by MPs in their personal capacity. These latter bills are on a topic of interest to MPs, but are normally defeated for lack of parliamentary time or support. However, some important private members' bills concerning homosexuality, abortion and sexual offences have survived the obstacles and become law.

Bills must pass through both Houses and receive the Royal Assent before they become law. The Commons is normally the first step in this process. The Lords, in its turn, can delay a non-financial bill. It can also propose amendments, and if amended the bill goes back to the Commons for further consideration. This amending function is an important power and has been frequently used in recent years. But the Lords' role today is to act as a forum for revision, rather than as a rival to the elected Commons. In practice, the Lords' amendments can sometimes lead to the acceptance of changes by the government, or even a withdrawal of the bill.

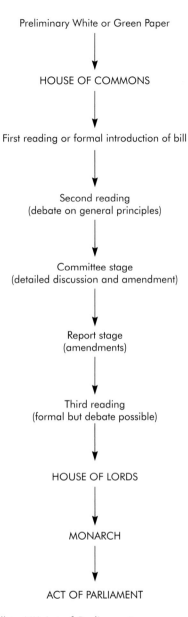

Preliminary White or Green Paper

HOUSE OF COMMONS

First reading or formal introduction of bill

Second reading
(debate on general principles)

Committee stage
(detailed discussion and amendment)

Report stage
(amendments)

Third reading
(formal but debate possible)

HOUSE OF LORDS

MONARCH

ACT OF PARLIAMENT

FIGURE 3.3 From bill to UK Act of Parliament

When the bill has eventually passed through the Lords, it is sent to the monarch for the Royal Assent (or signature), which has not been refused since the eighteenth century. After this, the bill becomes an Act of Parliament and enters the statute-book as representing the law of the land at that time.

UK Parliament elections

The UK is divided for Westminster parliamentary elections to the House of Commons into 659 constituencies (geographical areas of the country containing an average of about 66,000 voters – though some have many more or fewer). Each returns one MP to the House of Commons at a general election. Constituency boundaries are adjusted to ensure fair representation and to reflect population movements.

General elections are by ballot, but voting is not compulsory. British, Commonwealth and Irish Republic citizens may vote if they are resident in Britain, included on a constituency register of voters, are aged eighteen or over and not subject to any disqualification. People not entitled to vote include members of the House of Lords; mentally ill patients who are detained in hospital or prison; and persons who have been convicted of corrupt or illegal election practices.

Each elector casts one vote at a polling station set up on election day in a constituency by making a cross on a ballot paper against the name of the candidate for whom the vote is cast. Those who are unable to vote in person in their local constituency can register postal or proxy votes.

The turnout of voters has often been about 70 per cent at general elections out of an electorate of 42 million. The candidate who wins the most votes in a constituency is elected MP for that area. This system is known as the simple majority or the 'first-past-the-post' system. There is no voting by the various forms of proportional representation (PR), except for EU Parliament and devolved government elections, which have a mixture of first-past-the-post and party-list voting.

Some see the Westminster electoral system as undemocratic and unfair to smaller parties. The Liberal Democrats campaign for PR voting, which would create a wider selection of parties in the House of Commons and cater for minority political interests. The two big parties (Labour and Conservative) have preferred the existing system since it gives them a greater chance of achieving power. The Labour government will now examine the PR systems in Scotland and Wales to see whether they can be applied to Westminster elections.

It is argued that the British people prefer the stronger government which can result from the first-past-the-post system. PR systems are alleged to have weaknesses, such as party control of lists, coalition or minority government, frequent break-down, a lack of firm policies, power-bargaining between different parties in order to achieve government status and tension afterwards. But weak and small-majority government can also result from first-past-the-post.

The party-political system

British elections at parliamentary, devolved and local levels depend upon the party political system, which has existed since the seventeenth century. For UK parliamentary general elections, the parties present their policies in the form of manifestos to the electorate for consideration during the few weeks of campaigning. A party candidate (chosen by a specific party) in a constituency is elected to the Westminster Parliament on a combination of party manifesto and the personality of the candidate. But party-activity continues outside the election period itself, as the politicians battle for power and the ears of the electorate at all levels.

Since 1945 there have been eight Labour and eight Conservative UK governments in Britain. Some have had large majorities in the House of Commons, while others have had small ones. Some, like the Labour government in the late 1970s and the Conservatives in the 1990s, had to rely on

TABLE 3.1   British governments and Prime Ministers since 1945

Date	Government	Prime Minister
1945–51	Labour	Clement Attlee
1951–55	Conservative	Winston Churchill
1955–59	Conservative	Anthony Eden (1955–57)
		Harold Macmillan (1957–59)
1959–64	Conservative	Harold Macmillan (1959–63)
		Alec Douglas-Home (1963–64)
1964–66	Labour	Harold Wilson
1966–70	Labour	Harold Wilson
1970–74	Conservative	Edward Heath
1974–(Feb.)	Labour	Harold Wilson
1974–(Oct.)	Labour	Harold Wilson
1974–79	Labour	Harold Wilson (1974–76)
		James Callaghan (1976–79)
1979–83	Conservative	Margaret Thatcher
1983–87	Conservative	Margaret Thatcher
1987–92	Conservative	Margaret Thatcher (1987–90)
		John Major (1990–92)
1992–97	Conservative	John Major
1997–2001	Labour	Tony Blair
2001–	Labour	Tony Blair

the support of smaller parties, such as the Liberals and Ulster Unionists, to remain in power. Most of the MPs in the House of Commons belong to either the Conservative or the Labour Party. This continues the traditional two-party system in British politics, in which power alternates between two major parties.

The Labour Party has historically been a left-of-centre party with its own right and left wings. It emphasized social justice, equality of opportunity, economic planning and the state ownership of industries and services. It was supported by the trade unions (who had been influential in the party's development), the working class and some of the middle class. Its electoral strongholds are historically in Scotland, south Wales and the Midland and northern English industrial cities.

But traditional class-based support has changed with more social and job mobility. In the 1990s, the Labour Party tried to appeal to middle-class voters in southern England and to take account of changing economic and social conditions. Its leader (and current Prime Minister), Tony Blair, modernized the party by moving to the centre, captured some voters from the Conservatives and distanced himself from the trade unions and the party's doctrinaire past. As a result, the party had landslide victories in the 1997 and 2001 general elections.

The Conservative Party is a right-of-centre party, which also has right- and left-wing sections. It regards itself as a national party and appeals to people across class barriers. It emphasizes personal, social and economic freedom, individual ownership of property and shares and law and order. The Conservatives became more radical in their eighteen years of government power (1979–97). But splits in the party on policy (particularly Europe, the Euro and immigration) have deepened.

The party's support comes mainly from business interests and the middle and upper classes, but a sizeable number of skilled workers and women vote Conservative. The party's strongholds are in southern England, with scattered support elsewhere in the country. However, at the 2001 general election, it gained no seats in Wales, only one in Scotland and did not greatly increase its support in England. The party's defeat led to the resignation of its previous leader, William Hague, and the election of Iain Duncan Smith. The party, which has been accused of a right-wing move, needs to reorganize, strive for unity, cultivate an image which is more attractive to voters and develop policies which are more in tune with the changing face of British society.

The Liberal Democrats were formed in 1988 when the old Liberal Party and the Social Democratic Party merged into one party. Under their present leader, Charles Kennedy, they see themselves as an alternative political force to the Conservative and Labour Parties, based on the centre-left of British politics. Their strengths are in local government, constitutional reform and civil liberties, and opinion polls suggest that they are the most effective opposition to the Labour government at present.

They are relatively strong in south-west England, Wales and Scotland and increased their number of MPs at the 2001 general election to become the biggest third party in Parliament since 1929. But they lack a clearly defined identity. The Liberal Democrats have won some dramatic by-elections and have success in local government elections. But they have not made a large breakthrough into the Commons or the EU Parliament. Electoral reform to a form of PR might increase the number of their MPs.

Smaller parties are also represented in the House of Commons, such as the Scottish National Party; Plaid Cymru (the Welsh National Party); the Ulster Unionists and the Democratic Unionists (Protestant Northern Irish parties); the Social Democratic and Labour Party (moderate Roman Catholic Northern Irish Party); and Sinn Fein (Republican Northern Irish party). Other small parties, such as the Greens and fringe groups, may also contest a general election. A party which falls below a certain number of votes in the election loses its deposit (the sum paid when parties register for elections).

Social class and class loyalty used to be important factors in British voting behaviour. But these have now been replaced by property- and share-owning, job status and other considerations. A more volatile political situation exists as voters switch between Labour, Conservatives and Liberal Democrats and employ 'tactical voting' in constituencies to prevent specific party candidates from being elected. The changing character of the electorate has moved political parties to the centre ground and forced them to adopt policies which are more representative of people's wishes and needs.

The party which wins most seats in the House of Commons at a general election usually forms the new government, even if it has not obtained a majority of the popular vote (the votes actually cast at an election). A party will have to gather more than 33 per cent of the popular vote before winning a large number of seats, and 40 per cent in order to expand that representation and form a government with an overall majority (a majority over all the other parties counted together). This majority enables it to carry out its election manifesto policies (the mandate theory).

Election success often depends on whether support is concentrated in geographical areas, for a party gains seats by its local strength. Smaller parties, which do not reach the percentages above and whose support is scattered, do not gain many seats in the Commons. It is this system of representation that PR supporters wish to change, in order to reflect the popular vote and the appeal of minority parties.

The situation may be illustrated by the 2001 general election results (see table 3.2). On a very low turnout of voters of 59 per cent (the lowest since 1918) Labour became the government with 41 per cent of the popular

TABLE 3.2 General election results, 2001

Party	Popular vote (%)	Members elected
Labour (including speaker)	41.0	413
Conservative	31.9	166
Liberal Democrat	18.4	52
Scottish National Party	1.8	5
Plaid Cymru	0.7	4
Ulster Unionists		6
Social Democratic and Labour		3
Sinn Fein	6.2	4
Democratic Unionists		5
Independent (Richard Taylor)		1
Total	100	659
Turnout of voters:	59%	
Overall Labour majority:	167	
Non-Labour vote:	59%	

vote, while the opposition parties together obtained 59 per cent. Labour gained 413 seats with its share of the popular vote, the Conservatives received 166 seats with 31.9 per cent, while the Liberal Democrats with 18.4 per cent received 52 seats. Labour had a large 167-seat overall majority in the House of Commons. But only 25 per cent of the total electorate voted for Labour

The main reasons for this result were the low turnout; the 'first-past-the-post' system; the Liberal Democrats' popular support being spread widely (and thinly) over the country, resulting in them coming second in many constituencies; the Labour and Conservative Parties traditionally having specific geographical areas in which most of their votes are concentrated; the Conservatives being unable to improve their position from the 1997 election; and some 'tactical voting' to defeat Conservative candidates.

The result of a general election may be a 'hung Parliament', where no one party has an overall majority. A minority or coalition government would have to be formed, in which the largest party would be able to govern only by relying on the support of smaller parties in the Commons.

The largest minority party becomes the Official Opposition with its own leader and 'shadow government'. It plays an important role in the parliamentary system, which is based on adversarial politics and the two-party tradition of government. Seating arrangements in the House of

Commons reflect this system. Leaders of the government and opposition parties sit on facing 'front benches', with their supporting MPs, or 'backbenchers', sitting behind them. Some parties, such as the Liberal Democrats, dislike this confrontational style and advocate more consensus politics. Traditionally, the effectiveness of parliamentary democracy is supposed to rest on the relationship between the government and opposition parties and the observance of procedural conventions.

The opposition parties may try to overthrow the government by defeating it in a vote. But this is not usually successful if the government has a majority and can count on the support of its MPs. The opposition parties consequently attempt to influence the formation of national policies by their criticism of pending legislation; by trying to obtain concessions on bills by proposing amendments to them; and by increasing support for their policies outside the Commons. They take advantage of any publicity and opportunity which might improve their chances at the next general election.

Inside Parliament, party discipline rests with the Whips, who are chosen from party MPs by the party leaders and who are under the direction of a Chief Whip. Their duties include informing members of forthcoming parliamentary business and maintaining the party's voting strength in the Commons by seeing that their members attend all important debates. MPs receive notice from the Whips' office of how important a particular vote is and the information will be underlined up to three times. A 'three-line whip' signifies a crucial vote and failure to attend or comply with party instructions is regarded as a revolt against the party's policy.

The Whips also convey backbench opinion to the party leadership. This is important if rebellion and disquiet are to be avoided. Party discipline is very strong in the Commons and less so in the Lords. A government with a large majority (like Labour at present) should not become complacent, nor antagonize its backbenchers. If it does so, a successful rebellion against the government or abstention from voting by its own side may destroy the majority and the party's policy.

Outside Parliament, control rests with the national and local party organizations, which can be influential. They promote the party at every opportunity, but especially at election time, when constituencies select the party candidates and are in charge of electioneering on behalf of their party.

UK government

The UK government is elected by and serves the whole of Britain. It is centred on Whitehall in London where its ministries and the Prime Minister's official residence (10 Downing Street) are located. It consists of some hundred ministers who can be chosen from both Houses of Parliament and who are appointed by the monarch on the advice of the Prime Minister. They belong to the majority party in the Commons, from which they derive their authority and are collectively responsible for the administration of national affairs.

The *Prime Minister* is appointed by the monarch and is usually the leader of the majority party in the Commons. His or her power stems from majority support in Parliament; the authority to choose and dismiss ministers; the leadership of the party in the country; and control over policy-making. The Prime Minister sits in the Commons, as do most ministers, where they may be questioned and held accountable for government actions. The Prime Minister was historically the connection between the monarch and Parliament. This convention continues in the weekly audience with the monarch, at which the policies and business of the government are discussed.

The Prime Minister has great power within the British system of government and it is suggested that the office has become like an all-powerful executive presidency, which bypasses Parliament and government departments. But there are checks on this power, inside and outside the party and Parliament. However, there is a greater emphasis upon prime ministerial government today, rather than the traditional constitutional notions of Cabinet government.

The *Cabinet* is a small executive body in the government and usually comprises twenty-one senior ministers, who are chosen and presided over by the Prime Minister. Examples are the Chancellor of the Exchequer (Finance Minister), the Foreign Secretary, the Home Secretary and the Secretary of State for Education and Skills. The Cabinet originated in meetings that the monarch had with ministers in a royal Cabinet. As the monarch withdrew from active politics with the growth of party politics and Parliament, this developed into a parliamentary body.

Constitutional theory has traditionally argued that government rule is Cabinet rule because the Cabinet collectively initiates and decides government policy at its weekly meetings in 10 Downing Street. But this notion has weakened. Since the Prime Minister is responsible for Cabinet agendas and controls Cabinet proceedings, the Cabinet can become a 'rubber-stamp' for policies which have already been decided by the Prime Minister or smaller groups.

Much depends upon the personality of Prime Ministers and the way in which they avoid potential Cabinet friction. Some are strong and like to take the lead. Others work within the Cabinet structure, allowing ministers to exercise responsibility within their own ministerial fields. Much of our information about the operation of the Cabinet comes from 'leaks' or information divulged by Cabinet ministers. Although the Cabinet

PLATE 3.4   Prime Minister Tony Blair meets with his new cabinet for the first time since the June 2001 General Election (© *Popperfoto/Reuters*)

meets in private and its discussions are meant to be secret, the public is usually and reliably informed of Cabinet deliberations and disputes by the media.

The mass and complexity of government business and ministers' concern with their own departments suggest that full debate in Cabinet on every issue is impossible. But it is felt that broad policies should be more vigorously debated. The present system arguably concentrates too much power in the hands of the Prime Minister; overloads ministers with work; allows crucial decisions to be taken outside the Cabinet; and reduces the notion of collective responsibility.

Collective responsibilty is that which all ministers, but mainly those in the Cabinet, share for government actions and policy. All must support a government decision in public, even though some may oppose it during private deliberations. If a minister cannot do this, he or she may feel obliged to resign.

A minister also has an individual responsibility for the work of his or her government department. The minister is answerable for any mistakes, wrongdoing or bad administration, whether personally responsible for them or not. In such cases, the minister may resign, although this is not as common today as in the past. This responsibility also enables Parliament to maintain some control over executive actions because the minister is answerable to Parliament.

Government departments (or ministries) are the chief instruments by which the government implements its policy. A change of government does not necessarily alter the number or functions of departments. Examples of government departments are the Foreign Office, Ministry of Defence, Home Office and the Treasury (headed by the Chancellor of the Exchequer).

UK government departments are staffed by the *Civil Service*, consisting of career administrators (civil servants). They work in London and throughout Britain in government activities and are responsible to the minister of their department for the implementation of government policies. A change of minister or government does not require new civil servants, since they are expected to be politically neutral and to serve the government impartially. Restrictions on political activities and publication are imposed upon them in order to ensure neutrality.

There are some five hundred thousand civil servants in Britain today. Nearly half of these are women, but few of them achieve top ranks in the service. Many aspects of departmental work have now been transferred to executive agencies in London and throughout the country, which have administrative rather than policy-making roles, such as the Driver and Vehicle Licensing Agency (DVLA) in Cardiff and Social Security offices.

The heart of the Civil Service is the Cabinet Office, whose Secretary is the head of the Civil Service. The latter is responsible for the whole Civil Service, organizes Cabinet business and co-ordinates high-level policy. In each ministry or department the senior official (Permanent Secretary) and his or her assistants are responsible for assisting their minister in the implementation of government policy.

There have been accusations about the efficiency and effectiveness of the Service, and civil servants do not have a good public image. There have been attempts to make the system more cost-effective and to allow a wider category of applicants than the traditional entry of Oxford and Cambridge University graduates. Departments have been broken down into executive agencies and posts may be advertised in order to attract older people from industry, commerce and the professions.

It is alleged that the Civil Service imposes a certain mentality upon its members, which affects implementation of government policies and which ministers are unable to combat. There is supposed to be a Civil Service way of doing things and a bias towards the *status quo*. But much depends upon ministers and the way in which they manage departments. There may be some areas of concern, of which the latest is the alleged politicization of the Service by ministers and unelected advisers. But the stereotyped image of civil servants is not reflected in the many who serve their political masters and work with ministers for departmental interests. The Civil Service is highly regarded in other countries for its efficiency and impartiality.

UK parliamentary control of government

Most British governments in the past governed pragmatically. The emphasis was on whether policies worked and were generally acceptable. Governments were conscious of how far they could go before displeasing their supporters and the electorate, to whom they were accountable at general elections. The combination of the two-party system, Cabinet government and party discipline in the Commons seemed to provide a balance between efficient government and public accountability. But both Conservative and Labour governments have become more intent on pushing their policies through Parliament.

Constitutional theory suggested that Parliament should control the executive government. But unless there is small-majority government, rebellion by government MPs or public protest, a government with an overall majority in the Commons (such as Labour since 1997) can carry its policies through Parliament, irrespective of Parliament's attempts to restrain it. Critics argue for stronger parliamentary control over the executive, which has been described as an elective dictatorship. But there seems little chance of this without, for example, moving to a PR electoral system, more consensus politics, a strengthening of Parliament's constraining role and much more independent stances from MPs themselves.

Opposition parties can only oppose in the Commons and hope to persuade the electorate to dismiss the government at the next election. Formal devices such as votes of censure and no confidence are normally inadequate when confronting a government with a large majority. Even rebellious government MPs will usually support the party on such occasions, out of a self-interested desire to preserve their jobs and a need to prevent the collapse of the government.

Examinations of government programmes can be employed at Question Time in the Commons (30 minutes on Wednesdays), when the Prime Minister is subjected to oral questions from MPs. But the government can prevaricate in its answers and, while reputations can be made and lost at Question Time, it is a rhetorical and political occasion rather than an in-depth analysis of government policy. However, it does have a function in holding the executive's performance up to public scrutiny. The opposition parties can also choose their own topics for debate on a limited number of days each session, which can be used to attack the government.

A 1967 attempt to restrain the executive was the creation of the Parliamentary Commissioner for Administration (Ombudsman), who can investigate alleged bad administration by ministers and civil servants. But the office does not have strong watchdog powers and the public have no direct access to it, although its existence does serve as a warning.

In an attempt to improve the situation, standing committees of MPs were established, which examine bills during procedural stages. Such committees have little influence on actual policy. But in 1979 a new select committee system was created, which now has fourteen committees. They comprise MPs from most parties, who monitor the administration and policy of the main government departments and investigate proposed legislation. MPs previously had problems in scrutinizing government activity adequately, and party discipline made it difficult for them to act independently of party policy.

It is often argued that the real work of the House and parliamentary control of the executive is done in the select committees. Their members are now proving to be more independent in questioning civil servants and ministers who are called to give evidence before them (but who may refuse to attend). Select committees can be effective in examining proposed legislation and expenditure, and their reports can be damaging to a government's reputation. Although opinions differ about their role, it does seem that they have strengthened Parliament's authority against government and critics would like to see their power enhanced. Nevertheless, although parliamentary scrutiny is important, a government is elected (or mandated) to carry out its declared policies.

Attitudes to politics

Polls reveal that British politicians, political parties and Parliament do not rate highly in people's esteem. A *National Opinion Poll (NOP)* in 1997 found that politicians were the least admired group and a *MORI* poll in June 2001 found that 75 per cent of respondents agreed with the proposition that politicians never answer the questions people put to them. They are criticized and satirized in the media and allegations of sleaze, corruption and unethical behaviour in both Labour and Conservative Parties have led to stricter controls on politicians and their outside interests. The Labour government has faced accusations of 'cronyism' (favouring political supporters for public and official positions) since 1997.

A *MORI* poll in May 1997 showed an increase in political apathy, particularly among the young, and a distrust in politicians to rectify social ills. This partly resulted in a 59 per cent turnout at the 2001 general election, the lowest in any general election since 1918. A *MORI* poll in July 2001 found that 47 per cent of respondents were dissatisfied with the Labour government's performance (42 per cent satisfied).

But *MORI* opinion research in 2001 showed that in fact interest in politics has remained stable in Britain for thirty years; civic duty and habit are key motivators to voting (less so for the young); and people have positive attitudes to voting. They would prefer it to be made more convenient by phone or mobile phone, online and by post (the latter is now available). The research also found that low turnout is not a result of declining interest in politics or elections but rather a failure of campaigns to connect with the electorate. This suggests that people want more accurate information and a greater focus on the issues that directly concern them.

People therefore appear to be more interested in the political process and issues than is popularly assumed. But the *Independent Television Commission's Election 2001* survey found that interest in television election coverage fell to its lowest level; 70 per cent of viewers expressed little or no interest; and 25 per cent ignored all campaign coverage. None of the political parties, in spite of frequent drifts to the centre ground, individually encompasses all the basic views and sense of contemporary reality of the people, who may vary between egalitarian economic views and authoritarian social and moral positions. They desire economic freedom and personal liberty but also want state interventionist policies in some social areas, such as education, health and law and order.

Exercises

Explain and examine the following terms:

Whigs	executive	'three-line whip'
constitution	minister	life peers
Cabinet	manifesto	Oliver Cromwell
Magna Carta	conventions	Question time
civil servant	secret ballot	backbenchers
Lords Spiritual	Tories	constitutional monarchy
the Speaker	legislature	'hung Parliament'
Whitehall	sovereignty	select committees
White Paper	'cronyism'	sleaze

Write short essays on the following topics:

1   Describe what is meant by the 'two-party system', and comment upon its effectiveness.
2   Does Britain have an adequate parliamentary electoral system? If not, why not?
3   Critically examine the role of the Prime Minister.
4   Discuss the position and powers of the monarch in the British constitution.

Further reading

Birch, A.H. (1998) *The British System of Government* London: Routledge

Bogdanor, V. (2001) *Devolution in the United Kingdom* Oxford: Oxford University Press

Childs, D. (2001) *Britain since 1945: A Political History* London: Routledge

Foley, M. (2000) *The British Presidency* Manchester: Manchester University Press

Jones, B. *et al.* (2000) *Politics UK* London: Prentice-Hall

Kavanagh, D. (2000) *British Politics: Continuities and Change* Oxford: Oxford University Press

Ludlam, S. and Smith, M.J. (2000) *New Labour in Government* London: Macmillan

Websites

UK government: www.open.gov.uk and www.ukonline.gov.uk

Houses of Parliament: www.parliament.uk

Monarchy: www.royal.gov.uk

Privy Council Office: www.privy-council.org.uk

Cabinet Office: www.cabinet-office.gov.uk

Prime Minister's Office: www.number-10.gov.uk

Wales Office: www.wales.gov.uk

National Assembly for Wales: www.wales.gov.uk

Scotland Office: www.scottishsecretary.gov.uk

The Scottish Parliament: www.scottish.parliament.uk

Northern Ireland Assembly: www.ni-assembly.gov.uk

Northern Ireland Office: www.nio.gov.uk

International relations

Britain's historical position as a colonial, economic and political power was in relative decline by the early decades of the twentieth century. Some large colonies had already achieved self-governing status, and the growth of nationalism in African and Asian nations later persuaded Britain to decolonialize further. The effects of global economic competition, two World Wars, the emergence of Cold War politics (dominated by the USA and the former Soviet Union) and domestic economic and social problems forced Britain to recognize its reduced international status. It sought with difficulty to find a new identity and to establish different priorities, particularly in relation to Europe. Some of the previous overseas links continue in altered form, while other relationships are new. But, in spite of these fundamental changes, Britain still experiences uncertainties about its potential influence and appropriate role on the world stage.

Foreign and defence policy

Britain's international position today is that of a medium-sized country which ranks economically behind Germany, the USA and Japan. Yet some of its leaders still believe that it can have international influence and a global role. For example, the Labour government had earlier developed a foreign policy with an 'ethical dimension' which focused on human rights and shifted away from aggressive unilateral action to persuasive partnership. This could be applied to Britain's dealings with other countries, particularly in terms of arms sales and nationalist conflicts. But the policy was heavily criticized and there has been a return to issues of national self-interest in the context of international co-operation.

It is argued that Britain's foreign policy and self-image do not reflect the reality of its world position and conflict with domestic matters. Britain has engaged in joint military actions (for example the Gulf, the Balkans and Afghanistan). But, while it has gradually reduced its defence expenditure and overseas commitments, some critics feel that the current costs in these areas should be directed to domestic problems in Britain.

Nevertheless, Britain's foreign and defence policies still reflect its traditional position as a major trading nation, the world's fourth largest economy and a global finance centre. It is therefore self-interestedly concerned to maintain stable economic and political conditions through global co-operation. Although its domestic manufacturing base has declined, manufactures are 86 per cent of exported goods and it is the world's fifth largest exporter of products and services, amounting to 25 per cent of GDP in 1999. It has substantial overseas investments (being the world's second biggest foreign investor in 1998) and imported 9 per cent of its food in 1999 and 3 per cent of its basic manufacturing requirements. Britain is therefore dependent upon maintaining global commercial connections, although it is increasingly committed to Europe, where EU countries are Britain's biggest export and import markets. Other European countries, the USA and Japan are also leading export fields.

Britain's *foreign policy* and membership of international organizations is based on the principle that overseas objectives can be best attained by persuasion and co-operation with other nations on a regional or global basis. The imperial days of unilateral action are now largely past, although Britain did take such action in the 1982 Falklands War. But its foreign policy can reflect particular biases, with support for one country outweighing that for another. The USA has been Britain's closest ally in recent years; it is often considered, rightly or wrongly, that a 'special relationship' exists between the two; and a majority of Americans regard Britain as a close ally of the USA. But this association varies according to circumstances, although Britain is concerned to maintain the American military presence in Europe and NATO. The USA sees Britain partly as a bridge to Europe while Britain wants to maintain the Atlantic connection in its own bargaining with EU countries.

However, a *MORI* poll in November 2001 showed that British people feel the USA is now of relatively less importance to Britain than Europe is: 53 per cent of respondents thought that Britain's closest relationship should be with Europe (36 per cent for the USA). Britain's membership of the EU means that it is to some extent dependent upon EU foreign policy. But, although the EU is moving to more unified policies, member states have conflicting interests and Britain follows its own policy when necessary. EU foreign policy is still very much in its infancy and many critics doubt its potential validity.

Britain has diplomatic relations with over 160 nations and is a member of some 120 international organizations, ranging from bodies for economic co-operation to the United Nations (UN). Support for the UN and the principles of its charter has been part of British foreign policy since 1945, although there has sometimes been a scepticism about its effectiveness as a practical body.

But, as a permanent member of the UN Security Council, Britain has a vested interest in supporting the UN. It sees a strong UN as a necessary

PLATE 4.1   Prime Minister Tony Blair with US President George W. Bush at the G8 summit in July 2001 (© *Popperfoto/Reuters*)

framework for achieving many of its own foreign policy objectives, such as the peaceful resolution of conflict, arms control, disarmament, peacekeeping operations and the protection of human rights. UN agencies also provide important forums for discussing issues in which Britain is involved, such as disaster relief, the use of the sea-bed, terrorism, the environment, energy development and world resources. Yet Britain, like other nations, is ready to ignore the UN when it sees its own vital interests challenged.

Britain's major *defence* alliance is with the North Atlantic Treaty Organization (NATO). This comprises Belgium, Canada, Denmark, Iceland, Italy, Luxembourg, the Netherlands, Norway, Spain, Portugal, Britain, the USA, Greece, Turkey, Germany, Poland, Hungary, the Czech Republic and France (the latter is outside NATO's military wing). The original justification for NATO was that it provided its members with greater security than any could achieve individually and was a deterrent against aggression by the now-defunct Warsaw Pact countries.

All the major British political parties are in favour of retaining the NATO link and, according to opinion polls, the public would not support any party which tried to take Britain out of the alliance. Membership of NATO also allows Britain to operate militarily on the international stage. Its defence policy is based on NATO strategies and it assigns most of its armed forces and defence budget to the organization.

Despite changes in Eastern Europe since 1989 and moves to transform NATO into a more flexible military association, the British government has taken such developments cautiously and is concerned to maintain its own military defence with both conventional and nuclear forces. It fears global instability and the risk to its own security if it were to reduce its and NATO's armed defences substantially. It also supports in principle the USA's missile shield defence programme and will probably contribute early-warning facilities in Britain.

However, in 1998 Britain argued that the EU must have a credible military and security capability to support its political role. The EU is now working towards the creation of its own 'rapid deployment force'. The problem is whether this should be seen as an independent force outside NATO or whether it should operate within NATO frameworks. It would respond to international crises, but without prejudice to NATO (which would continue to be the foundation of collective security). Some critics argue that this development will weaken the NATO structure and could lead to American withdrawal from Europe.

The British government has progressively cut its defence expenditure (6 per cent of government spending in 2000–01) by reducing the number of armed forces personnel, ships, aircraft and equipment. It aims to depend on leaner, more flexible forces, although there have been strenuous objections to these policies from the military. The primary objectives of defence policy are to ensure the country's security and the NATO commitment and to allow British forces to engage in high-intensity war as well as in peace-keeping roles. However, defence spending is still higher than in other European countries and it is asked whether the money could be better spent in other areas of national life. On the other hand, the armed forces are understaffed for their global commitments and military equipment is often out-of-date and in short supply.

Nuclear weapons, which account for a large part of the defence budget, continue to be fiercely debated. Britain's independent nuclear deterrent consists mainly of long-range American-built Trident missiles carried by a fleet of four submarines (although only one is on patrol at any given time). Governments have committed themselves to upgrading nuclear weapons while critics want cheaper alternatives, or the cancellation of the nuclear system. But it seems that the British nuclear stategy will continue. All the major political parties are multilateralist (keeping nuclear weapons until they can be abolished on a global basis).

Britain can operate militarily outside the NATO and European area, although this capacity is becoming increasingly expensive and limited. Military garrisons are stationed in Brunei, Cyprus, the Far and Middle East, the Falkland Islands and Gibraltar. The 1982 Falklands War, the 1991 Gulf War and Afghanistan in 2001 showed that Britain was able to respond to challenges outside the NATO area, although the operations did draw attention to defects and problems in such commitments.

The total strength of the professional armed forces, which are now all volunteer following the abolition of conscription in 1960, was 207,600 in 2000. This was made up of 42,800 in the Royal Navy and Royal Marines, 110,100 in the Army and 54,700 in the Royal Air Force. Women personnel in the Army, Navy and Air Force are integral parts of the armed services. They were previously confined to support roles, but may now be employed in some front-line military activities. Reserve and volunteer forces, such as the Territorial Army (TA), support the regular forces, reinforce NATO ground troops and help to maintain security in Britain.

Empire and Commonwealth

The British Empire was built up over eight centuries. It began with the attempted internal domination of the British-Irish Isles by the English, together with military conquests in Europe. These were followed by trading activities and colonization in North and South America. Parts of Africa, Asia and the West Indies were also exploited commercially over time and many became colonies. Emigrants from Britain settled in countries such as Australia, Canada, South Africa and New Zealand. By the nineteenth century, British imperial rule and possessions embraced a quarter of the world's population.

The Empire developed into the British Empire and Commonwealth in the late nineteenth and early twentieth centuries when Canada, Australia, New Zealand and South Africa became self-governing dominions and achieved independence. Many of their people were descendants of those settlers who had emigrated from Britain in earlier centuries. They regarded Britain as the 'mother country' and preserved a shared kinship. But this relationship has changed as national identities in these countries have become more firmly established.

In the mid twentieth century, the British Empire and Commonwealth became the British Commonwealth as British governments granted independence to other colonies. India and Pakistan became independent in 1947, followed by African territories in the 1950s and 1960s and later many islands of the West Indies. The British Commonwealth then developed into the Commonwealth of Nations, as most of the remaining colonies became independent. They could choose whether they wanted to break all connections with the colonial past or remain within the Commonwealth as independent nations. Most of them decided to stay in the Commonwealth. Only a few small British colonies, dependencies and protectorates now remain and are scattered widely, such as the Falklands and Gibraltar.

The present Commonwealth is a voluntary association of some fifty-four independent states (including Britain). It does not have written laws,

PLATE 4.2   Prince Charles on walkabout in Saskatchewan, Canada, in April
2001 (© *Popperfoto/Reuters*)

an elected Parliament, or one political ruler. There is evidence of colonial rule in many of the countries, such as educational and legal systems. But few have kept the British form of parliamentary government. Some have adapted it to their own needs, while others are one-party states or have constitutions based on a wide variety of models, with varying records on civil and democratic rights.

The Commonwealth has nearly a third of the world's population and comprises peoples of different religions, races and nationalities, who share a history of struggles for independence from colonialism. The Commonwealth is sometimes described as a family of nations. But there are occasional wars, tensions and quarrels between these family members.

The British monarch is its non-political head and has varying constitutional roles in the different countries. The monarch is a focal point of identification and has an important unifying and symbolic function, which has often kept the Commonwealth together in times of crisis and conflict.

The Prime Ministers, or heads of state, in Commonwealth countries meet every two years under the auspices of the monarch for Commonwealth Conferences in different parts of the world. Common problems are discussed and sometimes settled, although there seem to have been more arguments than agreements in recent years, with Britain having a minority position on some issues (such as opposing trade sanctions against the former apartheid regime in South Africa).

There is a Commonwealth Secretariat in London which co-ordinates policy for the Commonwealth, in addition to many Commonwealth societies, institutes, libraries, professional associations and university exchange programmes. Commonwealth citizens still travel to Britain as immigrants, students and visitors, while British emigration to Commonwealth countries continues in reduced numbers. English in its many varieties remains the common language of the Commonwealth, and the Commonwealth Games are held every four years. There are many joint British/Commonwealth programmes on both official and voluntary levels in agriculture, engineering, health and education, in which some vestiges of the old relationship between Britain and the Commonwealth are still apparent.

But British attempts to enter Europe since the 1960s have reduced the importance to Britain of the organization. There is no longer the traditional sense of Commonwealth solidarity and purpose, and Britain has little in common with some Commonwealth nations. It is argued that, unless member countries feel there are valid reasons for continuing an association which represents historical accident rather than common purpose, the long-term future of the Commonwealth must be in doubt. Opinion polls reveal that Europe is now more important for British people than the Commonwealth is.

Britain had preferential trading arrangements with the Common-wealth before it joined the European Union in 1973 and the Commonwealth question formed part of the debate on membership. EU entry was seen as ending the relationship between Britain and the Commonwealth. But economic co-operation and trading between the two has continued, and Britain contributes a considerable amount of its overseas aid to developing countries in the Commonwealth. However, Britain has a declining share of this market and its economic priorities are now more with the European Union and other world partners.

Nevertheless, the Labour government feels that the Commonwealth is a success and is committed to raising its profile. Indeed, a number of countries wish to join the organization, not all of which have been previous British colonies. But it is argued that the value of the Commonwealth in the contemporary world must be based on a concrete and realistic role which is distinctive from other global organizations. It should function as a worldwide political forum which emphasizes accountable govern-ment, democratic concerns, anti-corruption reform and civil and human rights.

The European Union (EU)

The ideal of a united Europe, strong in economic and political institutions, became increasingly attractive to European statesmen after the Second World War (1939–45). There was a desire to create a peaceful and pros-perous Europe after the destruction of two World Wars and after centuries of antagonism and mutual distrust between the European powers.

The foundations for a more integrated Europe were established in 1957 when six countries (West Germany, France, Belgium, the Nether-lands, Luxembourg and Italy) signed the Treaty of Rome and formed the European Economic Community (EEC). Britain did not join, but instead helped to create the European Free Trade Association (EFTA) in 1959. Britain distanced itself from closer European connections in the 1950s and saw its future in the trading patterns of the Commonwealth and an assumed 'special relationship' with the USA. It regarded itself as a commercial power and did not wish to be restricted by European relationships. An ancient suspicion of Europe also caused many British people to shrink from membership of a European organization, which they thought might result in the loss of their identity and independence.

However, a European commitment grew among sections of British society in the 1960s. But attempts by Britain to join the EEC were vetoed by the French President, Charles de Gaulle. He was critical of Britain's rela-tionship with the USA (particularly on nuclear weapons policies), queried the extent of British commitment to Europe and arguably did not want Britain as a potential rival to the leadership of the EEC.

De Gaulle resigned from the French presidency in 1969, and new British negotiations on membership began in 1970 under the pro-European Conservative Prime Minister, Edward Heath. In 1972, Parliament voted in favour of entry, despite widespread doubts and the strong opposition of a politically diverse group of interests among the British people. Britain, together with Denmark and the Irish Republic, formally joined the EEC on 1 January 1973, having left EFTA in 1972.

But a new Labour government (1974) under Harold Wilson was committed to giving the British people a referendum on continued membership. After further renegotiations of the terms of entry, the referendum was held in 1975, the first in British political history. The pro-marketeers won by a margin of 2 to 1 (67.2 per cent in favour, 32.8 per cent against).

The EEC was based initially on economic concerns and instituted harmonization programmes, such as common agricultural and fisheries policies, abolition of trade tariffs between member states and development aid to depressed areas within its borders. Britain's poorer regions have benefited considerably from regional funds. In 1986 the member-states formed an internal or Single European Market, in which goods, services, people and capital could move freely across national frontiers within what was then called the European Community. Today, 59 per cent of British exports go to the EU and Britain receives 54 per cent of its imports from EU countries.

Some politicians had always hoped that increased economic integration would lead to political initiatives and a more integrated Europe. The Maastrict Treaty (1992) was a step in this process as a result of which the European Community became the European Union (EU). The Treaty provided for the introduction of a common European currency (the Euro), a European Bank and common defence, foreign and social policies. Further treaties have also increased the integration momentum.

There are now fifteen EU members with a total population of 360 million people (Britain, Denmark, Germany, Greece, Spain, Belgium, Ireland, Luxembourg, the Netherlands, France, Italy, Portugal, Sweden, Finland and Austria). Since 1994, most of the EU single market measures have also been extended to Iceland, Norway and Liechtenstein through the creation of the European Economic Area (EEA). The actual and potential growth of the EU (to include Eastern European nations) has been seen as providing an important political voice in world affairs and a powerful trading area in global economic matters. Today, EEA member-states account for 40 per cent of world trade.

The institutions involved in the running of the EU are the European Council, Council of Ministers, European Commission, European Parliament and European Court of Justice.

1 Irish Republic	6 The Netherlands	11 Spain
2 Britain	7 Belgium	12 Portugal
3 Denmark	8 France	13 Sweden
4 Luxembourg	9 Italy	14 Finland
5 Germany	10 Greece	15 Austria

FIGURE 4.1   The European Union, 2001

The European Council consists of government leaders who meet several times a year to discuss and agree on broad areas of policy. The Council of Ministers is the principal policy-implementing body and is normally composed of Foreign Ministers from the member-states.

The Commission (under an appointed President) is the central administrative force of the EU, proposing programmes and policy to the Council of Ministers. It comprises commissioners (with two from Britain) chosen

PLATE 4.3 The European Parliament in Brussels (© *Popperfoto/Reuters*)

from member-states to hold certain portfolios, such as agriculture or competition policy, for a renewable five-year period. Their interests then become those of the EU and not of their national governments. It is argued that the unelected Commission has too much power and should be more democratically accountable.

The European Parliament (in which Britain has 87 seats – see table 4.1) is directly elected for a five-year term on a party-political basis from the EU-wide electorate. It advises the Council of Ministers on Commission proposals, determines the EU budget and exerts some control over the Council and the Commission. It is argued that the Parliament, as the only elected body in the EU, should have more power, and its veto over EU policy has now been extended. In the 1999 British EU Parliament elections (held under a partial PR arrangement with party lists) the Labour Party did badly compared with the Conservatives. The Liberal Democrats increased their seats and the UK Independence Party (which wants British withdrawal from the EU) did relatively well.

The Court of Justice comprises judges from the member-states. It settles disputes concerning EU law and is a very influential factor because it also determines the application of EU law in the domestic systems of the member-states.

British membership of the EU is difficult. It has complained about its contribution to the EU budget (which was eventually reduced); objected to the agricultural and fisheries policies; and opposed movements towards

TABLE 4.1 European Union Parliament
election results, 1999 (Britain)

Party	Seats
Conservative	36
Labour	29
Liberal Democrats	10
UK Independence Party	3
Northern Irish parties	3
Scottish National Party	2
Plaid Cymru	2
Greens	2

greater political and economic integration. Critics argue that Britain's sovereignty and independence are threatened by EU developments. Some British politicians want economic and political integration on federal lines, while others see the EU as a free-trade area in which national legal rights and interests are firmly retained. But all the major political parties are pro-European in the sense of wanting to be in Europe, although there are opposition groups (Eurosceptics) in the Labour and (particularly the) Conservative parties. The country is now so closely tied to Europe in economic and institutional ways that withdrawal would be difficult in practical terms, although it is possible constitutionally.

There are divided views about the pace and direction of future developments. The Labour government wants a Europe of nation states (as now) in which Britain can play a central role and is against the concept of a 'superstate'. It favours the Council of Ministers as the key decision-making body and is against enhancing the powers of the European Parliament, an elected president or a written constitution for the EU. But it supports enlargement, a second chamber of representatives from national parliaments and favours moves towards common European defence. However, it did not take Britain into the first wave of the common currency (the euro) in 1999. Its policy is wait and prepare, waiting until Britain's economy is in line with other members, seeing how the currency develops and putting the issue to a referendum (possibly in the current Parliament). Successive polls in 2000 and 2001 suggested that 70 per cent of Britons were against joining a common currency. But it seems that some may be persuadable on economic grounds.

British support for the EU peaked in the 1980s but has since eroded. A *MORI* poll in 2001 found that 52 per cent of respondents wished to leave the EU immediately; 71 per cent wanted a referendum on Britain's continued membership; and 75 per cent believed that Britons had not been given enough information about the arguments for and against membership. An *NOP* poll in 2001 showed that 61 per cent of respondents felt that holding a referendum on EU membership is as important as holding a general election. But a 2001 *MORI* poll found that barely 28 per cent of British respondents felt that EU membership was a good thing.

Public support for the EU tends therefore to be lukewarm and indifferent. The turn out for British EU Parliament elections is the lowest in Europe and there is ignorance about the EU, its benefits and its institutions. But polls show that 'Europe' is considered to be relatively more important to Britain than the USA and the Commonwealth are. Europeanism (rather than an EU institutional entity) seems to be more easily and naturally accepted by younger people.

Irish Republic and Northern Ireland

Northern Ireland (also known as 'the six counties', or Ulster after the ancient kingdom in the north-east of the island) is constitutionally a part of the United Kingdom. But its (and British) history is inseparable from that of the Republic of Ireland (Ireland or Eire). Historically, mainland Britain has been unable to accommodate itself successfully to its next-door neighbours. During the twentieth century, as Britain has detached itself from empire and entered the European Union, its relationship with Northern Ireland and the Irish Republic was problematic. But the latter is now more closely involved politically with the UK as a result of the 1998 Good Friday Agreement on Northern Ireland and later legislation.

A basic knowledge of the island's long and troubled history is essential in order to understand the current role of the Irish Republic and the actual situation in Northern Ireland itself, for any solution to the problems there cannot be simplistic. Ireland was first controlled by England in the twelfth century. Since then there have been continuous rebellions by the native Irish against English colonial, political and military rule.

The situation worsened in the sixteenth century, when Catholic Ireland refused to accept the Protestant Reformation, despite much religious persecution. The two seeds of future hatred, colonialism and religion, were thus early sown in Irish history. A hundred years later, Oliver Cromwell crushed rebellions in Ireland and continued the earlier 'plantation policy', by which English and Scottish settlers were given land and rights over the native Irish. These colonists also served as a police force to put down any Irish revolts. The descendants of the Protestant settlers became a powerful political minority in Ireland as a whole and a majority in Ulster. In 1690, the Protestant William III (William of Orange) crushed Catholic uprisings at the Battle of the Boyne and secured Protestant dominance in Northern Ireland.

Ireland was then mainly an agricultural country, dependent upon its farming produce. But crop failures were frequent, and famine in the middle of the nineteenth century caused death and emigration, with the result that the population was reduced by a half by 1901. The people who remained demanded more autonomy over their own affairs. Irish MPs in the Westminster Parliament called persistently for 'home rule' for Ireland (control of internal matters by the Irish through an assembly in Dublin). The home rule question dominated late nineteenth- and early twentieth-century British politics. It led to periodic outbreaks of violence as the Northern Irish Protestant majority feared that an independent and united Ireland would be dominated by the Catholics.

Eventually in 1921–22 Ireland was divided (or partitioned) into two parts as a result of uprisings, violence and eventual political agreement. This attempted solution of the historical problems has been at the root of troubles ever since. The twenty-six counties of southern Ireland became the Irish Free State and a dominion in the Commonwealth. This later developed into the Republic of Ireland (Eire), remained neutral in the Second World War and left the Commonwealth in 1949. The six counties in the north became known as Northern Ireland and remained constitutionally part of the United Kingdom. Until 1972, they had a Protestant-dominated Parliament (at Stormont outside Belfast), which was responsible for governing the province.

After the Second World War, Northern Ireland developed agriculturally and industrially. Urban centres expanded and more specifically Catholic districts developed in the towns. But the Protestants, through their ruling party (the Ulster Unionists) in Parliament, maintained an exclusive hold on all areas of life in the province, including employment, the police force, local councils and public services. The minority Catholics suffered systematic discrimination in these areas.

Conflicts arose again in Northern Ireland in 1968–69. Marches were held to demonstrate for civil liberties and were initially non-sectarian. But the situation deteriorated, fighting erupted between Protestants and Catholics and violence escalated. The Northern Ireland government asked for the British army to be sent in to restore order. The army was initially welcomed, but was soon attacked by both sides. Relations between Catholics and Protestants worsened and political attitudes became polarized. Violence continued after 1968 with outrages from both sides of the sectarian divide.

On one side of this divide is the Provisional wing of the Irish Republican Army (IRA), which is supported by some republicans and

Catholics. The IRA is illegal in both Eire and Northern Ireland and is committed to the unification of Ireland, as is its legal political wing, Provisional Sinn Fein. The IRA wants to remove the British political and military presence from Northern Ireland. Prior to the Peace Agreement in 1998, they had engaged in a campaign of bombings, shootings and murders.

Protestant paramilitary groups and Unionist Parties, such as the Democratic Unionists under the leadership of Ian Paisley, are equally committed to their own views. They are loyal to the British Crown and insist that they remain part of the United Kingdom. Protestant paramilitaries, partly in retaliation for IRA activities and partly to emphasize their demands, have also carried out sectarian murders and terrorist acts. British troops and the Northern Ireland Police Service are supposed to control the two populations and to curb terrorism. But they are also targets for bullets and bombs and have been accused of perpetrating atrocities themselves.

From 1972, responsibility for Northern Ireland rested with the British government in London (direct rule) after the Northern Ireland Parliament was dissolved. There have been various assemblies and executives in Northern Ireland, which were attempts to give the Catholic minority political representation in co-operation with the Protestant majority (power-sharing). But these efforts failed, largely because of Protestant intransigence, although most injustices to Catholic civil liberties were removed.

The level of violence in the province fluctuated from 1968. But emergency legislation and the reduction of legal rights for suspected terrorists continued. Moderates of all political persuasions, who were squeezed out as political polarization grew, were appalled by the outrages and the historical injustices. Outsiders often felt that a rational solution should be possible. But this was to underestimate the deep emotions on both sides, the historical dimension and the extremist elements. There was also little agreement over the cause of the problems, with views including ethnic, national, religious, political and economic reasons.

British governments have often launched initiatives to persuade Northern Irish political parties to discuss the realistic possibilities of power-sharing in Northern Ireland. They have also tried to involve the Irish government, and the Anglo-Irish Agreement of 1985 was a joint attempt to resolve the situation. It aimed to solve difficulties (such as border security and extradition arrangements) in order to achieve a devolved power-sharing government for Northern Ireland. The Republic of Ireland had to make some concessions as the price for the agreement, but was given a significant role to play in the resolution of the Northern Irish situation. However, the Republic's co-operation with Britain was seen by Northern Irish Protestants as a step to reunification of the island and they opposed the agreement. The Republic now sees unification as a long-term aim and the British government insists that no change in Northern Ireland will take place unless a majority of the inhabitants there agree (consent). In this connection, the population of Northern Ireland consists of a majority of those who would consider themselves to be Protestants (61.5 per cent in 2001) and a growing minority of Catholics (38.5 per cent).

The Downing Street Declaration of 1993 by the Irish and British governments was a further attempt to halt the violence and bring all parties to the conference table to discuss the future of the whole country. It largely restated existing positions. But, building on a Protestant paramilitary cease-fire, the Labour government in 1997 set out conditions and a schedule for peace talks between all the political parties. An IRA ceasefire was called which allowed Sinn Fein into the peace process beginning in September 1997.

Multi-party talks held in Belfast in April 1998 concluded with the 'Good Friday Agreement'. Legislation was passed in Dublin and London for referendums on the Agreement and provided for elections to a new Northern Ireland Assembly. In May 1998 referendums on the Agreement were held. Northern Ireland voted 71.1 per cent in favour and 28.8 per cent against, while in the Irish Republic the result was 94.3 per cent and 5.6 per cent respectively.

A new Northern Ireland Assembly of 108 members was elected by proportional representation (single transferable vote) in June 1998. A Northern Ireland Act sets out the principle of consent to any change in constitutional status in Northern Ireland, provides for its administration and contains arrangements for human rights and equality.

In December 1999, some political power was devolved by the Westminster Parliament to the Northern Ireland Assembly and its Executive. It has legislative and executive authority to make laws and take decisions in Northern Ireland, except for reserved UK powers over policing, security matters, prisons and criminal justice.

A North/South Ministerial Council, North/South Implementation Bodies, a British-Irish Council and a British/Irish Intergovernmental Conference were also established. These organizations bring together significant UK and Irish elements in the context of both islands.

It is argued that the British-Irish Council is a very positive step and a political expression of the mixed ethnic and cultural history of the British-Irish Isles. The Council comprises the UK and Irish governments, the Northern Ireland Assembly, the Welsh Assembly, the Scottish Parliament, the Isle of Man, the Channel Islands and provision for the English regions. It could promote participation in one democratic, representative British-Irish body for the first time.

However, in February 2000, following a report from the Independent International Commission on Decommissioning, the Assembly was suspended owing to a lack of progress on the decommissioning of illegally held weapons, mainly by the IRA. Direct rule from London was reimposed. Although a settlement was eventually reached and devolved powers were restored to the Assembly in May 2000, there were further suspensions in 2001 because no progress had been made on decommissioning. The Peace Agreement was in danger of collapse. But a partial IRA decommissioning in 2001 allowed the Assembly to continue.

Profound difficulties remain in the path of progress. The Protestant Unionists want to remain part of the United Kingdom, oppose union with the Republic of Ireland, insist upon the decommisioning of all IRA weapons and argue that any future solution for Northern Ireland must lie in consent by a majority of the people living there. Sinn Fein and the IRA are committed to a united Ireland and argue that a majority of all people (Northern Ireland and the Republic) must consent to any eventual proposed solution. In addition, dissident groups from the Republican and Unionist paramilitaries protest against the Good Friday Agreement and continue violent acts in both Ireland and mainland Britain. The 2001 general election resulted in increased representation in the UK Parliament for Sinn Fein and the anti-peace agreement Democratic Unionist Party, with reduced support for the Ulster Unionists and the moderate SDLP. This could indicate more extreme and hardline positions being taken in Northern Ireland, and the original euphoria over the Peace Agreement has been reduced.

Opinion polls in recent years indicate a weariness by a majority of the mainland British population with both sides in Northern Ireland. They are in favour of Irish unification and do not accept the Labour government's strategy of British withdrawal only with the consent of the majority in Northern Ireland. A *MORI* poll in August 2001 of people in mainland Britain found that 26 per cent of respondents believed that Northern Ireland should remain in the UK and 41 per cent believed that the province should join the Irish Republic.

 # Exercises

Explain and examine the following terms:

Commonwealth	Falklands	Treaty of Rome
decolonialization	Boyne	NATO
direct rule	Stormont	referendum
power-sharing	Trident	'special relationship'
Sinn Fein	Maastricht	European Commission
EFTA	IRA	pro-marketeer
euro	Unionists	EEA
'consent'	decommissioning	British-Irish Council

Write short essays on the following topics:

1   Should Northern Ireland be reunited with the Irish Republic? Give your reasons.
2   Does the Commonwealth still have a role to play today?
3   Discuss possible future developments in the European Union.
4   Does Britain still have a world role?

Further reading

Chapters in Black, J. (2000) *Modern British History from 1900* London: Macmillan

Dixon, P. (2001) *Northern Ireland: The Politics of War and Peace* London: Palgrave/ Macmillan

Warner, G. (1994) *British Foreign Policy since 1945* Oxford: Blackwell

Young, J.W. (2000) *Britain and European Unity 1945–1999* London: Macmillan

Websites

Foreign and Commonwealth Office: www.fco.gov.uk

Department for International Development: www.dfid.gov.uk

The Commonwealth: www.thecommonwealth.org

Ministry of Defence: www.mod.uk

NATO: www.nato.int

European Union: http://europa.eu.int/

Chapter 5

The legal system

LAW AND ORDER and the workings of the legal system are of concern to British people. They regularly appear near the top of public opinion polls about the state of the country.

Britain does not have a common legal system. Instead, there are three separate elements – those of England and Wales, Scotland and Northern Ireland. They often differ from each other in their procedures and court names. Some laws are only applicable to one of the nations. But, despite devolution, much Westminster legislation still applies to all of Britain.

In order to simplify matters, this chapter concentrates on the largest element – that of England and Wales – with comparative references to Scotland and Northern Ireland. The Northern Irish legal system is similar to that of England and Wales. But Scotland has historically maintained its independent legal apparatus despite being part of the UK.

British court cases are divided into civil and criminal law. Civil law involves private rights and settles disputes between individuals or organizations. It deals with claims for compensation (financial or otherwise) by a person (plaintiff) who has suffered loss or damage (such as a breach of contract or a negligent act) at the hands of another (defendant). Civil cases may be decided by settlement before trial or by a judge (and sometimes a jury) after trial.

Criminal law protects society by punishing those (the accused or defendants) who commit crimes against the state, such as theft or murder. The state usually prosecutes an individual or group at a trial in order to establish guilt. The result may be a fine or imprisonment. Such punishment is supposed to act as a deterrent to potential offenders, as well as stating society's attitudes on a range of matters.

Legal history

The legal system is among the oldest and most traditional of British institutions. Its authority and influence are due to its independence from the executive and legislative branches of government. It is supposed to serve citizens; control unlawful activities against them and the state; protect civil liberties; and support legitimate government.

But it has historically been accused of harshness; of supporting vested and political interests; favouring property rather than human rights; maintaining the isolation and mystique of the law; encouraging the delay and expense of legal actions; and showing a bias against the poor and disadvantaged. It has been criticized for its resistance to reform and the maintenance of professional privileges which can conflict with the public interest.

It is felt that the law today has still not adapted to changing conditions, nor understood the needs of contemporary society. Recent miscarriages of justice have embarrassed the police, government and judiciary and increased public concern about the quality of criminal justice. Similar misgivings are also felt about the expense and operation of the civil law.

But the legal system has changed over the centuries in response to changing structures and social philosophies. Today, consumer demands, professional pressures and government reforms are forcing it to develop, sometimes rapidly and sometimes slowly. Most people in the past were unaffected by the law. But it now involves citizens more directly and to a greater extent than before. Increased demands are made upon it by individuals, the state and corporate bodies. Concern about crime has emphasized the control role of the criminal law, while increased divorce, family break-down and a more litigious society have led to a heavier workload for the civil law.

To some extent, the differences in the various elements of the legal system are due to the events of history and the political development of the British state. English (and gradually British) legal history has been conditioned by two basic concerns: first that the law should be administered by the state in national courts and second that judges should be independent of royal and political control.

State centralization of the law in England meant that the same laws should be applicable to the whole country. But the early courts were centred mainly in London, where they dealt with canon (or church), criminal, civil and commercial law. There was an increasing need for courts in local areas outside London to apply the national law. By the end of the twelfth century, London judges travelled throughout England and decided cases locally. In 1327, Edward III appointed magistrates (Justices of the Peace) in each county who could hold alleged criminals in gaol until their later trial by a London judge. The powers of the magistrates were gradually extended and they ran a system of local criminal courts with the London judges. But there was no adequate provision for local civil courts. These were not established until 1846, and an integrated apparatus of local civil and criminal law was only gradually established at a later stage.

Over the centuries, a growing population, an expanding volume of legal work and increased social and economic complexity necessitated more courts and specialization. But the number of local and London courts in this haphazard historical development resulted in an overlapping of functions in England and Wales and diverse procedures, which hindered implementation of the law. The two periods of major reform to correct this situation were in 1873–75, when there was a complete court revision, and in 1970–71, when further changes produced the present court system in England and Wales. Similar developments occurred also in Scotland and Ireland.

The second concern was that the judiciary should be independent of the executive and legislative branches of government. Monarchs were responsible for the law in earlier centuries and later interfered in the legal process and dismissed unsympathetic judges. Judicial independence was achieved in 1701, when the Act of Settlement made judges virtually irremovable from office. This principle has now been relaxed for junior judges, who may be dismissed, and all judges convicted of criminal offences are expected to resign.

Sources of British law

The three main sources of *English/Welsh* law are the common law, statute law and European Union law. The oldest is the *common law*, based on the customs of early settlers and invaders. After the Norman Conquest, it became a body of rules and principles which was decided and written down by judges in court cases. These judgements were the law of the land. The same rules still guide judges in their interpretation of statutes and in the expansion of the common law.

Common law decisions form precedents from which judges can find the principles of law to be applied to new cases. Normally today, the creation of new precedents in England and Wales lies with the House of Lords, as the supreme court of appeal. Its rulings state the current law to be applied by all courts. The tradition of following precedent maintains consistency and continuity. But it can create conservative law and fail to take account of changing social conditions.

Statute law was originally made by the monarch. But the Westminster Parliament gradually became the legislating authority because of its growing power against the monarch. Statutes (Acts of Parliament which create new law) multiplied in the nineteenth and twentieth centuries because rules were needed for a changing society. Much British law today is in statute form and shows the influence of the state in citizens' lives. Acts of the Westminster Parliament are applicable to England, Wales and often the UK as a whole and are supreme over most other forms of law (except for some EU law).

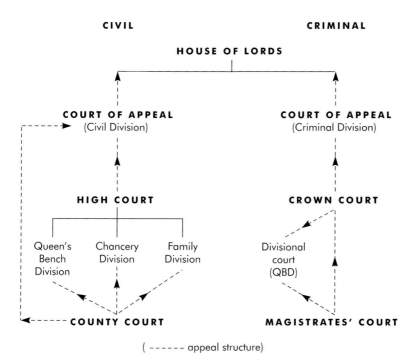

CIVIL   **CRIMINAL**

HOUSE OF LORDS

COURT OF APPEAL
(Civil Division)

COURT OF APPEAL
(Criminal Division)

HIGH COURT   **CROWN COURT**

Queen's Bench Division   Chancery Division   Family Division   Divisional court (QBD)

COUNTY COURT   **MAGISTRATES' COURT**

(------ appeal structure)

FIGURE 5.1   Civil and criminal courts in England and Wales

European Union law became part of English (British) law following Britain's entry into the European Economic Community in 1973. EU law takes precedence over British domestic law in certain areas and judges must apply EU law when there is a conflict with Acts of Parliament. EU law and British domestic law now coexist and Britain plays its part in creating EU law.

Scottish law derives from legal principles and rules modelled on both Roman and English law. The sources of Scots law are judge-made law, authoritative legal treatises, EU law and legislation. The first two are the common law of Scotland and are similar to the English common law. Legislation consists of relevant Westminster Acts of Parliament and Scottish Parliament Acts on devolved matters in Scotland.

Northern Ireland has a similar common law tradition to England and Wales. In addition to UK statutes affecting Northern Ireland, the Northern Ireland Assembly from 2000 has legislative and executive authority for all devolved matters and can thus make laws in Northern Ireland.

The court system in England and Wales

The principal court system is divided into criminal and civil courts at various levels (see figure 5.1), although the Labour government intends to reform this structure.

Criminal courts

There are two levels of criminal courts. The lower and busiest is the magistrates' court, which deals with summary (less serious) cases and handles over 95 per cent of all criminal matters. The more serious (indictable) criminal offences, such as murder, are tried by the higher court, the crown court.

Magistrates' courts serve urban and rural local areas in England and Wales. Two types of magistrates sit in the courts: Justices of the Peace (JPs) and stipendiary magistrates.

Most magistrates' courts are presided over by thirty thousand lay magistrates (JPs). They are part-time judicial officials chosen from the general public; hear cases without a jury; receive no salary for their services (only expenses); and have some legal training before they sit in court. Magistrates may be motivated by the desire to perform a public service or the supposed prestige of the position. They sit daily in big cities and less frequently in rural areas. They date from 1327 and illustrate a legal system in which the ordinary person is judged by other citizens, rather than by professionals.

Magistrates are appointed by the Crown on the advice of the Lord Chancellor, who receives suitable names from county committees. This procedure has been criticized for its secrecy and exclusivity. Magistrates in the past were white middle- or upper-class males who were prominent in the local community, such as landowners, doctors, retired military officers and businessmen. But they are now recruited from wider and more representative social, ethnic and gender backgrounds.

The magistrates' court has an average of three JPs when hearing cases, composed usually of men and women. They decide a case on the facts and decide the punishment (if any). They are advised on points of law by their clerk, who is a legally qualified, full-time official and a professional element in the system. The clerk is restricted to an advisory role and must not be involved in the magistrates' decision-making, but is now able to handle some minor judicial tasks.

Everyone accused of a criminal offence (defendant) must usually appear first before a magistrates' court. The court can itself try summary offences and some indictable/summary offences ('either-way offences'). The

PLATE 5.1 Inside a magistrates' court (*Priscilla Coleman*)

magistrates also decide whether there is a case to answer in indictable offences. If so, they commit the person for trial at the crown court.

Magistrates have limited powers of punishment. They may impose fines up to £5,000 for each offence, or send people to prison for six months on each offence up to a maximum of one year. They prefer not to imprison if a fine or other punishment is sufficient, and the majority of penalties are fines.

There is a need for uniform punishments in magistrates' courts. But sentences vary in different parts of the country. This factor, in addition to alleged bias and the amateur status of JPs, has led to criticism of the system. There have been proposals to replace magistrates with lawyers or other experts. But these suggestions are criticized by those who oppose the professionalization of the legal process and who argue that such changes would not necessarily result in greater competence or justice. It may be that magistrates will work in court with district judges in future.

An important function of magistrates is to decide cases involving young persons under eighteen in Youth Courts. Media reports of these cases must not normally identify the accused, and there is a range of punishments for those found guilty. Youth Courts play a central role, particularly at a time when many crimes are committed by young people under sixteen. The Labour government proposes tougher treatment for young offenders.

PLATE 5.2 The Old Bailey, London (© *Rupert Horrox/CORBIS*)

Magistrates' courts also handle limited civil matters involving family problems and divorce; road traffic violations; and licence applications for public amenities such as restaurants, clubs, public houses (pubs) and betting shops.

Stipendiary magistrates are qualified lawyers and full-time officials, are paid by the state, usually sit alone to hear and decide cases and work mainly in the large cities. They relieve the magistrates of some of their caseload, and generally deal with the more serious or difficult summary offences. Since the magistrate system is divided between JPs and professional stipendiaries, it is sometimes argued that the latter should be used to replace the amateurs on a national basis. But this proposal has been resisted by those who wish to retain the civilian element in the magistrates' courts.

The higher *crown courts*, such as the Central Criminal Court in London (popularly known as the Old Bailey), are situated in about ninety cities in England and Wales and are administered by the Lord Chancellor's Department in London.

The crown court has jurisdiction over all indictable criminal offences, and innocence or guilt after a trial is decided by a jury of twelve citizens. After it has reached its decision on the facts of the case, sentence is passed by the judge who is in charge of proceedings throughout the trial.

In *Scotland*, minor criminal cases are tried summarily by lay Justices of the Peace in district courts (equivalent to English magistrates' courts).

Sheriffs' courts deal with more serious offences, where the sheriff sits alone to hear summary offences and is helped by a jury (fifteen members) for indictable cases. The most serious cases (such as murder and rape) are handled by the High Court of Justiciary in major urban centres and are heard by a judge and a jury of fifteen lay people. *Northern Irish* criminal courts follow the system in England and Wales with lower magistrates' courts and higher crown courts. Jury trials have the same place in the system, except in the case of offences involving acts of terrorism, where a single judge may hear and decide the case without a jury.

Criminal appeal courts

The appeal structure (see figure 5.1) is supposed to be a safeguard against mistakes and miscarriages of justice. But the number of such cases has increased, resulting in much publicity and concern. They have been caused by police tampering with or withholding evidence; police pressure to induce confessions; and the unreliability of forensic evidence. Appeal courts are criticized for their handling of some appeals, and an independent authority (the Criminal Cases Review Commission) was created (1995). It reviews alleged miscarriages of justice and now receives many applications.

Appeals to a higher court can be expensive and difficult and permission must usually have been granted by a lower court. Appeals may be made against conviction or sentence and can be brought on grounds of fact and law. If successful, the higher court may quash the conviction, reduce the sentence or order a new trial. The prosecution can also appeal against a lenient punishment and a heavier sentence may be substituted.

The crown courts hear appeals from the magistrates' courts and both may appeal on matters of law to a divisional court of the Queen's Bench Division. Appeals from the crown court are made to the Criminal Division of the Court of Appeal. Appeals may then go to the House of Lords as the highest court in England and Wales. But permission is granted only if a point of law of public importance is involved. Up to five Law Lords hear the case and their decisions represent the current state of the law.

In *Scotland*, the High Court of Justiciary in Edinburgh tries criminal cases and is the supreme court for criminal appeals. *Northern Ireland* has its own appeal courts, but the House of Lords in London may also be used.

Civil courts

Civil law proceedings are brought either in the county court (which deals with 90 per cent of civil cases) or in the High Court (see figure 5.1). Less expensive and complex actions are dealt with in the county court, rather than the High Court, and most civil disputes do not reach court at all.

England and Wales are divided into 250 districts with a *county court* for each district. The county court handles a range of money, property, contract, divorce and family matters and a district judge usually sits alone when hearing cases.

The *High Court of Justice* has its main centre in London, with branches throughout England and Wales. It is divided into three divisions which specialize in specific matters. The *Queen's Bench Division* has a wide jurisdiction, including contract and negligence cases; the *Chancery Court Division* is concerned with commercial, financial and succession matters; and the *Family Division* deals with domestic issues such as marriage, divorce, property and the custody of children.

In *Scotland*, the sheriff court deals with most civil actions, because its jurisdiction is not financially limited, although the higher Court of Session may also be used for some cases. The *Northern Irish* High Court handles most civil cases.

Civil appeal courts in England and Wales

The High Court hears appeals from magistrates' courts and county courts. But the main avenue of appeal is to the Court of Appeal (Civil Division), which deals with appeals from all lower civil courts on questions of law and fact. It can reverse or amend decisions, or sometimes order a new trial.

Appeals from the Court of Appeal may be made to the House of Lords. The appellant must normally have obtained permission either from the Court of Appeal or the House of Lords. Appeals are usually restricted to points of law where an important legal issue is at stake. In *Scotland* at present, civil appeals are made first to a sheriff-principal, then to the Court of Session and finally to the House of Lords in London. The *Northern Irish* Court of Appeal hears appeal cases.

Civil and criminal proceedings

Many features of civil and criminal procedure in Scotland and Northern Ireland are similar to those in England and Wales.

Civil procedure

A civil action in the county court or the High Court begins when the plaintiff serves documents with details of a claim on the defendant. If the defendant defends the action, documents are prepared and circulated to all parties and the case proceeds to trial and judgement. A decision in civil cases is reached on the balance of probabilities. The court also decides the

PLATE 5.3   The Royal Courts of Justice, London (*John Oakland*)

expenses of the action, which may be considerable, and the loser usually pays both his or her own and the opponent's costs.

Civil law procedures have been reorganized and simplified (1999) because of concern about the efficiency of the system, with its delays and expense. Much of the High Court's work has been transferred to the county court, procedural rules between the two courts have been unified, active court management is now in place and cheaper, quicker alternative forms of settlement in other courts have been implemented, particularly those dealing with smaller matters. Nevertheless, it is often advisable that disputes be settled by negotiation out of court to avoid high costs and any uncertainty about a trial result.

Criminal procedure

Crimes are offences against the laws of the state and the state usually brings a person to trial. Prior to 1985, the police in England and Wales were responsible for prosecuting criminal cases. But a Crown Prosecution Service (CPS) now does this job. It is independent of the police, financed by the state and staffed by state lawyers. There is criticism of the performance of the CPS, which suffers from understaffing and underfunding. The CPS and its head (the Director of Public Prosecutions – DPP) have the final word in deciding whether to proceed with difficult cases. In *Scotland*, prosecution duties rest with the Crown Office and Procurator-Fiscal Service and in *Northern Ireland* with the police and the DPP.

Arrests for most criminal offences are made by the police, although any citizen can make a 'citizen's arrest'.

After criticism of the police for their arrest, questioning and charging practices, they now operate under codes of practice, which lay down strict procedures for the protection of suspects. The police cannot formally interrogate people, nor detain them at a police station, if they have not been arrested or charged. Once a person has been arrested and charged with an offence, he or she must be brought before a magistrates' court, normally within twenty-four hours. This period can be extended up to ninety-six hours without charge in serious cases. After ninety-six hours, the suspect must be released if no charges are brought.

When a person appears before a magistrates' court prior to a trial, the magistrates can grant or refuse bail (freedom from custody). If bail is refused, a person will be kept in custody in a remand centre or in prison. If bail is granted, the individual is set free until a later court appearance. The court may require certain assurances from the accused about conduct while on bail, such as residence in a specific area and reporting to a police station.

Application for bail is a legal right, since the accused has not yet been found guilty of a crime, and there should be strong reasons for refusing it.

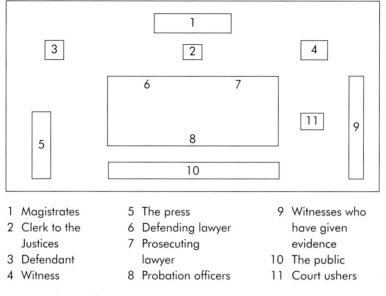

1 Magistrates
2 Clerk to the Justices
3 Defendant
4 Witness
5 The press
6 Defending lawyer
7 Prosecuting lawyer
8 Probation officers
9 Witnesses who have given evidence
10 The public
11 Court ushers

FIGURE 5.2 A typical magistrates' court in action

There is concern that people who are refused bail are, at their later trial, either found not guilty or are punished only by a fine. The system thus holds alleged criminals who have been refused bail (60 per cent) on remand to await trial and increases overcrowding in prisons. But there is also public concern about accused persons who commit further serious offences while free on bail.

Criminal trials in the magistrates' and crown courts are, with a few exceptions, open to the public. But the media can only report the court proceedings and must not comment upon them while the trial is in progress (the *sub judice* rule).

The accused enters the dock, the charge is read and he or she pleads 'guilty' or 'not guilty'. On a 'guilty' plea, the person is often sentenced after a short presentation of the facts by the prosecution. On a 'not guilty' plea, the trial proceeds in order to establish the person's innocence or guilt. An individual is innocent until proved guilty, and it is the responsibility of the prosecution to prove guilt beyond a reasonable doubt. If proof is not achieved, a 'not guilty' verdict is returned by magistrates in the magistrates' court or by the jury in the crown court. In Scotland, there is an additional possible verdict of 'not proven'.

The prosecution and defence of the accused are usually performed by solicitors in magistrates' courts and by barristers and solicitor-advocates in crown courts. But it is possible to defend oneself. British trials are adversarial contests between defence and prosecution. Both sides call witnesses

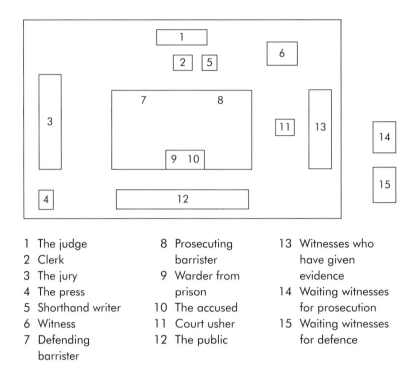

1 The judge
2 Clerk
3 The jury
4 The press
5 Shorthand writer
6 Witness
7 Defending
   barrister

8 Prosecuting
   barrister
9 Warder from
   prison
10 The accused
11 Court usher
12 The public

13 Witnesses who
    have given
    evidence
14 Waiting witnesses
    for prosecution
15 Waiting witnesses
    for defence

FIGURE 5.3 A typical crown court in action

in support of their case, who may be questioned by the other side. The rules of evidence and procedure in this contest are complicated and must be strictly observed. The accused may remain silent when arrested and charged and at the trial and need not give evidence. However, the right to silence has now been limited. This means that the police must warn arrestees that their silence may affect their later defence. The judge at the trial may comment on silence and it may influence the decision of juries and magistrates.

It is argued that the adversarial nature of criminal trials can result either in the conviction of innocent people or the guilty escaping conviction. It is suggested that the inquisitorial system of other European countries would be better. This allows the prior questioning of suspects and establishing of facts to be carried out by professional impartial interrogators rather than the police.

The judge in the crown court and the magistrates in the magistrates' court are controlling influences in the battle between defence and prosecution. They apply the rules of the court and give directions on procedure and evidence. But they should not interfere too actively, nor show bias. After the prosecution and the defence have concluded their cases, the magistrates decide both the verdict and sentence. In the crown court, the jury

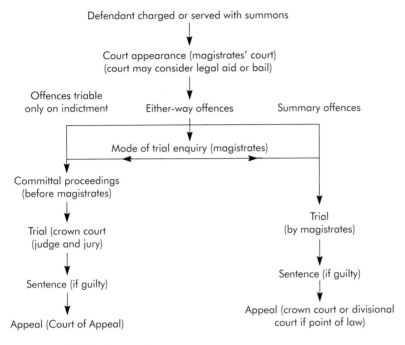

FIGURE 5.4 Criminal procedure

delivers the verdict after the judge has given a summing-up and the judge then pronounces sentence.

The jury

Trial by jury is an ancient and important feature of British justice. It has declined in civil cases (except for libel and fraud), but is the main element in criminal trials in the crown court for indictable offences. Most British residents are obliged to undertake jury service when summoned and there has been a clampdown on those seeking to avoid the duty.

Before the start of a criminal trial in the crown court, twelve jurors are chosen from a list of thirty names randomly selected from local electoral registers. They listen to the evidence at the trial and give their verdict on the facts, after having been isolated in a room for their deliberations. If a jury cannot reach a decision, it will be discharged and a new one sworn in. The accused can thus be tried twice for the same offence (as in appeals which order a new trial or in the re-hearing of cases where new evidence appears). Such results are an exception to the principle that a person can be tried only once for the same offence. In most cases, the jury reaches a decision. The judge accepts a majority (rather than a unanimous) verdict after the jury has deliberated for more than two hours, if there are no more than two dissentients (ten to two). The jury does not decide the punishment or sentence, except in some civil cases, where it awards damages.

The jury system is the citizen's link with the legal process. It is supposed to safeguard individual liberty and justice because a common-sense decision on the facts either to punish or acquit is taken by fellow citizens. But the system has been criticized because of high acquittal rates; allegedly unsuitable or subjective jurors; intimidation of jurors; and need to save time and expense. Some critics wish to replace the jury with 'experts' and the Labour government intends to reduce the right to jury trial in some 'either-way' offences.

Legal aid

Legal aid (created in 1949) enables persons who cannot afford legal representation and advice in criminal and civil matters to have their bills paid by the state. Applicants must prove that they have a suitable case and that their income falls below certain financial limits. Only those with very low incomes or who are receiving welfare benefits qualify. There are demands to raise the income limits to include more people. But governments have reduced the legal aid fund and reformed its operation so that fewer people are eligible for help. This is seen as a serious development in the provision of justice, especially when demand is constantly rising. Given the high costs of legal actions, only the poor or the very rich can afford to take on litigation costs without hardship.

A recent reform may help those people who wish to start personal injury civil actions but who cannot afford the cost. Clients can enter into conditional agreements with lawyers, in which payment of legal fees on the basis of a percentage of the amount awarded is made only if the client wins. The Labour government may extend this scheme to most civil disputes which involve money or damages. But critics argue that such work will appeal only to lawyers if there is a reasonable chance of winning and it will not solve the problem of insuring against the cost of losing.

Law and order

Crime and punishment

The overall cost of crime to Britain (including the expense of the criminal justice system) is considerable, amounting to 5 per cent of government spending. Law and order in Britain are serious issues, which are of great concern to people and on which political parties base their claims for public support.

Central problems here are the reliability of official statistics and the non-reporting of offences such as burglary and rape. Government figures show that there was a 3.8 per cent increase in overall reported crime in 2000 in England and Wales (1 per cent in Scotland), with rises in violent crimes such as assaults, robberies and sexual offences. But the number of unsolved crimes remains high, with a clear-up rate of 24 per cent.

It is estimated that only one in fifty crimes results in a conviction, and the Home Office itself admits that only 23 per cent of all crimes are recorded. *MORI* polls suggest that 50 per cent of victims do not report incidents to the police because they lack confidence that criminals would be caught.

However, contrasting crime figures are found in victim-based statistics such as the *British Crime Survey*, which covers people who actually experience crime. Figures for 2000 suggest a decrease of 12 per cent. Violent crimes fell by 19 per cent and the proportion of people who were victims of some type of crime once or more during 2001 fell to 27 per cent.

Disturbing aspects of these statistics are the greater use of firearms in criminal acts (leading to demands that the police should be armed), the increased amount of drug- and alchohol-related crime and the number of offences committed by young people. Britain has a serious problem with young offenders: the peak age for committing crime is fifteen and one in four criminal offences is committed by teenagers under sixteen.

Respondents to polls think that the causes of crime in Britain are lack of parental discipline; drugs; alcohol; lenient sentencing; unemployment; lack of school discipline; poverty; television; and poor policing. The Labour government has tried to ease public concern by promising 'zero tolerance' for crime and being 'tough on crime and the causes of crime'. There would be stricter punishment (particularly for young people), curfews and restrictions on persistent offenders, longer gaol terms and greater protection for the public. But polls in 2000 and 2001 show that people do not think that the government has delivered on its law and order promises.

A person found guilty of a first criminal offence may receive no punishment, or be placed on probation for a period under supervision of probation officers. Other punishments for adults are often fines or imprisonment (for those over twenty-one), which vary according to the severity of the offence and any previous convictions. Stricter sentencing will lead to more prisoners, and 18 per cent of convicted persons are imprisoned, a higher rate than in other European countries. Britain has one of the largest prison populations in Western Europe with 105,000 prisoners in 2001 (4 per cent women).

Alternatives to prison are community service (serving the community in some capacity for a number of hours) and prison sentences which are suspended, i.e. not served if no further offences are committed for a specified period. A successful experiment is 'tagging' (arm or leg bracelets connected electronically to local police stations) whereby non-violent offenders are confined to a specific area and have to observe a curfew. The tag is activated if these conditions are broken.

Young people may be punished by fines (if under seventeen), taken into local authority care, confined in a young offenders' institution (Youth Prison) for those between seventeen and twenty, or undergo supervision in the community. Re-offending among young people after a custodial sentence is high, but supervision outside institutions leads less often to re-offending.

The death penalty by hanging for murder was abolished in 1965. The House of Commons has since voted on several occasions against its re-imposition. Polls show that only one Briton in four wants the restoration of the death penalty for murder. But the public seem to support harsh treatment of criminal offenders and argue that more sympathy and aid should be given to the victims of crime. The government has tried to support such victims with financial compensation, but its programmes have not satisfied the critics or the victims.

Many British people feel that the penalties for criminal offences are inadequate as deterrents to prevent crime. But many prisons are old and decayed, lack humane facilities, are unfitted for a modern penal system and their personnel are understaffed and overworked. Prison conditions have resulted in serious disorder and riots in recent years and low morale among prisoners and prison staff. Debates about punishment as opposed to the rehabilitation of offenders continue. But proposals to improve the situation usually encounter the problems of expense, although the government is building more courts and prisons. Some prisons and prison services (such as escorting prisoners to court) have now been privatized.

The majority of prisoners are not reformed by their sentences, nor does fear of prison or punishment seem to act as a deterrent. Some critics argue that gaol terms should be cut (with weekend-only prisoners) and that institutions should be humanized and prisoners given a sense of purpose. Alternatives to custodial sentences, such as supervised housing, probation hostels and supervised work projects, are also advocated. But others argue that the main concern of the criminal system should be punishment and not rehabilitation.

Law enforcement and the police

The armed forces in Britain are subordinate to the civilian government and are used only for defence or civil emergency purposes. An exception has been the deployment of the army in Northern Ireland since 1969, where they support the police force (the Police Force of Northern Ireland).

But there are proposals that the military could help the police to counter organized crime in drugs, illegal immigration and computer hacking.

However, the maintenance of law and order rests mainly with the civilian police. The oldest police force is the Metropolitan Police, founded in 1829 by Sir Robert Peel to combat crime in London, and from which the modern forces have grown. Today there is no one national police force. Instead, there are fifty-two independent forces, which undertake law enforcement in local county or regional areas, with the Metropolitan Police being responsible for policing London. The regional forces are under the political control of local police committees, although their direct influence is small. Authority rests with the head of each regional force (Chief Constable), who has organizational independence and responsibility for the actions of the force. But the Home Secretary is responsible for the Metropolitan Police, which is centred on New Scotland Yard in London.

There are about 126,000 policemen and women in Britain, or one officer for every 460 people. But the forces have lost officers, are under-staffed and recruitment is difficult. Only a disproportionately small number are from ethnic communities. Many members of these communities are hostile to or sceptical of the police, although there have been attempts to recruit more of them to the forces, with varying degrees of success. There are government proposals to involve traffic wardens, special constables and a new London auxiliary force to help in some police duties and to give a greater street presence.

The police are not allowed to join trade unions or strike. But they do have staff associations to represent their interests. They are subject to the law, and can be sued or prosecuted for any wrongdoing in the course of their work. But it is difficult to bring successful prosecutions against them, although individuals can appeal to the Police Complaints Authority. However, this body is largely composed of police representatives and lacks independence. It is argued that complaints procedures are unsatisfactory and that democratic control of the police in practice does not exist.

The police, with their peculiar helmets and lack of firearms, are often regarded as a typical British institution. They used to embody a presence in the local community by 'walking the beat' and personified fairness, stolidity, friendliness, helpfulness and incorruptibility. These virtues still exist to a degree, and the traditional view is that the police should control the community by consent rather than force and that they should be visible in local areas.

But, in recent years, the police have been taken off foot patrols and put into cars to increase effectiveness and mobility; more are now armed and trained in riot-control programmes. They have been accused of insti-tutional racism, corruption, brutality, excessive use of force, perverting the course of justice and tampering with evidence in criminal trials. Some of

PLATE 5.4   British riot police in action in London (© *Alan Copson*)

these accusations have been proved in a number of cases. They have lowered the image of the police as well as their morale and have contributed to a loss of public confidence. The Labour government is concerned to reform the police forces and some of their practices.

The police tread a thin line in community activities, strikes and demonstrations. They are in the middle of opposing forces, much is expected of them and uncertain law sometimes hinders their effectiveness. The problems of violent crime, relations with ethnic communities and an increasingly complex society have made their job more difficult. The police are trying to find ways of adequately and fairly controlling a changing society. They are concerned about their image, but insist that their primary duty is to maintain law and order.

The legal profession

The legal profession in England and Wales is divided into two types of lawyer: barristers and solicitors. Each branch has its own vested interests and jurisdiction and fiercely protects its position. This system is criticized because of duplication of services, delay and expense. But reforms have occurred in legal services in order to benefit consumers, promote competition and give easier access to the law.

There are some 90,000 *solicitors*, who practise mainly in private firms, but also in local and central government, legal centres and industry. Most are now organized by their self-regulating professional body, the Law Society. The solicitors' branch is a middle-class profession, but it is increasingly attracting members from a relatively wide spectrum of society.

Solicitors deal with general legal work, although many now specialize in one area of the law. Their firms (or partnerships) offer services such as conveyancing (the buying and selling of property); probate (wills and succession after death); family matters; criminal and civil litigation; commercial cases; and tax and financial affairs.

Complaints by dissatisfied clients against solicitors, of which there are an increasing number (some 16,000 a year), are investigated by the Office for the Supervision of Solicitors. This body is supposed to provide an impartial investigation into complaints but has been criticized by consumers and has now been brought under the direct control of the Law Society.

The client with a legal problem will first approach a solicitor, who can often deal with all aspects of the case. But solicitors were once able to appear (rights of audience) for their clients only in the lower courts (county and magistrates' courts) and cases in higher courts had to be handed to a barrister. This expensive practice has now been reformed and solicitor-advocates can appear in higher courts.

In order to become a solicitor, it is necessary to have a university degree, not necessarily in law. After passing further professional examinations organized by the Law Society, the student serves a practical apprenticeship as a trainee solicitor with an established solicitor for some two years. After this total period of about six years' education and training, the new solicitor can practise law.

There are 10,000 *barristers* in private practice, who have the right to appear before any court in England and Wales. They belong to the Bar, which is an ancient legal institution controlled by the self-regulating Bar Council and four Inns of Court in London (Gray's Inn, Lincoln's Inn, Middle Temple and the Inner Temple). Barristers have two functions: to give specialized advice on legal matters and to act as advocates in the courts. Most of the general public cannot approach a barrister directly, but must be introduced by a solicitor.

In order to become a barrister, one must usually have a university degree, pass professional examinations and become a member of an Inn of Court. The student must dine in the Inn for a number of terms before being 'called to the Bar', or accepted as a barrister. He or she must then serve for a one-year period (pupillage) under a practising barrister. After this total training period of about five years, the new barrister can practise alone.

Barristers are self-employed individuals who practise from chambers (or offices), together with other barristers. The barrister's career starts as

PLATE 5.5 Outside a barrister's chambers in Middle Temple, London
(© *Adam Woolfit/CORBIS*)

a 'junior' handling minor briefs (or cases). He or she may have difficulty in earning a living or in becoming established in the early years of practice, with the result that many barristers drop out and enter other fields. Should the barrister persist and build up a successful practice as a junior, he or she may 'take silk' and become a Queen's Counsel (QC). A QC is a senior barrister who can charge higher fees for his or her work, but who is then excluded from appearing in lesser cases. Appointment as a QC may lead to a future position as a judge and it is regarded as a necessary career step for the ambitious.

The *judges* constitute the judiciary, or independent third branch of the constitutional system. There are a relatively small number of judges at various levels of seniority, who are located im most large cities and in the higher courts in London. They are chosen from the ranks of senior barristers, although solicitors are now eligible for some of the lower posts. The highest appointments are made by the Crown on the advice of the Prime Minister and lower positions on the advice of the Lord Chancellor. This appointments procedure has been criticized because it rests with the Lord Chancellor and the senior judiciary, who consequently hold much power and patronage. In an attempt to combat 'elitism', more judgeships are now advertised for open competition.

The Lord Chancellor is a political appointee of the sitting government; effective head of the legal system and profession; a member of the Cabinet; presiding officer (or Speaker) of the House of Lords; and a law lord. It is argued that this office should be abolished because of its political connections. Other judgeships are supposedly made on non-political grounds. Senior judges cannot be removed from office until the retirement age of seventy-five, although junior judges can be dismissed by the Lord Chancellor for good reasons before the retirement age at seventy-two. There have been proposals that complaints against judges and their dismissal should be handled by a complaints board and that judges should be more easily removable from office. But the existing measures have been designed to ensure the independence of the judiciary and its freedom from political involvement.

Critics feel that judges are socially and educationally elitist, remote from ordinary life and overwhelmingly male. They are seen as people who will not cause embarrassment to the establishment and who tend to support the accepted wisdom and *status quo*. However, they do rule against government policies and their powers of independence have arguably been increased by the Human Rights Act. The judiciary is gradually changing to admit more women, ethnic minorities and people with lower-class and educationally diverse backgrounds. But, although over half of law students are female, there are few women judges, QCs, or senior partners in solicitors' firms.

The judiciary tends to be old in years because judgeships are normally awarded to senior practising lawyers and there is no career structure that people may join early in life. A lawyer's income may be greatly reduced on accepting a judgeship, but the honour and added security are supposed to be some compensation. There are promotional steps within the judiciary from recorder to circuit judge to High Court judge, and thence to the Court of Appeal and the House of Lords.

The legal professions in *Scotland* and *Northern Ireland* are also divided. Scotland has some 400 practising advocates (barristers) and 8,250 solicitors. Advocates practise as individuals, do not work from chambers and are independent of each other. Scottish solicitors usually operate in partnership with other solicitors. Northern Ireland has solicitors and about 450 barristers.

Attitudes to law and order

Britain is not usually thought of as a litigious society. People avoid the difficulty and cost of legal actions if possible and regard the law and lawyers as a last resort. Polls frequently show that while the police (perhaps surprisingly) are the most admired professional group after doctors and nurses, lawyers are the least admired. But, in recent years, more Britons have been using the civil law to gain satisfaction and large damages for matters ranging from libel cases to complaints about the school and health systems.

Polls reveal consistently that many British people have little confidence in the legal system. A *MORI* poll in 2000 showed that 47 per cent of respondents were dissatisfied with the courts and their work, while 32 per cent were satisfied. There is support for legal reforms and a desire to see more government action on the law's delays, risks and costs. But a *Property Litigation Association* survey in 2001 reported that continuing delays, inefficiencies and lack of resources in civil courts were hindering reforms. Nevertheless, a 1999 *British Council/MORI* poll found that 58 per cent of overseas respondents thought that the British legal system ensures that everyone gets a fair trial.

Crime, vandalism and violence are a main concern for many Britons. In June 2001, a *MORI* poll showed that in a list of worries 33 per cent of respondents worried about law and order, an increase since 1996. A *NatWest* survey in 1997 indicated that 70 per cent of respondents would accept tax rises if significant cuts in crime would result. Nearly 50 per cent considered drugs and drug-related offences to be the biggest crime problems, far ahead of burglary and assault.

In spite of the fact that fear of crime is arguably greater than its actuality, polls reveal that many people are afraid: feel unsafe walking alone after dark; believe that worries about crime affect their everyday life; and think that the police are handicapped in the fight against crime by the criminal justice system. The *Crimestoppers Trust* reported in September 2001 that three-quarters of British people believe that the country has become a more dangerous place to live in over the past ten years. In terms of neighbourhood crime, 56 per cent said they feared burglary and 35 per cent car crime; and 20 per cent would not go to the police if they had information about a crime.

In a 2000 *MORI* poll, 44 per cent of interviewees were fairly satisfied and 9 per cent very satisfied with the way their areas were policed. When asked how confident they were that the police would arrive in an emergency within ten minutes, 37 per cent were fairly and 13 per cent very confident. But 44 per cent were not confident.

Some 72 per cent of respondents strongly agreed that people should have the right to defend their property and 24 per cent tended to agree. Some 64 per cent strongly agreed that the law is too lenient on criminals who commit property theft and 22 per cent tended to agree.

Exercises

Explain and examine the following terms:

civil law	plaintiff	conveyancing
barrister	legal aid	Crown Prosecution Service
indictable	Inns of Court	common law
solicitor	Lord Chancellor	Metropolitan Police
jury	crown court	county court
JP	statute law	bail
'tagging'	summary	stipendiary magistrate

Write short essays on the following topics:

1   Describe and comment critically on the structure of the legal profession in Britain.
2   How is the courts system in England and Wales organized?
3   Discuss the role of the police in law enforcement.

Further reading

Berlins, M. and Dyer, C (2000) *The Law Machine* London: Penguin

Robertson, G. (1993) *Freedom, the Individual and the Law* London: Pelican

White, Robin (1999) *The English Legal System in Action: Administration of Justice* Oxford: Oxford University Press

Websites

Lord Chancellor's Department; www.lcd.gov.uk

Law Officers: www.lslo.gov.uk

Home Office: www.homeoffice.gov.uk

Police: www.police.co.uk

New Scotland Yard: www.open.gov.uk/police/mps/home.htm

Amnesty International: www.amnesty.org.uk

Scottish Executive: www.scotland.gov.uk

Northern Ireland Office: www.nio.gov.uk

The economy

Fluctuations in the british economy affect people directly and are of concern to them. They influence employment, income levels, taxation, investment and government programmes.

Historically, the British economy has been conditioned by agricultural and industrial revolutions; the growth and later reduction of manufacturing industry; the expansion of service industries; government policies and intervention; and a decline from the late nineteenth century relative to other competitor countries. It experienced both recession and growth throughout the twentieth century, but developed successfully from 1994 with low inflation, unemployment and interest rates. However, there were again signs of weakness in 2001 due to a domestic and global economic downturn.

Economic history

Britain was a largely rural country until the end of the eighteenth century and its economy was based on products generated by agricultural revolutions. But there had also been industrial and manufacturing developments over the centuries, which were mainly located in the larger towns. Financial and commercial institutions, such as banks, insurance houses and trading companies, were gradually founded in the City of London and throughout the country to finance and service the expanding and increasingly diversified economy.

The growth of an overseas colonial empire from the sixteenth century contributed to national wealth as Britain capitalized on its worldwide trading connections. Colonies supplied cheap raw materials, which were converted into manufactured goods in Britain and exported. Overseas markets grew quickly because merchants and traders were protected at home and abroad. They exploited the colonial markets and controlled foreign competition. By the nineteenth century, Britain had become an economic power. Its wealth was based on international trade and the payments that it received for its exported products. Governments believed that a country increased its wealth if exports exceeded imports.

This trading system and its financial institutions benefited industrial revolutions, which began in the late eighteenth century. Manufacturing and industrial inventions, together with a rich supply of domestic materials and energy sources, such as coal, steel, iron, steam power and water, stimulated production and the economy. Manufacturers, who had gained by foreign trade and demand for British goods, invested in new industries and technology. Industrial towns expanded, factories were built and a transport system of roads, canals and railways developed. Efficient manufacturing produced competitively priced goods for foreign markets and Britain was transformed into an urban and industrialized country.

But industrialization was opposed by some people. The Luddites in the nineteenth century, for example, destroyed new machinery in an attempt to halt progress and preserve existing jobs. Industrial and urban development had negative effects, such as long working hours for low wages and bad conditions in mines and factories. They also resulted in the depopulation of rural areas and the decline of traditional home and cottage work. Industrial conditions caused social and moral problems in towns and the countryside, and mechanization was often regarded as exploitative and dehumanizing. The situation was worsened by the indifference of many manufacturers, employers and politicians to the human cost of industrialization.

However, the industrial changes did transform Britain into a rich nation, despite economic slumps, unemployment, growth of urban slums and hardship in the nineteenth century. Manufacturing output was now the chief generator of wealth; production methods and technology advanced; and domestic competition improved the quality of goods and services.

But this industrial dominance of world trade did not last. It declined relatively by the end of the nineteenth century as countries such as Germany and the USA industrialized and became competitive. However, British financial expertise continued to be influential in global commercial dealings.

The modern economy: policies, structure and performance

It is argued that British economic performance and world status declined further in the twentieth century, although some research queries whether decline has been as substantial in relative terms as is popularly assumed. But Britain was affected by economic problems created by two World Wars; international recessions; global competition; structural changes in the economy; a lack of industrial competitiveness; alternating government policies; and a series of 'boom-and-bust' cycles in which economic growth fluctuated greatly.

Economic policies

Governments became more involved in economic planning from the 1940s, and the performance of the economy has been tied to their fiscal and monetary policies. All British governments have variously intervened in economic life in attempts to manage the economy and stimulate demand and growth.

The Conservative Party, however, has traditionally advocated a minimum interference in the economy and favoured the workings of the market. But, in practice, government intervention was necessary as global competition grew and domestic demands became more complex. The Labour Party argued that the economy should be centrally planned and its essential sectors should be owned and managed by the state. This policy in Clause 4 of its constitution was dropped only in 1995.

Labour governments from 1945 consequently nationalized (moved to public ownership) railways, road transport, water, gas, electricity, shipbuilding, coal-mining, the iron and steel industries, airlines, the health service, the Post Office and telecommunications. Public industries and services were run by the state through government-appointed boards. They were responsible to Parliament and subsidized by taxation for the benefit of all, rather than for private owners or shareholders. But they were expensive to run and governments were expected to rescue any which had economic problems.

This policy was gradually reversed by the Conservatives. They argued that public industries and services were too expensive and inefficient; had outdated technology and bad industrial relations; suffered from lack of investment in new equipment; were dependent upon tax subsidies; and were run as state services with too little attention paid to profit-making, consumer demand or market forces. They denationalized some state industries and returned them to private ownership.

Conservative denationalization was later (1979–97) called 'privatization'. Ownership of state industries such as British Telecom, British Airways, British Petroleum, British Gas, water and electricity supplies, British Coal and British Rail was transferred from the state to private owners mainly through the sale of shares. These industries are run as profit-making concerns and are regulated in the public interest by independent regulators. The aim was to 'deregulate' the economy so that restrictions on businesses were removed to allow them to operate freely and competitively. For example, the stock market and public transport were deregulated, resulting in greater diversity in the City of London and local authority bus companies competing with private bus firms.

Conservatives believe that privatization improves efficiency, reduces government spending, increases economic freedom and encourages share ownership. The public bought shares in the new private companies, and share-owning by individuals and financial institutions increased. But there was concern about privatization. Private industries became virtual monopolies (although there is now more competition) and there is criticism of the independent regulators' abilities to supervise them. There have been complaints about their services, prices and products, although some of them are now profitable and many initial problems have been solved.

The Labour government (1997–) accepted privatization and is controversially part-privatizing UK air traffic control and the London Tube. It also wants to introduce the private sector into public services such as education and health. 'Public–private partnerships' can mean, for example, private companies managing public concerns or even building and running state schools and hospitals. The policy is attacked by trade unions, and a *MORI* poll in July 2001 found that only 8 per cent of respondents thought that hiring private sector managers to run public services would lead to big improvements. Only 11 per cent believed that using private companies to provide public services will improve them. A *MORI* poll in September 2001 showed that large majorities considered that schools, hospitals, trains, public utilities (water and electricity) and pensions should be provided by the public sector.

However, the major parties have now accepted 'market economics', deregulation, a mobile workforce and economic liberalization. The problem is how to manage this economy effectively, while satisfying demands for public services.

Economic structure

Government policies have created a mixed economy of public and private sectors. The public sector includes the remaining state-run industries and public services, which now amount to under one-third of the economy. Over two-thirds is in the private sector and will increase with further privatization.

Unlike public-sector concerns which are owned and run by the state, the private sector belongs to people who have a financial stake in a company. It consists of small businesses owned by individuals; companies whose shares are sold to the public through the Stock Exchange; and larger companies whose shares are not offered for sale to the public. Most companies are private and small or medium-size. They are crucial to the economy and generate 50 per cent of new jobs. Some 10 per cent of the economy is controlled by foreign corporations, which employ 10 per cent of the workforce. Britain (even outside the Euro) has been seen as an attractive low-cost country for foreign investment in areas such as electronic equipment and cars, although such investment has recently been reduced.

The shareholders are the real owners of those companies in which they invest their money. However, the daily organization of the business is left to a board of directors under a chairman(woman) or managing director. In practice, most shareholders are more interested in receiving profit dividends on their shares from a successful business than in being concerned with its running. But shareholder power is occasionally mobilized if the company is performing badly.

National and foreign companies are sometimes involved in takeovers and mergers in the private sector. A takeover occurs when a larger company takes over (or buys) a smaller, often loss-making, firm. Mergers are amalgamations between companies of equal standing. Such battles for control can be fiercely fought and have resulted in sections of the economy, such as cars, hotels, media concerns and food products, being dominated by a relatively small number of major groups.

Takeovers and mergers can cause concern to the target companies and their workforces. A Competition Commission is supposed to monitor this situation by preventing any one group forming a monopoly or creating unfair trading conditions. It examines the plans and reports to the Director General of Fair Trading, who may rule against the proposed takeover or merger. Some decisions have stopped undesirable developments. But others have allowed near-monopolistic situations, and the performance of the Commission is criticized.

Economic performance

Since the Second World War Britain's economic problems (caused by domestic and global factors) have resulted in recession and boom cycles; high unemployment, inflation and interest rates; trade weaknesses; poor growth; a fluctuating pound; and industrial relations problems. There have also been structural changes in the economy, such as a growth in service industries and a decline in industrial and manufacturing trades.

The location of British industry, which was dictated by the industrial revolutions, has been a factor in manufacturing and industrial decline. Industries were situated in areas where there was access to natural resources and transport systems and where there was often only one major industry. They could be easily damaged in a changing economic climate, unless they managed to diversify. But even regions which had diversified successfully in the past were affected by further deindustrialization and recession from the 1970s to the 1990s.

Many manufacturing industries did not adapt to new markets and demands; did not produce goods efficiently and cheaply enough to compete; lacked competitiveness; and priced themselves out of the world market. In 1938, Britain produced 22 per cent of global exports of manufactured

PLATE 6.1   Textile factory, Inverness, Scotland (*The Hutchison Library*)

goods. This figure slumped to 6.5 per cent by 1989, owing to world competition and the run-down of manufacturing industries.

Industrial decline badly affected northern England, the English Midlands, Scotland, Northern Ireland and South Wales. Traditional trades such as textiles, steel, ship-building, iron and coal-mining were greatly reduced. Governments, helped by European Union grants, tried to revitalize depressed areas with financial aid and the creation of new industry. These policies have only slowly had a positive effect in places such as Liverpool, Glasgow, Newcastle, Birmingham and Belfast.

But Britain is still the world's fourth largest economy and a significant industrial and manufacturing country. It is the fifth largest exporter of goods and services, despite its reduced share of the global market and fluctuations in manufacturing since the 1980s. But manufactured goods, such as food, drink and tobacco, engineering and transport machinery, electronics and chemicals, are 86 per cent of exports and 22 per cent of the gross domestic product (a third in 1950).

Structural change in industry and manufacturing forced adjustments to different markets. New production methods and technology led to a growth in specialized industries and the service sector (banking, insurance, catering, leisure, finance and information), which is now 70 per cent of gross domestic product, although it also suffered in the 2001 downturn.

The discovery of North Sea oil and gas in the mid-1970s has contributed greatly to the British economy and made it less dependent upon imported energy. But gas and oil are finite; Britain has problems in finding alternative sources; it already has to import some gas and oil; and must fill the financial gap with new revenues. It is argued that energy income has been unwisely spent on social targets, rather than being used more positively for investment in new industry and in creating a modern economic infrastructure.

Britain's trading patterns have also changed and its partners are now the European Union (59 per cent), North America (17) and other countries (24), with non-EU exports increasing. But it has had a balance-of-payments problem since 1983, and a trade deficit results when exports do not exceed imports. However, 'invisible exports', such as financial and insurance services, are not calculated in this equation and contribute significantly to the economy.

The economy is affected by fluctuations in the value of the pound. Devaluation (reducing the pound's exchange value) was earlier used by governments as an economic weapon. This boosted exports by making them cheaper on the world market, but raised the cost of imports and dissuaded people from buying foreign goods. Devaluation has not been used recently. Instead, the pound was allowed to 'float' from 1972 and find its own market value in competition with other currencies.

Conservative governments (1979–97) addressed inherent weaknesses in the British economy, but opinions differ on their record. They tried to reduce inflation by high interest rates and cuts in public spending. Industry and commerce were expected to restructure themselves; increase their growth rates and productivity; cut down overstaffing in the workforce; and become more efficient under market forces. Privatization was also gradually applied in many areas of the public sector.

Such measures and a world recession resulted in the 1980 British economy falling to very low levels with high interest rates, unemployment and inflation. Although it improved by 1986, it overheated from mid-1988. There were record balance-of-payments deficits, the pound was attacked, inflation increased, and interest rates were raised. Domestic and international factors caused Britain to have its worst recession (1989–93) since the 1930s world depression.

In an attempt to boost economic strength, Britain in 1990 joined the European Exchange Rate Mechanism (ERM) which, by linking European moneys, is supposed to stabilize currencies and improve national economies. But, after speculation against the pound in 1992, Britain withdrew from the ERM and allowed the pound to float. The economy recovered outside the ERM. At present (2001), the pound is strong, although this has created problems for British exporters and businesses.

In 1993–94, Britain came slowly out of recession, with improved manufacturing and financial performance and a fall in inflation, unemployment and interest rates. By 1997 the economy, which the Labour government inherited, was one of the most successful in the world. It is continuing similar policies to the Conservatives; is prudently managing the economy; and is determined to avoid traditional boom and bust cycles. But the government has had to spend considerably on services such as health, education and transport. This illustrates the problem of trying to combine a 'market economy' with public services.

Britain in 2001 suffered mixed fortunes from a global economic downturn. Manufacturing was in recession and there was weakness in

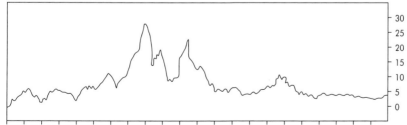

FIGURE 6.1   Inflation rate (%), 1960–2001
Source: *The Times*

other sectors. Consumer spending boosted the economy but consumer confidence was waning. Unemployment, after falling since 1993, rose in October 2001 to 951,100 or 3.2 per cent of the labour force. But interest rates were very low at 4.0 per cent, as was inflation at 2.6 per cent. *OECD* forecasts suggested that Britain would avoid an international recession and have above-average growth through 2002.

Social class, the workforce and employment

Social class

Class in Britain has been variously defined by material wealth; ownership of the means of production as against the sellers of labour; education and job status; accent and dialect; birth and breeding; and sometimes by lifestyle.

Historically, the British class system was divided into upper, middle and working classes. Earlier, hierarchies based on wealth, the ownership of property, aristocratic privilege and political power were rigidly adhered to. But a middle class of traders, merchants and skilled artisans began to make inroads into this system. Industrialization in the nineteenth century further fragmented class divisions. The working class divided into skilled and unskilled workers and the middle class split into lower, middle and upper sections, depending on job classification or wealth. The upper class was still largely defined by birth, property and inherited money.

The spread of education and expansion of wealth to greater numbers of people in the twentieth century allowed more social mobility (moving upwards out of the class into which one was born). The working class was more upwardly mobile, the upper class (owing to a loss of aristocratic privilege) merged more with the middle class and it was felt that the old rigid class system was breaking down. But class structures still exist, although the proportions of people belonging to the various levels have changed substantially.

Some researchers now employ a six-class model based on occupation, income and property ownership, such as:

1   Higher-grade professional, managerial and administrative workers (e.g. doctors and lawyers)
2   Intermediate professional, managerial and administrative workers (e.g. school teachers and sales managers)
3   Non-manual skilled workers (e.g. clerks)
4   Manual skilled workers (e.g. coal-miners)
5   Semi-skilled workers (e.g. postmen)
6   Unskilled workers (e.g. refuse collectors, cleaners and labourers)

PLATE 6.2 Rover car plant, Oxfordshire (© *Jacky Chapman/Format*)

In addition, a further group (the underclass) has been used in recent years. This consists of people who fall outside the usual classes and includes the unemployed, single-parent families, the very poor and those with alternative lifestyles.

This model indicates two social/occupational groupings in contemporary Britain: a 'middle class' made up of classes 1, 2 and 3 and a 'working class' consisting of classes 4, 5 and 6. Research indicates that the British population today largely consists of a middle class (60 per cent) and a working class (40 per cent). The working class has shrunk and there has been more upward mobility, with people advancing socially due to economic progress and changes in occupational structures.

Polls suggest that the British themselves feel that they are becoming more middle-class and it is argued that many people have the sort of lifestyle, jobs and income which classify them as middle-class. It also seems that class is now as much a matter of different social habits and attitudes as it is of occupation and money. The old gaps between the classes have lessened and class today is a more finely graded hierarchy dependent upon a range of characteristics. But inequalities of wealth, difficulties of social mobility for some people, poverty and questions of prestige remain.

The workforce and employment

The potential workforce in 2001 was 29.6 million, of whom 27.9 million were in employment. The first figure also includes the self-employed

(3.2 million), the unemployed, the armed forces and people on work-related training programmes.

Despite twentieth-century occupational changes, the majority of British people, whether part-time or full-time, are employed by an organization. It may be a small private firm, a large company, a public sector industry or service, or a multinational corporation. Most people are workers who sell their labour in a market dominated by concerns which own and control production and services. The class-defining boundaries of employees and employers have remained constant and the top 1 per cent of British society still own more than 18 per cent of marketable wealth and the top 10 per cent have 49 per cent.

But the deregulated and mobile economy has created very different work patterns. Manufacturing has declined; service trades have increased; self-employment has risen; managerial and professional fields have expanded; and there are more part-time (6.8 million in 2001) and temporary jobs. Manual jobs have decreased in number; non-manual occupations have increased; the working class has been eroded by salaried jobs; and the workforce has become more 'white-collar' and better educated.

Women in 2001 were 45 per cent of the labour force and are the principal breadwinner in 30 per cent of households. But a majority of female workers are low-paid, part-time and often unprotected by trade unions or the law. Although women form a 52 per cent majority of the population and are increasing their numbers in higher education (where they are a majority of students), the professions and white-collar jobs, they have problems in progressing to the senior ranks. Yet in 1996, three out of every ten new businesses were started by women and in the service sector it was almost five out of ten.

Since the 1960s, women have campaigned for greater equality with men in job opportunities and rates of pay. Legislation has attempted to redress the balance with varying degrees of success. Equal Pay Acts stipulate that men and women who do the same or similar kinds of work should receive the same wages. The Sex Discrimination Act makes it unlawful for the employer to discriminate between men and women when choosing a candidate for most jobs. The Equal Opportunities Commission monitors this legislation and brings cases when there have been breaches of the Acts. But the average weekly wage of women is still only 79 per cent of the average paid to men, particularly in industry and the service sector.

There has been a recent need for more women to enter the workforce at all levels, in order to compensate for a reduced birth-rate and the shortage of labour. This situation requires improved financial, social and child-care benefits for women to enable them to work, as well as more flexible employment arrangements. Some employers and the government are responding positively in these areas and Britain now seems to be more egalitarian on women's work than it has been.

PLATE 6.3 An open-plan office (© *Paula Solloway/Format*)

Unemployment has dropped steadily from 1993 (although rising in 2001 to 3.2 per cent of the workforce). But it is proportionally high in Northern Ireland, the English Midlands, Merseyside, north-east England, Scotland, South Wales and localized areas of the big cities and countryside. Since the late 1980s it has also affected the normally affluent south of England and includes professional and higher-grade workers.

The creation of jobs is important for political parties. The Labour government introduced (1997) a Welfare to Work programme. Companies willing to create jobs for the unemployed are given subsidies, and the unemployed may also be placed in training and employment-related schemes under bodies such as the Training and Enterprise Councils. These train the workforce, in the hope that permanent jobs may be found for them. Young people between the ages of sixteen and eighteen, who become unemployed on leaving school, do not receive Social Security benefits and must undertake a training scheme or further education. The training programmes have been criticized and there is no guarantee that trainees will obtain a job afterwards. But the government argues that their policies have succeeded in getting more people into stable employment.

Although the British workforce is now more mobile, deregulated and flexible, many vacant jobs are low-paid and part-time. Others are in technical and skilled areas, for which the educational systems have not adequately provided. Traditional apprenticeships have been greatly reduced and technical education suffers from a lack of investment and facilities.

FIGURE 6.2 Unemployment rate (% of labour force), 1960–2001
Source: *The Times*

Although Conservative governments established technological colleges in the major cities (financed jointly by government and private companies), firms in 2001 were experiencing skills shortages and many had unfilled vacancies. Despite the success of some programmes, Britain lacks adequate training schemes for the unemployed and young people in those technical areas which are essential for a modern industrial state. According to the World Economic Forum's 1997 global competitiveness report, Britain ranked 23rd out of 53 countries for the quality of its employee training.

Traditional manufacturing industry has been progressively reduced in Britain. But an industrial infrastructure will continue to be important. It will not be as labour-intensive as in the past, because of technical advances. High-technology industry and service trades are set to expand. It is also likely that opportunities for professional and skilled workers in managerial, supervisory, personal and financial services will increase. But employment and a trained workforce will still be problems in this post-industrial society and will entail revisions of the work ethic and concepts of leisure, as well as more flexible employment and child-care arrangements. At present, only 13 per cent of parents can afford to use formal child-care services all the time, and parents themselves have to pay three-quarters of the cost of care.

Financial institutions

Financial institutions are central actors in the economy. In the 1980s, they responded to a deregulated and freer economy. Banks, building societies, insurance firms, money markets and the London Stock Exchange expanded, merged and diversified. They entered new fields and reorganized their traditional areas of expertise, as competition between institutions increased. But they also had problems when the economy fluctuated in the late 1980s, the early 1990s and 2001. However, despite unemployment in financial businesses, the weak performance of the Stock Market and European competition, London has retained its status as a global financial centre.

Many major financial institutions have their headquarters in London, with branches throughout Britain. The square mile of the *City of London*, with its banks, insurance houses, legal firms and financial dealers' offices, has always been a centre of British and world finance. Its resources have financed royal wars, military and colonial exploration and trading companies. Today it provides financial and investment services for commercial interests in Britain and overseas. Many City institutions were founded in the seventeenth and eighteenth centuries, as Britain's prosperity and overseas trade grew, such as the insurance firm Lloyd's (1680s), the London Stock Exchange (1773) and the Bank of England (1694). The City is now being seriously challenged in financial dealings by the London Docklands redevelopment centred on Canary Wharf.

The Bank of England ('the old lady of Threadneedle Street') is the country's central bank. Although previously nationalized, it is now independent (1997) of government and sets interest rates to control inflation. Other institutions adjust their interest rates accordingly. It is organized by a governor and directors who are appointed by the government. It is the government's banker; the agent for British commercial and foreign central banks; prints money for England and Wales; manages the national debt and gold reserves; and supports the pound by buying pounds on foreign currency exchanges.

The other main banks which provide banking services throughout Britain are the *central clearing banks*, of which the most important are HSBC, Lloyds TSB, The Royal Bank of Scotland (including National Westminster) and Barclays. They provide their customers with current and deposit (savings) accounts, loans and financial advice. But they have been criticized for their banking charges to clients, their treatment of customers and their unwillingness to provide funds for small businesses. They are involved in international finance and have expanded their traditional activities. Building societies, which now offer banking facilities and Internet banking, offer competition to the high street banks.

In addition to these high street banks, there are the long-established *merchant banks*, which are mainly located in London. They give advice and finance to commercial and industrial businesses, both in Britain and overseas; advise companies on takeovers and mergers; provide financial assistance for foreign transactions; and organize a range of financial services for individuals and corporations.

The London Stock Exchange is a market for the buying and selling of quoted (listed) stocks and shares in British public companies and a few overseas. Dealings on the Stock Exchange reflect the current market trends and prices for a range of securities, which may go up as well as down. In recent years, the performance of the stock market has been weak.

The Stock Exchange was revolutionized in 1986 by new developments, known popularly as the 'Big Bang'. The changes deregulated the financial market and gave greater freedom of operation. New members were allowed, financial dealers were given greater powers of dealing and competition increased. However, some companies were too ambitious, over-expanded and suffered from the effects of the world stock market crash of 1987. The London market returned to earlier profitability levels only after many redundancies among dealers and closure of some companies. From 1997 financial transactions have been organized directly from computer screens in corporate offices by an order-driven system which automates the trading process, rather than traditional dealing on the floor of the Exchange.

The Foreign Exchange Market is also based in London. Brokers in corporate or bank offices deal in the buying and selling of foreign currencies. The London market is the largest in the world in terms of average daily turnover of completed transactions. Other money markets arrange deals on the Euromarkets in foreign currencies; trade on financial futures (speculation on future prices of commodities); arrange gold dealings on the London Gold Market; and transact global deals in the commodity, shipping and freight markets.

Lloyd's of London is a famous name in the insurance market and has long been active in the fields of shipping and maritime insurance. But it has now diversified and insures in many other areas. Lloyd's operates as a market, where individual underwriters (or insurers), who are all members of Lloyd's, carry on their business. Underwriters normally form groups to give themselves greater security, because they have to bear any loss which occurs. But many underwriters have suffered in recent years owing to heavy insurance losses.

In addition to the Lloyd's market, there are many individual insurance companies with headquarters in London and branches throughout the country. They have international connections and huge assets. They play an important role in British financial life because they are the largest investors of capital. Their main activity has traditionally been in life insurance. But many have now diversified into other associated fields, such as pensions and property loans. However, their handling of customers' investments (particularly pension mis-selling) has been heavily criticized in recent years.

British financial institutions have traditionally been respected for their honesty and integrity. But, as money markets have expanded and become freer, there have been fraud cases, collapse of financial organizations and financial scandals. These give the City a bad image and have forced it to

PLATE 6.4   Lloyd's of London (*Clive Dixon/Rex Features, London*)

PLATE 6.5 Canary Wharf, London (© *Popperfoto/Reuters*)

institute self-regulatory provisions in order to tighten the controls on financial dealings.

But some critics have argued for stronger independent supervision of the City's business. The Labour government, although now more friendly towards the business world than in the past, created a watchdog (the Financial Services Authority) in 2000 and a Financial Ombudsman in 2001 to oversee all financial dealings. But these institutions have been criticized for their lack of adequate control. It is also argued that the City should be more nationally and socially conscious and forced to invest in British industry rather than overseas. The City insists that it should be allowed to invest how and where it likes in order to make a profit. However, it seems that City organizations are conscious of the negative criticisms and are prepared to put their houses in order.

The composition of those who create and control wealth in Britain has changed since the Second World War. Bankers, aristocrats, land-owners and industrialists were the richest people in the nineteenth and early twentieth century. Today the most affluent are retailers and those who service the consumer society, although holders of inherited wealth are still numerous. Many millionaires are self-made, with lower-middle-class and working-class backgrounds.

The Labour Party in opposition felt that anyone earning more than £27,000 a year should be classified as rich (and taxed accordingly), while polls suggest that the public considers earnings above £30,000 a year to be reasonable wealth. Talking about what one earns and about money gener-ally has been traditionally regarded as unseemly in Britain and too much involved with the cruder elements of existence and survival. But this mentality has slowly changed, particularly since the expansion of the busi-ness and money markets.

Industrial and commercial institutions

The trade unions

Trade unions obtained legal recognition in 1871 after long and bitter strug-gles. The fight for the right of workers to organize themselves originated in the trade guilds of the fourteenth century and later in social clubs which were formed to give their members protection against sickness and unemployment.

The modern trade unions are associated (if no longer closely) with the Labour Party and campaign for better pay, working and health condi-tions for their members. The trade union movement is highly organized, with a membership of 7.1 million people. But this is a fall from 12 million in 1978.

Today there are some 243 trade unions and professional associations of workers, which vary considerably in size and influence. They represent not only skilled and unskilled workers in industry but also white-collar workers in a range of businesses, companies and local and central govern-ment. Other professional associations such as the Law Society, the Police

Federation and the British Medical Association carry out similar representational roles for their members.

Members of trade unions pay annual subscriptions to their unions and frequently to the Labour Party, unless they elect not to pay this latter amount. The funding provides for union activities and services, such as legal, monetary and professional help. The richer unions are able to give strike pay to members who are taking part in 'official strikes', which are those legally sanctioned by members. Trade unions vary in their wealth and in their political orientation, ranging from the left to the right wing of the political spectrum.

Some unions admit as members only those people who work in a specific job, such as miners or teachers. Other unions comprise workers who are employed in different areas of industry or commerce, such as the Transport and General Workers' Union. Some unions have joined with others in similar fields to form new unions, such as Unison (public service workers) which is now the largest in Britain with 1.4 million members. Workers may choose, without victimization, whether they want to belong to a particular union or none at all.

Many trade unions are affiliated to the Trades Union Congress (TUC), which was founded in 1868, serves as an umbrella organization to co-ordinate trade union interests and tries to promote worker co-operation. It can exert some pressure on government and seeks to extend its contacts in industry and commerce and with employers as well as workers.

But the influence of the TUC and trade unions (as well as their membership) has declined. This is due to unemployment; changing attitudes to trade unions by workers; the reduction and restructuring of industry; and Conservative legislation. Laws were passed to enforce secret voting by union members before strikes can be legally called and for the election of union officials. The number of pickets (union strikers) allowed outside business premises has been reduced, secondary (or sympathy) action by other unionists is banned and unions may be fined by the courts if they transgress legislation. Such laws (which the Labour government accept) and the economic climate have forced trade unions to be more realistic in their wage demands. But pay claims are escalating again and there are also arrangements for legal recognition of unions in those workplaces where a majority of workers want them and for consultation with workers in matters such as redundancy.

Legislation has controlled extreme union practices and introduced democratic procedures into union activities. The grassroots membership has become more independent of union bosses and activists; is more determined to represent its own wishes; and is concerned to cure abuses in the labour movement. The initiative in industry has shifted to employers and moderate unions, who have been moving away from the traditional 'class-war' image of unionism and are accepting new technology and working patterns in an attempt to improve competitiveness and productivity.

Public opinion polls in the past found that, while a large majority of respondents believed that unions are essential to protect workers' interests, a sizeable number felt that unions had too much power in Britain and that they were dominated by extremists. Half of trade unionists themselves agreed with this latter point of view and half disagreed. The concern over trade unions and their close relationship with Labour governments has declined in recent years.

Strike action by unions can be damaging to the economy and has been used as an economic and political weapon in the past. In some cases, strikes are seen as legitimate and find public support. But others, which are clearly political, are unpopular and are rejected. Britain historically seemed to be prone to industrial disputes. However, statistics show that fewer working days are lost in Britain each year than in other industrial nations, although the number has increased recently. On average, most manufacturing plants and businesses are free of strikes, and media coverage is often responsible for giving a distorted picture of industrial relations.

Industrial problems should be placed in the context of financial rewards. Britain has a low-wage economy, compared with major European countries, although the Labour government has set a minimum wage of £4.61 an hour to help the lowest-paid workers over twenty-one, to the dismay of many companies. The average gross weekly wage in 2000 was £411 per week. Many workers (women at £338) receive less than this. Personal income is taxed at 10 per cent for the first £2,000 of taxable income, 22 per cent up to £28,000 and 40 per cent above this figure. The British tend to believe that they are over-taxed. But their basic and top rates of taxation are in fact lower than in many other western countries. However, the Labour government has significantly raised indirect or 'stealth' taxes, and income tax may increase to pay for public services.

Employers' organizations

There are some 101 employers' and managers' associations in Britain, which are mainly associated with companies in the private sector. They promote good industrial relations between businesses and their workforces; try to settle disputes; and offer legal and professional advice.

Most are members of the Confederation of British Industry (CBI). This umbrella body represents its members nationally; negotiates on their behalf with government and the TUC; campaigns for greater investment and innovation in industry and technology; and is often more sympathetic to Conservative governments than Labour ones. However, it can be very critical of Conservative policies. It also acts as a public-relations organization; relays the employers' points of view to the public; and has considerable economic influence and authority.

Industrial relations

Complaints are often raised about the quality of industrial relations in Britain. This has tended to be confrontational rather than co-operative and based on notions of 'class warfare' and 'us-and-them'. Trade union leaders can be extremist and stubborn in pursuing their members' interests. But the performance of management and employers is also criticized. Insensitive managers can be responsible for strikes arising in the first place, and relations between management and workers still leave much to be desired although industrial unrest is not as common as it once was. Opinion polls have found that a majority of respondents believe that bad management is more to blame than the unions for poor industrial relations and Britain's economic problems.

The Advisory, Conciliation and Arbitration Service (ACAS)

ACAS is an independent, government-financed organization, which was created in 1974 to improve industrial relations. It may provide, if requested, advice, conciliation and arbitration services for the parties involved in a dispute. But ACAS does not have binding power and the parties may disregard its advice and solutions. Industrial relations in Britain consist of free collective bargaining between employers and workers. It has been argued that arbitration should be made compulsory and that findings should be binding on the parties. However, strike action is not illegal for most workers if legally called and the government has no power to intervene. Nevertheless, ACAS has performed much valuable work and has been responsible for settling many disputes.

ACAS also oversees the operation of employment law and abuses of workers' rights under legislation. These may involve complaints of unfair and unlawful dismissal; claims under Equal Pay Acts; grievances under Sex Discrimination Acts; and unlawful discrimination under Race Relations Acts. There is now a large body of employment and regulatory law, which makes conditions of work more secure and less arbitrary than they have been in the past, particularly in the cases of women, ethnic minorities and the low-paid. But there is still concern about the real effectiveness of such legislation.

Consumer protection

In a competitive market, consumers should have a choice of goods and services; information to make choices; and laws to safeguard their purchases. Statutory protection for consumers has grown steadily in Britain and is harmonized with European Union law. The public can complain to tribunals and the courts about unfair trading practices, dangerous and unsafe goods, misrepresentation, bad service, misleading advertising and personal injuries resulting from defective products.

The Office of Fair Trading is a government department which oversees the consumer behaviour of trade and industry. It promotes fair trading, protects consumers, suggests legislation to government and has improved consumer awareness. It has drawn up codes of practice with many industrial and commercial organizations; keeps a close watch for any breaches of the codes; and publishes its findings, often to the embarrassment of the manufacturers and companies concerned.

Organizations which provide help on consumer affairs at the local level are Citizens Advice Bureaux, Consumer Advice Centres and consumer protection departments of local councils. Private consumer-protection groups, which investigate complaints and grievances, also exist in some localities.

The independent National Consumer Council monitors consumers' attitudes, although its effectiveness is queried. A more active body is the Consumers' Association. Its magazine *Which?* champions the consumer and applies rigorous tests to anything from television sets to insurance and estate agents. *Which?* is the 'buyers' bible' and its reports have raised the standards of commercial products and services in Britain.

Much still needs to be reformed in the consumer field, such as cowboy builders preying on gullible consumers and mis-selling by financial organizations, to achieve minimum standards and adequate protection. But there are signs that a British reluctance to complain about goods and services is breaking down as litigation and compensation claims increase.

Attitudes to the economy

Opinion polls echo the changing economic climate. The electorate was dissatisfied with the Conservative government in the mid-1990s, despite a booming economy. General elections in 1997 and 2001 showed that voters were willing to trust the Labour Party to run the economy efficiently because it had adopted centrist, pragmatic and low-taxation policies. But polls in 2000 and 2001 showed disillusionment with the Labour government on public service issues.

The economy still concerns British people in areas such as unemployment, industrial decline, inflation, interest rates, prices and taxation. Polls suggest that, in a mobile and deregulated market, job security (or the ability to get another job if one is lost) is a priority of job seekers, ranked ahead of work satisfaction, promotion and working conditions. Britain also has a reputation as a country of workaholics, where people work the longest hours in Europe (despite an EU maximum working week of 48 hours which will probably be obligatory in 2003). This may be out of choice, enjoyment, ambition, coercion or desperation not to lose one's job. However, it seems that a majority of British people are very or fairly satisfied with their jobs and only a small minority are either fairly or very dissatisfied.

A *CBI* poll in 2001 showed that flexible working was now a key part of British employment patterns: 81 per cent of businesses use part-time workers; 62 per cent operated subcontracting; and 39 per cent use teleworking to allow their employees to work at home for at least some of the time.

Nevertheless, respondents to polls believe that business and economic arrangements in Britain are unfair; the values of managers and workers are opposed; the country's wealth is unfairly distributed; this favours the owners and the rich at the expense of employees and the poor; the gap between rich and poor is growing; there are no longer 'jobs for life' and businesses do not care about the community, the environment or customers. It is felt that workers should be given more control over and say in the organization of their workplaces (now covered by the Social Chapter of the Maastrict Treaty).

A *MORI Corporate Image* survey in August 2001 showed that public hostility towards profitability and business success had waned slightly after rising from 1980 to 1999. In 1999 only 25 per cent of respondents supported corporate profit while 52 per cent were against. In 2001 the figures were 29 per cent and 43 per cent respectively. Stakeholders or shareholders want their companies to make a profit but not at the expense of their staff or the community. The public now thinks that caring for employees should be the top priority for business. Providing more jobs, the safety of workers and the training of the workforce are also more emphasized.

It is often argued that Britain's economic ills are due to cultural factors and attitudes. Traditionally, educated and upper-class people were reluctant to enter trade and industry; the workforce has a lower productivity rate than comparable competitors; there has been insufficient investment in industry and training; management is weak and unprofessional; and there has been too little investment in and encouragement of the technical, scientific and research fields.

But a *MORI/British Council* poll in 1999 found that 81 per cent of overseas respondents rated British goods and services as 'good' overall and 74 per cent thought that British managers are good. However, the country ranks behind the USA, Japan and Germany when it comes to having world-beating companies, and British business is seen as too risk-averse.

Exercises

Explain and examine the following terms:

diversify	privatization	GDP	invisible exports
merger	Lloyd's	shares	balance of payments
private sector	deficit	TUC	service industries
ACAS	Canary Wharf	HBSC	'market economy'
the City	inflation	*Which?*	mixed economy
devaluation	Stock Exchange	CBI	deregulation
monopoly	Clause 4	ERM	deindustrialization

Write short essays on the following topics:

1 Examine modern British economic policies and performance.
2 Discuss the role of the trade unions in British life.
3 Consider the financial institutions in Britain. Should they be more closely regulated by government? If so, why?

Further reading

Booth, A. (2001) *The British Economy in the Twentieth Century* London: Palgrave

Buxton, T., Chapman, P. and Temple, P. (1997) *Britain's Economic Performance* London: Routledge

Gregg, P. and Wadsworth, J (eds) (1999) *The State of Working Britain* Manchester: Manchester University Press

McIlroy, J. (1995) *Trade Unions in Britain Today* Manchester: Manchester University Press

Websites

Department of Trade and Industry: www.dti.gov.uk

HM Treasury: www.hm-treasury.gov.uk

National Statistics: www.statistics.gov.uk

British Trade International: www.brittrade.com

Bank of England: www.bankofengland.co.uk

Financial Services Authority: www.fsa.gov.uk

Lloyd's of London: www.lloydsoflondon.co.uk

Confederation of British Industry: www.cbi.org.uk

Trades Union Congress: www.tuc.org.uk

Business in the Community: www.bitc.org.uk

The Industrial Society: www.indsoc.co.uk

Social services

S TATE PROVISION FOR SOCIAL SECURITY, health care, personal social services and housing are very much taken for granted by the British today. They also feature prominently in lists of people's concerns and directly affect the daily lives of Britons of all ages. But it was not until the 1940s that the state accepted overall responsibility for providing basic help nationally for all its citizens. Previously, there had been few such facilities and it was felt that the state was not obliged to supply social services. British social amenities developed considerably from the mid twentieth century as society and government policies changed. They are now divided between state (public) and private sectors.

The state provides services and benefits for the sick, retired, disabled, elderly, needy and unemployed. They are organized by devolved and local authorities throughout Britain under the central direction of the UK Department of Health and the Department of Work and Pensions. The costs of this welfare state are funded mainly by taxation and partly by a National Insurance Fund to which employers and employees contribute.

In the private sector, social and health services are financed by personal insurance schemes and by those people able to pay for such facilities out of their own income or capital. There are also many voluntary organizations which continue the tradition of charitable help for the needy and depend for their funding upon donations from the public.

Conservative governments (1979–97) introduced reforms in the state sector in order to reduce expenditure, improve efficiency, encourage more self-provision and target benefits to those most in need. Such policies were widely attacked and it was argued that they were based on a market orientation and a return to the old mentality on social services.

The Labour government since 1997 has also tried to reform the hugely expensive welfare state by encouraging people to insure themselves against unemployment and sickness and to provide for their own pensions and care in old age. It has introduced reforms to help families, reduce poverty and exclusion, and made efforts to get the unemployed into work.

These policy changes suggest that the state in future may be unable (or unwilling) to meet the financial costs of social services without increases in income tax. People are being encouraged to build their own welfare plans, and government's role may lie in directing such aid rather than its funding and provision. This shows the difficulty of reconciling public services demand with a 'market economy' and of deciding how much dependence there should be upon the state. The Labour government also intends to involve the private sector more in the provision and management of public services. But there is public and trade union opposition to this policy, which is generally perceived as the 'privatization' of social services.

Social services history

Historically, state social services were non-existent for most of the British population. The churches, charities, the rural feudal system and town guilds (organizations of skilled craftsmen) did give some protection against poverty, illness and unemployment. But this help was limited in its application and effect. Most people were therefore thrown upon their own resources, which were often minimal, in order to survive.

In Elizabeth II's reign (1558–1603), a Poor Law was established in England, by which the state took over the organization of charity provisions from the church. Similar schemes existed in Wales, Scotland and Ireland. They operated at the local level, and parishes were responsible for their poor, sick and unemployed, providing housing, help and work relief. The Poor Law was the start of state social legislation throughout Britain. But it was grudging, limited in its effects and discouraged people from relying on it. Poverty and need were considered to be the result of an unwillingness to work and provide for oneself. The state was not supposed to have extensive responsibility for social services.

These attitudes persisted in later centuries. But urban and rural poverty and need continued. Conditions worsened in the eighteenth and nineteenth centuries under the industrial revolutions as the population increased rapidly. The urban workforce had to work long hours in often bad conditions in low-quality factories for low wages. Families frequently inhabited slums of overcrowded, back-to-back dwellings which lacked adequate sewerage, heating or ventilation. The situation of many rural agricultural workers was just as bad.

Public health became an inevitable problem, and the poor conditions resulted in infectious epidemics in the nineteenth century, such as diphtheria, typhoid, tuberculosis and smallpox. Some diseases remained endemic in the British population into the twentieth century because of bad housing and the lack of adequate health and social facilities.

The old Poor Law was replaced by the Poor Law Amendment Act of 1834 in England and Wales (later in Scotland). This was designed to prevent the alleged abuse of parish social relief. It created a system of work-houses in which the destitute and needy could live. But the workhouses were unpleasant places and people were discouraged from relying upon them. They were dreaded by the poor and accepted as a last alternative only when all else failed. Since nineteenth-century Britain was subject to economic slumps and unemployment, the workhouse system resulted in misery and the separation of families.

Successive governments until the nineteenth century also refused to allow workers to organize themselves into trade unions, through which they might agitate against their working and living conditions. This forced workers into establishing their own social and self-help clubs in order to provide basic protection for themselves. Some employers were more benevolent than others and provided good housing and health facilities for their workforces. But these examples were few, and life continued to be harsh for many people.

The social misery of the nineteenth century persuaded some towns to establish local boards to control public health and initiate health schemes. But a public health apparatus was not created until 1848 and an effective national system was not in place until 1875. Other legislation was passed to clear slum areas, but large-scale clearance was not achieved until the middle of the twentieth century. Reforms relating to housing, health, factory and mine conditions, sanitation and sewerage, town planning and trade unionism were implemented in the nineteenth century. But they were limited in their effects and have been described as paternalistic in their intention.

The social welfare problems of the nineteenth century were considerable, and the state's failure to provide major help against illness, unemployment and poverty made the situation worse. Social reformers, who promoted legislation which gave some relief from the effects of nineteenth-century industrialization, had to struggle against the apathy and hostility of vested interests in Parliament and the country.

However, small victories had been won and it was slowly admitted, if not universally, in the early twentieth century that the state had social responsibility for the whole of society. The progressive Liberal government between 1906 and 1914 introduced reform programmes on old age pensions, national insurance, health, employment and trade unionism. These formed the basic structures of the future welfare state. But they affected only a minority of people, and the state was unwilling or unable to introduce further provisions in the early twentieth century. The financial and physical exhaustion resulting from the 1914–18 World War and the economic crises of the 1920s and 1930s halted social services expansion.

But the underlying need for more state help continued. The model for a welfare state appeared in the Beveridge Report of 1942. It recommended that a comprehensive system of Social Security and free health care for all should be established to overcome suffering and need. It was intended that the system would be largely financed by a national insurance scheme, to which workers would contribute, and out of which they and their families would receive benefits when required. Although Conservative governments passed some of the legislation to implement these proposals, it was the Labour government from 1945 to 1951 that radically altered the social and health systems and created the present welfare state.

Changing family and demographic structures

The provision of contemporary social services, in both public and private sectors, is conditioned by changes in family structures, demographic factors (such as increases in life expectancy and an ageing population), governmental responses to social needs and the availability and cost of services.

It is argued that, as new social structures have emerged, the traditional British family is falling apart; failing to provide for its elderly and disabled; suffering from social and moral problems; lacking parenting skills; and looking automatically to the state for support. The nuclear family (two parents and children living together) has been reduced, but it still accounts for a majority of households.

Marriage has decreased in popularity in Britain and in 2000 it accounted for 55 per cent of the adult population. In 1998 there were 305,000 marriages (one of the lowest annual figures in the twentieth century) and two in five of these were remarriages of one or both parties. Only a quarter of first marriages now have a religious ceremony, while most remarriages are civil. More people are delaying marriage until their late twenties (average age twenty-eight for men and twenty-six for women) for a variety of reasons, such as career considerations.

Statisticians predict that, for the first time since 1801, married couples will in future be outnumbered by those people who never marry. The number of married adults will fall from 55 per cent at present to 48 per cent by 2011 and 45 per cent by 2021. The proportion of unmarried men will increase more than the proportion of unmarried women; the rise in cohabiting couples (heterosexual or lesbian and gay couples living together outside marriage) will not compensate for the decrease in married couples; and divorce rates will decline correspondingly.

This suggests that many more adults will be living alone. There has already been a significant increase in one-person households with no children. These are people of all ages who live alone and may be unmarried, divorced, separated, widows or widowers. They are nearly one in three (29 per cent) of all households, more than double the proportion in 1961.

Four out of ten marriages end in divorce, although there was a decrease in 1998 to 12.9 per 1,000 married people. Britain has the highest divorce rate in the European Union; remarriages are at greater risk than first marriages; and people who marry under twenty-one are the most susceptible to divorce. The average length of marriages ending in divorce is ten years; the average divorce age is thirty-seven for women and thirty-nine for men; and divorce affects a considerable number of children under sixteen. The trauma is increased by the confrontational nature of the divorce system, with conflicts over property, financial support and custody of children.

Over the past twenty years, there has been a big increase in cohabitation. There are 1.6 million cohabiting couples in England and Wales and the number is expected to rise to 2.93 million over the next twenty-five years. Many of these relationships are stable and long term and eight out of ten resulting births are registered by both parents, rather than by one as many previously were.

Non-matrial (or illegitimate) births arising from cohabitation and single mothers are 39 per cent of live births. This (particularly the number of under-eighteen mothers which is the highest in Europe) has caused controversy on moral and cost grounds. Illegitimacy retains some of its old stigma. But the legal standing of such children has been improved by removing restrictions in areas such as inheritance.

There were 700,000 live births in Britain in 1999 which outnumbered deaths at 629,000. But the average family size has declined and is below 2.1 children per family, or the level necessary to replace the population in the long term. Family size is expected to decline to 1.8 children per woman for women born after 1970 and pensioners will exceed the number of children in the population by 2008.

There are several reasons for the low birth rate. Child-bearing is being delayed, with women having their first child on average at twenty-eight. Some women are delaying even longer for educational and career reasons, and there has been an increase in the number of single women and married couples who choose to remain childless, or to limit their families. Contraception has become more widespread, voluntary sterilization of both sexes is more common and legal abortions have increased.

Increased divorce and individual lifestyles have led to a threefold growth in the number of one-parent families with dependent children since 1961. It is estimated that some 2 million children are being raised in 1.3 million one-parent units (22 per cent of all families with dependent children), where 89 per cent of the parents are women. Of the women bringing up one-parent families 16 per cent are single, 34 per cent are divorced, 22 per cent are separated and 17 per cent are widowed. Many of these families (with the highest proportion being in inner London) often have reduced living standards and are dependent upon Social Security benefits.

The proportion of married women in employment is now some 49 per cent, more women are returning to work more quickly after the birth of a child and women make up 45 per cent of the workforce. But although Britain has a high percentage of working mothers and wives, provisions for maternity leave and child-care are the lowest in Europe.

The nuclear, one-parent and cohabiting family units have to cope with increased demands upon them, which may entail considerable personal sacrifice. Families carry out most of the caring roles in British society, rather than state professionals. Only 5 per cent of people over sixty-five and 7 per cent of disabled adults live in state or private institutions. Most handicapped children and adults are cared for by their families and most of the elderly are cared for by families or live alone. This is a saving to the state without which the cost of state health and welfare care would rise. But the burden upon families will grow as the population becomes more elderly, state provision is reduced and the disabled (6 million adults) and disadvantaged increase in numbers. There are demands that more government aid should be given to carers, families and local authorities to lighten their burden.

Some one in six of the population are now over sixty-five and 7 per cent are over seventy-five. Life expectancy of men is 75 years and women eighty years, so that there are more women among the elderly. However, the number of older people in the population is expected to grow less quickly than in recent years.

The picture that emerges from these statistics is one of smaller families; more people living alone; an increase in one-parent families and non-matrial births; high divorce rates; more people living longer and contributing to an ageing population; more working mothers and wives; more cohabiting couples; and a decrease in marriage. These features influence the contemporary state and private provisions for Social Security, health, social services and housing.

Social Security

The Social Security system provides benefits for British people and is operated by Department of Work and Pensions agencies throughout the country. It is the government's most expensive programme (30 per cent of public spending – £101 billion) and is financed from taxation and contributions by employers and workers over sixteen to the National Insurance Fund.

This means that Social Security gives benefits to workers who pay contributions to the National Insurance Fund; income-related benefits to people who have no income or whose income falls below certain levels and who need assistance; and other benefits which are conditional on disability or family needs, such as non-contributory Disability and Attendance Allowances.

The contributory system gives, for example, state retirement pensions for women at sixty and men at sixty-five (to be equalized at sixty-five from 2010); maternity pay for pregnant working women; sick pay or incapacity benefit for people who are absent from work because of illness or who become incapable of work; and a Jobseeker's Allowance for those who become unemployed (dependent upon their actively seeking work).

Income-related benefits are also provided by the state. For example, *Income Support* depends upon savings and capital and is given to some 5.6 million people in financial need, such as one-parent families, the elderly and long-term sick, disabled and unemployed. It covers basic living requirements, although the sums are relatively low. It also includes free prescription drugs, dental treatment, opticians' services and children's school meals. The *Working Families' Tax Credit* is a benefit whereby families with children and at least one parent in low-paid work receive a tax credit through workers' pay packets to increase their earnings. It includes the same extra benefits as Income Support and is dependent upon income, savings and capital. *Housing Benefit* is paid to people on Income Support and other low-income claimants (4.2 million in 2001) and covers the cost of rented accommodation. A tax-free *Child Benefit* (£15 per week for the eldest child and £10 for other children) is paid to each mother for each of her children up to the age of eighteen, irrespective of family income.

In the past, people in great need were also able to claim non-contributory single payments, such as the cost of clothes, cookers and children's shoes, in the form of grants or loans. But these have now been sharply cut and replaced by a Social Fund, to which people have to apply. The Fund is being applied restrictively and has been widely attacked as an example of government's alleged reduction of Social Security aid.

Social Security does provide a degree of security. It is supposed to be a safety-net against urgent needs, but this does not prevent hardship. Some 27 per cent of British people are on income-related benefits of one kind or another. It is also estimated that a quarter of the population (including 4.5 million children) exist on the poverty line, which is sometimes measured as half the average national income. But accurate figures of poverty are difficult to find, because of the variable presentation of official statistics and because there are different definitions of what constitutes poverty.

Social Security is very expensive and will become more so as the population ages and as the numbers of the sick, poor, disadvantaged and unemployed persist. It is very complicated with its array of benefits and subject to fraud, particularly in the cases of Income Support and Housing Benefit.

The Labour government is trying to reform the system, attack fraud, cut expense and reduce benefits while still preserving the safety-net commitment and targeting those people with the greatest needs. It is committed to reducing poverty and exclusion. But it is also concerned that people should look after themselves more, without automatic recourse to the state for help and that they should seek employment more actively. They are encouraged to take out pensions (such as the new government-backed Stakeholder Pension) to add to their (relatively low) state pensions and to insure privately against health and other costs. But the inadequate record of the insurance companies in these areas has been criticized.

It is argued that such reforms mean a real reduction in Social Security, particularly the Social Fund, Housing Benefit, Income Support, Disability Allowance and unemployment aid. The young unemployed between sixteen and eighteen are now ineligible for benefits until they are eighteen and must follow training or education programmes. But the Labour government argues that the cost of Social Security is unsustainable and wants to encourage greater self-provision through work rather than dependency. However, it is difficult to create a simple and fair system which protects the genuinely needy and also encourages people to become more self-reliant and independent.

The National Health Service (NHS)

A Labour government created the National Health Service (NHS) in 1947. It was based on the Beveridge Report recommendations and replaced a private system of payment for health care by one of free treatment for all. The medical profession wished to retain private medicine and opposed the establishment of the NHS. But this was countered by the Labour government.

The NHS was originally intended to be completely free, and this ideal, to a large extent, has been achieved. Hospital and most medical treatment under the NHS is free for British and EU citizens. The NHS provides a range of medical and dental services for the whole country based on hospitals, doctors, dentists, nurses, midwives, ambulance services, blood transfusion and other health facilities.

But some charges are now made. For example, prescriptions, which are written notes from a doctor enabling patients to obtain drugs from a chemist, have to be paid for, as do some dental work, dental checks and eye tests. Such payments are dependent upon employment status, age and income. Children under sixteen, people on Social Security benefits and old age pensioners receive free prescriptions.

The NHS is financed from taxation. It costs £43.4 billion per year (15 per cent of government spending) and the NHS is the biggest single employer of labour in Western Europe. Yet state health expenditure in Britain is only 6 per cent of the gross domestic product (GDP) and lower than in many other major western countries, which have a greater mixture of the public and the private in their total health spending.

The UK government is responsible for the NHS through the Department of Health in England and devolved bodies in Wales, Scotland and Northern Ireland. At a lower level, the NHS used to be administered by local health authorities in England and Wales and health councils in Scotland and Northern Ireland. They identified the general healthcare needs of the people living in their area and secured hospital and community health services. But their functions are being changed.

The structure has now been more localized because the Labour government has created Primary Care Groups, controlling two-thirds of NHS budgets at local level. These bodies comprise health professionals (such as doctors) and hospitals; work with the local health authorities; and determine patient services. The aim is to achieve a system of integrated care by frontline medical professionals which is direct and effective.

Doctors

Most people who require healthcare will first consult their local NHS-funded doctor, who is a GP or non-specialist general practitioner: of these there are about 35,000 in Britain. Doctors have an average of about 2,000 registered patients on their panel (or list of names), although they will see only a small percentage of these on a regular basis. The majority of GPs are now members of group practices, where they share larger premises, services and equipment. However, a patient will usually be on the panel of one particular doctor, who will often be a personal choice. An alternative to seeing a doctor is to make use of the new NHS Direct service, which allows one to seek advice on the telephone from nurses. There are conflicting reports on this service's effectiveness.

Hospitals

If patients require further treatment or examination, the GP refers them to specialists and consultants, normally at local NHS hospitals (or NHS Trusts). NHS Trust hospitals are funded by contracts with the local Primary Care Groups. But they are 'self-governing' and largely manage their own affairs. These hospitals have about 370,000 beds and provide medical, dental, nursing and midwifery staff. Britain has some very modern hospitals and facilities, and more hospitals are being constructed. But it also has many buildings which were erected in the nineteenth century and which are in urgent need of modernization and repair. There is a shortage of beds

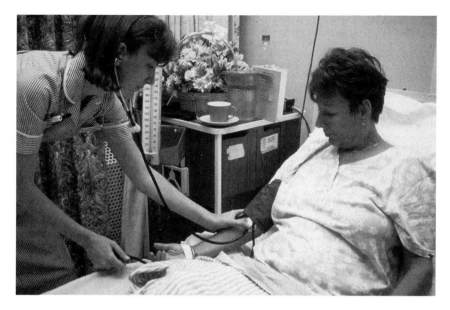

PLATE 7.1   A hospital nurse (© *Jacky Chapman/Format*)

in some hospitals, wards and hospitals are being closed, and waiting times for admission to hospital as well as for treatment in accident and emergency departments increased in 2001. The blame for this situation is variously placed on spending cuts, a government unwillingness to spend more money on health or managerial inability to organize the funds which do exist.

The state of the NHS

The NHS has an ambivalent position in the public mind. On the one hand, it is praised for its work as a free service and its achievements. It is considered a success in terms of consumer demand. Today people are in general receiving help when they need it and many who would previously have died or suffered are surviving and being cared for. Standards of living and medicine have risen, better diets have been devised and there is a greater health awareness in the population at large.

On the other hand, the NHS is criticized for its alleged inefficiency, inadequate standards, treatment discrepancies throughout the country and bureaucracy. Its objectives are considered too ambitious for the money spent on it. The media constantly draw attention to shortcomings and forecast breakdown. Workers in the NHS, such as doctors, nurses and non-medical staff, complain about low pay, long hours, management weaknesses, levels of staffing (with a severe shortage of doctors and nurses) and cuts in services. Such critics often seem to suggest that many of the problems could be solved simply by injecting more finance into the NHS.

Rising costs and increased demand arguably contribute to alleged underfunding. The NHS is in many ways a victim of its own success and of the demands that the British place upon it as of right. It is inevitable that a free, consumer-led service will require increasing levels of expenditure, better management of existing resources or alternative funding. Yet despite problems and undoubted pressures, much of the NHS works well and gives value for the money spent on it.

There are many suggestions as to how the NHS can be improved. Increasing government spending on the NHS may increase taxation. Charges could be made for some services, but this hits the principle of free health care, although a *MORI* poll in May 2001 showed that 66 per cent of respondents were prepared to pay for some NHS care if it meant an overall better service. Better management of existing funds might make some savings, but not enough. Combining a public service with private insurance would not include poorer people, who would still depend upon a free NHS. The Labour government is trying to involve the private sector more closely in the running of the NHS through Public–Private Partnerships. But many people regard this as privatization of the NHS. The government is committed to raising NHS spending to European levels; cutting down management costs; transferring money to medical care and staff; and reorganizing NHS administration. But the public see little actual improvement in the NHS and according to polls in 2000 and 2001 are disillusioned with Labour's attempts to revitalize it. However, the *World Health Organization* in August 2001 ranked Britain as 24th out of 191 countries in terms of the efficiency of international health systems, above countries such as Germany, the USA and Denmark.

The private medical sector

It is argued that health care should not be a question of who can pay for it, but a responsibility of the state. However, the public sector has problems, and attempts have been made to involve the private sector in providing health care.

The previous Conservative government encouraged the growth of private health institutions, private medical insurance and partnership between the public and private sectors on a commercial basis. Its Private Finance Initiative allowed new health facilities to be built, maintained and owned by the private sector. These are then leased to the NHS, which provides clinical services and controls planning and clinical decisions. The Conservatives saw the private sector as complementary to the NHS. It would release pressure on state funds; give choice to patients; allow the sharing of medical resources; provide flexible services; result in cost-effective co-operation with the NHS; and allow treatment of NHS patients at public expense in the private sector.

The Labour government, in a reversal of old Labour ideology, has embraced these ideas. It has an agreement with private healthcare providers to enable the NHS to make better use of facilities in private hospitals. Some NHS hospitals share expensive equipment with private hospitals, and NHS patients are treated (at public expense) in the private sector when it represents value for money. But the scale of private practice in relation to the NHS is small. Much private treatment is confined to minor medical cases, and expensive, long-term care is still carried out by the NHS.

A quarter of patients pay for private health care out of their income or capital. Some 6.9 million other individuals and 4.8 million people in company plans are covered by private medical insurance taken out with businesses such as the British United Provident Association (BUPA). Concern about waiting lists and standards of health care in the NHS persuade many to take out such insurance. The insurance policy pays for private care either in private hospitals and clinics, or in NHS hospitals which provide 'pay-beds' (beds for the use of paying patients, which still exist in NHS hospitals and were a concession in 1946 to those doctors who agreed to join the NHS but who wished to keep a number of private patients). A *Consumers' Association* report in August 2001 found that 40 per cent of respondents would consider going private to avoid lengthy NHS queues. But 84 per cent did not have medical insurance and many are likely to be deterred by the rising costs of insurance premiums and private treatment.

The personal social services

The social services provide facilities in the community for assisting people such as the elderly, the disabled, the mentally ill, families, children and young people. Trained staff, such as district visitors and social workers, cater for these personal needs. The services are organized by local government authorities with central government funding (£10 billion in England). But it is argued that social services need extra money to address the problems that they face.

An increasing pressure is being put upon the social services, families and carers as the elderly population grows and the ranks of the disadvantaged rise. For example, the number of public residential and nursing homes for the elderly is insufficient for the demand, and some private homes close because of cost. In both cases, people may be forced to sell their homes to cover the expense. Care services for the elderly and infirm face a severe staff shortage unless higher pay and better training for care workers are introduced.

The previous Conservative goverment introduced a 'Care in the Community' programme, parts of which are being developed by the Labour government. The aim is to give financial and material support to families and carers looking after elderly or disabled relatives in the latters' own homes, or for handicapped children and adults in the family home. It also allows mental hospital patients who do not need constant care to be moved to the community under social services supervision and for some elderly and disabled people to be cared for in their own homes by social services. The aim is to prevent the institutionalization of people and to give them independence.

The scheme is financed by central government and operated by local government authorities. But it has had difficulties, for example mentally ill and handicapped patients becoming homeless or housed in inadequate temporary accommodation and elderly people receiving inadequate attention and help. It is argued that local authorities need more support and that a greater awareness of implementation problems is required if the policy is to be more successful.

The personal social services also cater for people with learning disabilities, give help to families and provide day care facilities for children. Children in need are also supposed to be protected in residential care accommodation, and local authorities facilitate fostering and adoption services. But there have been a number of serious cases in recent years which have focused on abuse in children's homes.

The private social services (voluntary) sector

While there were substantial improvements in state social services in the twentieth century, there is still a shortage of finance and resources to support the needy in a comprehensive fashion. It is therefore important that voluntary charities and agencies have continued. They are a complementary welfare service to the state facilities and provide an essential element in the total aid pattern. The state system would be unable to cover all needs without them.

Most of the voluntary agencies have charitable status, which means that they receive tax concessions on their income, but receive no (or very little) financial support from the state. However, some groups, such as those dealing with drug and alcohol addiction, do receive financial grants from central and local government. There are many thousands of voluntary organizations in Britain, operating at national and local levels and varying considerably in size. Some are small and collect limited amounts of money from the public. Others are very large, have professional staffs and receive millions of pounds from many different sources. Some groups, such as Oxfam (for the relief of famine) and the Save the Children Fund, have now become international organizations.

The following are examples of the voluntary agencies. Barnado's provides care and help for needy children; The Church of England Children's Society cares for children in need and is Britain's largest adoption agency; the Cancer Research Fund gathers finance and carries out research into potential cures for cancer; the People's Dispensary for Sick Animals (PDSA) provides medical and veterinary aid for people's pets; the Samaritans give telephone help to the suicidal; women's groups have founded refuges for abused women; and Help the Aged campaigns for the elderly.

Housing

Housing in Britain is divided into public and private sectors. Of the 25 million domestic dwellings, the majority are in the private sector, with 68 per cent being owner-occupied and 11 per cent rented out by private landlords. Some 21 per cent are in the public, subsidized sector and are rented by low-income tenants from local government authorities or housing associations (non-profit-making bodies which manage and build homes for rent and sale with the aid of government grants).

In both public and private sectors, over 80 per cent of the British population live in houses or bungalows (one-storey houses) and the remainder in flats and maisonettes. Houses have traditionally been divided into detached (22 per cent), semi-detached (30) and terraced housing (28), with the greater prices and prestige being given to detached property.

Public-sector or social housing in England is controlled centrally by the Department of the Environment and by devolved bodies in Wales, Scotland and Northern Ireland. Much of this housing has historically been provided by local authorities with finance from local sources and central government. But the provision and organization of such properties by local government has declined in recent years and more has been taken over by housing associations.

The previous Conservative government encouraged the growth of home ownership in the housing market, as part of its programme to create a property- and share-owning democracy in Britain. In the public sector, it introduced (1980) a right-to-buy policy by which local government sells off council housing to sitting tenants at below-market prices. This policy has increased the number of home-owners by over one million and relieved local authorities of the expense of decoration, upkeep and repair. The Labour Party, after initially opposing the policy, accepted it, mainly

PLATE 7.2   A detached house (© *Sharon Baseley/Format*)

PLATE 7.3   A semi-detached house in Finchley, North London
(© *Robert Estal/CORBIS*)

PLATE 7.4 A terrace of houses (© *Joanne O'Brien/Format*)

because it proved attractive to tenants. The current Labour government has ploughed back the revenue from council sales into local government (which previously had not been able to spend it) so that it can provide more low-cost accommodation.

The Conservatives were critical of local government housing policies. They wanted local authorities to divest themselves of housing management. Instead, they would work with housing associations and the private sector to increase the supply of low-cost housing for rent without providing it themselves. However, the Labour government has returned some control over housing policies to local government.

But the construction of new publicly funded houses has been reduced and the private sector is not building enough low-cost properties. Critics argue that Conservative government housing policies contributed to a serious shortage of cheap rented accommodation in towns and rural areas for low-income groups, single people and the unemployed, at a time when demand is growing. The biggest increase is expected in the number of one-person households, which are projected to grow from 5.8 million in 1996 to 8.5 million by 2021 or 71 per cent of the total increase in the number of households.

Home ownership in the private sector has increased by 10 per cent since 1979. The normal procedure when buying a house or flat is to take out a loan on the security of the property (a mortgage) from a building society, bank or other financial institution. The amount of money advanced on a loan depends mainly on the borrower's salary and it is usual to borrow three times one's gross annual salary. This long-term loan is usually paid off over a twenty-five-year period and includes interest.

House prices can vary considerably throughout the country, with London and south-east England having the highest prices and northern England, Scotland and Wales having the lowest. Prices increased dramatically at the beginning of the 1970s and much property speculation occurred. Price increases then stabilized for some years at 7–10 per cent each year.

But there was a price boom from 1986 to 1988, followed by high interest rates and an increase in mortgage foreclosures. This means that, when people cannot afford to continue their repayments on the loan, the lending institution takes over the property and the occupier becomes homeless. The number of foreclosures has now been reduced. There was also a fall in house prices, a property slump and a growth in negative equity (where the loan or mortgage is higher than the value of the property) which was only slowly reversed from 1994 as interest rates were reduced and the property market slowly recovered. Since then, house prices have increased dramatically, particularly in south-east England, but slowed down in 2001.

British homes still have variable construction standards. Many are old and cold; are frequently badly built; and lack central heating and adequate insulation. But there has been some improvement in housing standards in recent years, and most new houses have a high percentage of the basic amenities. Greater attention has been paid to insulation, energy-saving and quality. However, as building costs rise and available land becomes scarcer, the trend in new property construction has been towards flats and smaller rooms in houses.

Nevertheless, there are still districts, particularly in the centres of the big cities, where living conditions are bad and the equivalent of contemporary slums. Nearly half of the property in the inner-city areas was built before 1919 and, in spite of large-scale slum clearance in the 1950s and 1960s, much existing housing here is in barely habitable shape. Some recently completed high-rise blocks of council flats and estates in the public sector have had to be demolished because of defective and dangerous structures. According to the National Housing Forum, one in thirteen British homes (or 1.8 million) is unfit for human habitation.

Twentieth-century town renovation and slum clearance policies from the 1930s were largely devoted to the removal of the populations of large city-centres to new towns, usually located in the countryside, or to new council estates in the suburbs. Some of the new towns, such as Crawley and Stevenage, have been seen as successes, although they initially had their share of social and planning problems. The same cannot be said of many

PLATE 7.5   A council estate in Thamesmead, London (© *Adam Woolfit/CORBIS*)

council estates, which have tended to degenerate very quickly. The bad design of some housing estates, their social deprivation and lack of upkeep are often blamed for the crime and vandalism which affect some of them. However, some local councils are now modernizing decaying housing stock, rather than spending on new development, in an attempt to preserve local communities. Similar work is also being done by housing associations (with government grants) and by private builders.

The provision of sufficient adequate and varied housing in Britain, such as one-bedroom properties for young and single persons, has been a problem for many years. People on low wages, whether married or single, are often unable to afford the cost of a mortgage for suitable private property. One of the factors causing the difficulty for young people in affording first homes, particularly in rural areas within (ever-increasing) commuting distance of London, is the desire of affluent people for homes – or second homes – in the country. It is also difficult for them to obtain council housing because of long waiting lists, which contain people with priority over them. The right-to-buy policy has reduced the number of available council houses and flats for low-income groups and the unemployed. An alternative for many was either to board with parents, or to rent property in the private sector. Young people in Britain tend to leave the family home at a relatively early age, and there is much more house-sharing among young people than in many other countries.

PLATE 7.6 Homeless (© *Ulrike Preuss/Format*)

But Rent Acts and other legislation have strictly controlled rents and security of tenure. These measures have resulted in the private rented sector being greatly reduced, because landlords could no longer charge market prices and were unwilling to put up with the restrictions. The previous Conservative government lessened the effects of the Rent Acts by introducing new lease structures and encouraged landlords and other agencies to provide more privately rented accommodation. But the relaxations have led to accusations of exploitation of tenants by landlords. The Labour government wants to see a healthy private rented sector. It is trying to improve the rights of leaseholders to purchase their freehold and protect themselves against abuse and exploitation by unscrupulous landlords.

The inadequate housing market has partly contributed to the number of homeless people, particularly in London and other large cities, which in turn has led to increased social problems. Officially, there are some 105,000 homeless people, who must be housed in temporary accommodation, which is usually inadequate. But unofficial figures put the real homeless total for all age groups at about 300,000, and some of them are visible on the streets of Britain's large cities, particularly London. The Labour government has established programmes and funds to combat 'rough sleeping' (people who sleep in the open) and there had been a reduction of one third in the numbers of rough sleepers by 2000. The causes of homelessness are complex and affect all age groups and types of people, but it is suggested that the problem could be better handled. There are some 700,000 homes (mainly in the Midlands and the north of England) in both private and public sectors which remain empty and unoccupied for various reasons. These could eradicate the problem of homelessness and the housing shortage if they were properly utilized.

Charities such as Shelter and religious organizations such as the Salvation Army provide accommodation for the homeless for limited periods and campaign on their behalf. Local organizations, such as Housing Advice Centres and Housing Aid Centres, also provide help. But the problem of housing in Britain is still a major one and a focus of public concern. The high prices of many private houses and the inadequacies of the public sector market suggest that the problem will remain. The number of new starts for construction in both the public and private sectors has decreased, although the slump in building did improve slightly from 1994.

Attitudes to the social services

Opinion polls consistently show that a large majority of British people feel a concern for and dissatisfaction with the condition of the National Health Service. They place a high priority for increased public spending on health and medical provisions. They do not consider that the NHS is as well run as other institutions and there has been growing support for a comprehensive, better-funded state healthcare service. There has also been opposition to reforms in the NHS, with fear expressed about the possible privatization of health services.

But a *MORI/British Council* poll in 1999 found that 65 per cent of overseas respondents believe that Britain has a good healthcare service. However, doctors and nurses always head the lists of those professionals with whom Britons are most satisfied (89 per cent in October 2001), despite recent medical scandals concerning negligence and incompetence.

Concern is also felt about the provision of public housing, Social Security benefits, the personal social services and community care. Most people, at least in response to poll questions, indicate that they would be willing to pay higher taxes in order to ensure better social and health welfare. There is also some support for the idea that a proportional amount of income tax could be earmarked as being directly applicable to the public services.

An alternative to public services being funded completely by taxation is the Public–Private Partnership schemes favoured by the Labour government. These involve the private sector in the organization of public services. A *MORI* poll in July 2001 found that only one in nine respondents believes that extending private sector involvement will improve public services. A *MORI* poll in September 2001 found that 64 per cent of respondents felt that public services, such as health, should be entirely or mostly provided by the public sector.

On being asked how public services could be improved, 64 per cent of respondents thought that better pay and conditions should be given to public sector workers; 43 per cent believed that there should be more public sector workers; and 42 per cent considered that there should be more investment in new buildings and equipment for public services.

These results show that a majority of British people support the idea of free public services funded by taxation. Trade union leaders suggest that the Labour government could be on a collision course with the public if it pushes ahead with public–private partnerships in the public services. A *MORI* poll in October 2001 found that only 42 per cent of respondents felt that Labour government policies in general would improve the state of public services.

Exercises

Explain and examine the following terms:

welfare state	chemist	flats	social services
Social Fund	benefits	GP	nuclear family
'pay-beds'	rent	Shelter	council housing
workhouses	landlord	Oxfam	Beveridge Report
Poor Law	bungalow	mortgage	Income Support
charities	homeless	cohabitation	building society

Write short essays on the following topics:

1 Describe the structure and condition of the National Health Service.
2 Does the Social Security system provide a comprehensive service for the needy in Britain?
3 Discuss the different types of housing in Britain and the mechanics of buying property.

Further reading

George, V. and Wilding, P. (1999) *British Society and Social Welfare* London: Palgrave/ Macmillan

Glennester, H. (2000) *British Social Policy since 1945* Oxford: Blackwell

Ham, C. (1999) *Health Policy in Britain* London: Palgrave/Macmillan

Ludlam, S. and Smith, M.J. (eds) (2000) *New Labour in Government* London: Macmillan

Page, R. and Silburn, R. (eds) (1999) *British Social Welfare in the Twentieth Century* London: Palgrave/Macmillan

Willman, J. (1998) *A Better State of Health* London: Profile Books

Websites

Department of Work and Pensions: www.dwp.gov.uk

Department of Health: www.doh.gov.uk

Home Office: www.homeoffice.gov.uk

Charity Commission: www.charity-commission.gov.uk

Women's Unit: www.womens-unit.gov.uk

National Assembly for Wales: www.wales.gov.uk

Northern Ireland Executive: www.nics.gov.uk

Scottish Executive: www.scotland.gov.uk

Education

BRITISH EDUCATION OPERATES ON THREE levels: schools, higher education and further/adult education. Schools are mainly mixed-sex, although there are some single-sex schools, and are divided into state (maintained from public funds) and independent (privately financed) sectors (the latter mainly in England). But there is no common educational organization for the whole country. Northern Ireland, Scotland and England/Wales have somewhat different school systems. Further/adult and higher education generally have the same structure throughout Britain and are mostly state-funded.

The quality of British education concerns parents, employers, politicians and students. School inspectors have criticized standards in English, Mathematics, Technology and writing and reading skills. In 1997, the *World Economic Forum* claimed that Britain ranked 32nd out of 53 countries in the quality of its primary and secondary schools. A 1997 *National Institute of Economic and Social Research* study showed that British thirteen-to-fourteen-year-olds were one year behind most European countries and even further behind Japan, Korea and Singapore.

Later, in 2001, the *Organization for Economic Cooperation and Development (OECD)* reported that Britain was slipping down the global league table of secondary schools (19th out of 28), defined by good passes in national examinations. Britain also had some of the worst pre-school education and child-care in the western world, with a lack of high-quality nurseries, low-qualified and underpaid staff and poor working conditions. A *National Skills Task Force* in 2000 reported that 7 million adults (nearly one in five) in Britain were functionally illiterate. It is argued that low standards of literacy and numeracy stem from decades of indequate school education.

But the *OECD* said that Britain leads the world in higher education, defined as having the highest proportion (35.6 per cent) of university graduates aged twenty-one, largely because of short (three-year) degree courses. However, in Britain itself there is criticism of degree standards, some university courses and varying performances between different universities.

But British education should not be seen in a wholly negative light. School examination results have improved in recent years, although some critics attribute this to lower standards. Many schools, teachers and students in the state and independent sectors produce excellent work, as do the universities. It is the failing and underperforming state schools and universities which catch the media headlines, although many of the schools have now improved. The Labour government in 1997 prioritized education, promised to focus on its quality and to make it a lifelong learning experience. But, while there has been improvement in literacy and at the primary school level, secondary school education still has weaknesses and the public are dissatisfied with Labour progress in raising educational standards.

School history

The complicated nature of British (particularly English) schooling and current educational controversies have their roots in school history. To simplify matters, this section concentrates on the largest school element, that of England and Wales, with comparative references to Scotland and Northern Ireland. State involvement in education was late and the first attempt to establish a national system of state-funded elementary schools came only in 1870 for England and Wales (1872 for Scotland and 1923 for Northern Ireland). But it was not until 1944 that the state supplied both primary and secondary schools nationally which were free and compulsory.

However, some church schools have long existed. After England, Scotland, Ireland and Wales were gradually converted to Christianity in the fifth and sixth centuries, the church's position in society enabled it to create the first schools. These initially prepared boys for the priesthood. But the church then developed a wider educational role and its structures influenced the later state system.

Other schools were also periodically established by rich individuals or monarchs. These were independent, privately financed institutions and were variously known as high, grammar and public schools: they were later associated with both the modern independent and state educational sectors. But such schools were largely confined to the sons of the rich, aristocratic and influential. Most people received no formal schooling and remained illiterate and innumerate for life.

In later centuries, more children benefited as the church created new schools; local areas developed secular schools; and schools were provided by wealthy industrialists and philanthropists for working-class boys and girls. But the minority of children attending such institutions received only a basic instruction in reading, writing and arithmetic. The majority of children received no adequate education.

By the nineteenth century, Britain had a haphazard school structure (except for Scotland). Protestant churches lost their domination of education and competed with the Roman Catholic Church, Nonconformist churches and other faiths. Church schools guarded their independence from state and secular interference and provided much of the available schooling. The ancient high, grammar and public schools continued to train the sons of the middle and upper classes for professional and leadership roles in society. But, at a time when the industrial revolutions were proceeding rapidly and the population was growing, the state did not provide a school system which could educate the workforce. Most of the working class still received no formal or adequate education.

However, local and central government did begin to show some regard for education in the early nineteenth century. Grants were made to local authorities for school use in their areas and in 1833 Parliament funded the construction of school buildings. But it was only in 1870 that the state became more actively involved. An Education Act (the Forster Act) created local school boards in England and Wales, which provided schools in their areas. State elementary schools now supplied non-denominational training and the existing religious voluntary schools served denominational needs.

By 1880 this system provided free and compulsory elementary schooling in most parts of Britain for children between the ages of five and ten (twelve in 1899). The Balfour Act (1902) later made local government responsible for state education and gave funding to voluntary schools. But, although schools provided elementary education for children up to the age of thirteen by 1918, this was still limited to basic skills.

Adequate secondary school education remained largely the province of the independent sector and a few state schools. But people had to pay for their services. After a period when the old public (private) schools had declined in quality, they revived in the nineteenth century. Their weaknesses, such as the narrow curriculum and indiscipline, had been reformed by progressive headmasters such as Thomas Arnold of Rugby and their reputations increased. The private grammar and high schools, which imitated the classics-based education of the public schools, also expanded. These schools drew their pupils from the sons of the middle and upper classes and were the training grounds for the established elite and the professions.

State secondary school education in the early twentieth century was marginally extended to children whose parents could not afford school fees. Scholarships (financial grants) for clever poor children and some state funding for secondary schools were provided, and more state secondary schools were created. But this state help did not appreciably expand secondary education, and in 1920 only 9.2 per cent of thirteen-year-old children in England and Wales were able to enter secondary schools on a non-fee-paying basis. The school system in the early twentieth century was still inadequate for the demands of society, working-class and lower-middle-class children lacked extensive education and hard-pressed governments avoided any further large-scale involvement until 1944.

The 1944 Education Act

In 1944, an Education Act (the Butler Act) reorganized state primary and secondary schools in England and Wales (1947 in Scotland and Northern Ireland) and greatly influenced future generations of schoolchildren. State schooling became free and compulsory up to the age of fifteen and was divided into three stages: primary schools (five–twelve years old), secondary schools (twelve–fifteen) and further post-school training. A decentralized system resulted, in which a Ministry of Education drew up policy guidelines and local education authorities (LEAs) decided which forms of schooling would be used in their areas.

Two types of state schools resulted from the Act: county and voluntary. Primary and secondary county schools were provided by LEAs in each county. Voluntary schools were mainly those elementary schools which had been founded by religious and other groups and which were now partially financed or maintained by LEAs, although they retained their religious affiliation. Non-denominational schools thus coexisted with voluntary schools. This situation continues today: most state non-denominational schools are controlled by LEAs and voluntary (faith) schools are controlled by religious groups.

Most state secondary schools in England, Wales and Northern Ireland were divided into grammar schools and secondary modern schools. Some grammar schools were new, while others were old foundations, which now received direct state funding. Placement in this secondary system depended upon an examination result. The eleven-plus examination was adopted by most LEAs, consisted of tests which covered linguistic, mathematical and general knowledge and was taken in the last year of primary school at the age of eleven. The object was to select between academic and non-academic children and introduced the notion of 'selection' based on ability. Those who passed the eleven-plus went to grammar school, while those who failed went to the secondary modern school. Although schools were supposed to be equal in their respective educational targets, the grammar schools were equated with a better (more academic) education; a socially more respectable role; and qualified children (through national examinations) for the better jobs and entry into higher education and the professions. Secondary modern schools were based on practical schooling, initially without national examinations.

The intention of the 1944 Act was to provide universal and free state primary and secondary education. Day-release training at local colleges was also introduced for employed people who wanted further education after fifteen, and local authority grants were given to students who wished to enter higher education. It was hoped that such equality of opportunity would expand the educational market, lead to a better-educated society, encourage more working-class children to enter university and achieve greater social mobility.

However, it was felt in the 1950s that these aims were not being achieved under the selective secondary school system. Education became a party-political battlefield. The Labour Party and other critics maintained that the eleven-plus examination was wrong in principle; was socially divisive; had educational and testing weaknesses; resulted in middle-class children predominating in grammar schools and higher education; and thus perpetuated the class system.

Labour governments from 1964 were committed to abolishing the eleven-plus, selection and the secondary school divisions. They would be replaced by non-selective 'comprehensive schools' to which children would automatically transfer after primary school. These would provide schooling for all children of all ability levels and from all social backgrounds.

The battle for the comprehensive and selective systems was fierce. Although more schools became comprehensive under the Conservative government from 1970, it decided against legislative compulsion. Instead, LEAs were able to choose the secondary education which was best suited to local needs. Some decided for comprehensives, while others retained selection.

But the Labour government in 1976 intended to establish comprehensive schools nationwide. Before this policy could be implemented, the Conservatives came to power in 1979. The state secondary school sector thus remains divided between the selective and non-selective options since a minority of LEAs in England and Wales do not have comprehensives and there are some 166 grammar schools left. Scottish schools have long been comprehensive, but Northern Irish schools are divided into selective grammars and secondary moderns.

The comprehensive/selection debate continues. Education is still subject to party-political and ideological conflict. Opinion polls suggest that only a minority of parents support comprehensive education and a majority favour a selective and diverse system of schools with entry based on continuous assessment, interviews and choice. It is often argued that the long-running arguments about the relative merits of different types of schooling have not benefited schoolchildren or the educational system. But reforms to the state school system are still being made by the Labour government (see below).

The state school system

State education in the UK is free and compulsory for children between the ages of five and sixteen. The vast majority of children are educated in state primary and secondary schools. But the state system is complicated by remnants of the 1944 Act and a diversity of school types throughout the country.

In England and Wales, the Department for Education and Skills (DfES) initiates policy (with Wales having some devolved responsibility) and the LEAs retain decentralized choice to organize school planning in their areas with finance provided by central government. The LEAs have traditionally left academic organization of schools to headteachers and staff. Many state schools have boards of unpaid governors, who are local citizens prepared to give help and guidance and who may be involved in the hiring of headteachers and teachers.

Following earlier Conservative reforms, headteachers now have financial control over and responsibility for their school budgets and management; school governors have greater powers of decision-making; and parents have a greater voice in the actual running of schools, as well as a right to choose a particular school for their children. These reforms have meant a shift from purely educational to management roles within state schools and involve increased burdens of time and administration. The LEAs have lost some authority in the state school sector but the Labour government has tried to find a new role for LEAs in England and Wales which would oversee admissions policies for all types of state schools.

State schooling before the age of five is not compulsory in Britain and there is no statutory requirement on the LEAs to provide such education. But more parents (particularly those at work) are seeking school provisions for young children and there is concern about the lack of opportunities. At present, 64 per cent of three- and four-year-olds benefit from a state nursery education, while others attend private playgroups. The Labour government wants to expand state nursery education.

Pupils attend primary school in the state sector from the age of five and then move to secondary schools normally at eleven until the ages of sixteen to eighteen. Over 87 per cent of state secondary pupils in England and all state secondary pupils in Wales attend comprehensives. There are only a small number of grammar (166) and secondary modern schools left in the state system. The continued existence of these schools depends partly upon local government decisions, partly upon parent power and partly upon Labour government policy.

Comprehensive school pupils are of mixed abilities and come from a variety of social backgrounds in the local area. There is still much

PLATE 8.1 A multi-ethnic class in a primary school (*Liba Taylor/The Hutchison Library*)

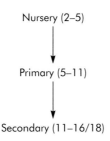

Nursery (2–5)

Primary (5–11)

Secondary (11–16/18)

FIGURE 8.1 The current state school system

argument about the quality and performance of the system. Some critics maintain that bright academic children suffer, although 'streaming' into different ability classes occurs and examination results can be excellent. The Labour government has introduced 'setting', which divides children into ability and interest classes. Arguably, therefore 'selection' continues within the comprehensives. There are some very good comprehensive schools, which are not necessarily confined to privileged areas. But there are also some very weak and failing ones, which suffer from a variety of social, economic and educational problems.

In an attempt to encourage diversity, the Conservative government established some fifteen secondary-level state-funded privately operated City Technology Colleges specializing in science, technology and mathematics. The Labour government from 1999 has also promoted school diversity and standards rather than having only one type of comprehensive school and has involved the private sector in school organization. It has created publicly funded privately operated City Academies which will replace failing and underperforming schools; some 530 secondary-level Specialist Schools which concentrate on the sciences, modern foreign languages or the arts; and Beacon Schools which are singled out as best-performing schools and are supposed to serve as examples of best practice for other schools. It also controversially intends to increase the number of voluntary schools controlled by faiths (for example, Church of England, Roman Catholic, Methodist, Jewish, Muslim and Sikh). It seems as if selective criteria for entry to some schools (particularly the specialist and faith schools) will be necessary. This is seen as a withdrawal from comprehensive principles and the creation of a two-tier school education.

Scotland has an ancient independent LEA educational system, with schools, colleges and universities which are among the oldest in Europe. Its state school system is comprehensive and non-selective. Children transfer from primary to secondary education at twelve and may continue until eighteen. The Scottish 'public schools' are state and not private institutions (although a few independent schools do exist).

In *Northern Ireland* the state schools are mostly divided on religious grounds into Catholic and Protestant and are often single-sex. However, there are some tentative movements towards integrated co-educational schools. The comprehensive principle has not been widely adopted and a selective system with an examination at eleven gives entrance to grammar schools, which 40 per cent of the age group attend. Performances at these schools have been generally superior to their counterparts in England and Wales, although examination results in the other secondary schools are comparatively poor.

The independent (fee-paying) school sector

The independent school sector exists mainly in England, is separate from the state school system and caters for some 6 per cent of all British children, from the ages of four to eighteen at various levels of education. There are 2,400 independent schools with over 563,500 pupils.

Its financing derives from investments and the fees paid by the pupils' parents for their education, which vary between schools and can amount to several thousand pounds a year. The independent sector is dependent upon its charitable and tax-exempt status to survive. This means that the schools are not taxed on their income if it is used only for educational purposes. There are a minority of scholarship holders, whose expenses are covered by their schools.

Some 250 public schools (private, not state), such as Eton, Harrow and Winchester, are the most famous of the independent schools, and are usually defined by their membership of the Headmasters' Conference. They were originally created (often by monarchs) to provide education for the sons of the rich and aristocratic. Such schools are mainly boarding establishments, where the pupils live and are educated during term time, although many of them now also take day-pupils who do not board in.

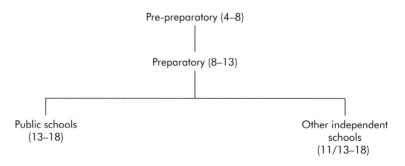

FIGURE 8.2 The independent school sector

PLATE 8.2   Girls in the classroom at Cheltenham Ladies College, a private school (© *Jacky Chapman/Format*)

Public and other independent schools play a significant role in British education, and many leading figures have been educated at them. Entry today is competitive, normally by an entrance examination, and is not confined to social class, connections or wealth, although the ability to pay the fees is important. Independent preparatory schools (primary level) prepare their pupils for independent secondary school entrance and parents who decide to send their children to an independent school will often give them a 'prep school' education first.

Independent schools can vary considerably in quality and reputation. The sector has grown and has an attraction despite its size and increasing school fees. Insurance schemes for the payment of fees give opportunities for independent education to the less affluent. But some parents make great financial sacrifices so that their children can be independently educated. Opinion polls often suggest that many parents would send their children to an independent school if they could afford it because of the quality of the education and because such schooling may give social advantages in later life.

The independent sector is criticized for being elitist, socially divisive and based on the ability to pay for education. In this view it perpetuates the class system. The Labour Party in opposition historically argued for the abolition of independent schools and the removal of their tax and charitable status, which the Labour government is currently evaluating. But independent schools are now firmly established and for many provide an element of choice in what would otherwise be a state monopoly on education.

School organization and examinations

The school day in state and independent schools usually runs from 9.00 a.m. until 4 p.m. and the school year is divided into three terms (autumn, spring and summer). Classes in British schools used to be called 'forms' and in secondary schools were numbered from one to six. But most schools have adopted year numbers from 7 to 11 in secondary schools, with a two-year sixth form for advanced work.

A reduced birth rate in recent years led to a decrease in the number of schoolchildren, resulting in the closure of schools in rural and urban areas. Numbers have since increased and the Labour government is committed to reducing average class size for primary schools to below thirty, although many secondary schools have classes with over thirty pupils.

Most teachers are trained at the universities and other colleges. There is a serious shortage of teachers in Britain in all subjects, but especially in mathematics, technology, physics and foreign languages. Potential teachers increasingly see the profession as unattractive and many practising teachers leave for better-paid jobs or retire early. Teachers at present are suffering from low morale after battles with the government over pay, conditions and educational reforms, and from what they perceive as the low status afforded them by government and the general public. The teaching profession has become very stressful and subject to greater pressures, such as assaults upon teachers by pupils and increased bureaucracy. The quality of teaching in state schools has attracted much criticism in recent years and the Labour government is committed to raising standards, removing incompetent and underperforming teachers and closing 'failing schools'.

However, the effect of alleged spending cuts in education has been considerable, with GDP public expenditure on education in Britain being below that of many comparable countries. This has prevented the building and modernization of schools, especially in inner-city areas. It has also resulted in reduced services and a shortage of books and equipment for pupils, teachers and libraries.

Previous Conservative governments introduced school reforms, which still remain under Labour. Attainment tests were set to establish what children should be reasonably expected to know at the ages of seven, eleven and fourteen. The progress of each schoolchild can then be measured against national standards, assessed and reported. But many teachers were opposed to the extra work involved, doubted the validity of the tests and have boycotted them in recent years.

Another radical reform was the creation of a National Curriculum in England and Wales (with similar developments in Northern Ireland but not

PLATE 8.3   Children in the playground of an inner-city primary school
(© *Jacky Chapman/Format*)

Scotland). The aim was to create a curriculum which was standardized, centrally devised and appropriate to the needs and demands of the contemporary world. It covers all age groups and includes the 'core subjects' of English, mathematics, science, technology, physical education and religious education. History, geography, music and art are taught in the earlier stages of the curriculum before becoming optional, while a modern foreign language is added later. This reform has generated much controversy, opposition, difficulties of implementation and problems about the content and scope of course material (such as a recent additional subject called 'citizenship').

The National Curriculum (which is not applicable to independent schools although they follow the subject structure) is tied to a system of examinations at the secondary level. They may be taken in all types of schools in England, Wales and Northern Ireland. The main examinations are the General Certificate of Secondary Education (GCSE), which is taken usually by sixteen-year olds; Advanced Subsidiary (AS) qualifications in the first year of the sixth form; and the General Certificate of Education at Advanced Level (GCE A-level), which is normally taken at the end of the second year in the sixth form by eighteen-year olds. Results in all exams tend to be better in single-sex girls' schools.

The GCSE is taken in a range of subjects, the questions and marking of which are undertaken by independent examination boards whose standards have attracted criticism in recent years. In addition to written examinations, project work and continuous assessment of pupils are taken into account in arriving at a final grade. It can be taken in any subject(s) according to individual choice. But most candidates will attempt six or seven subjects and the basic subjects required for jobs and further education are English, mathematics (or a science) and a foreign language. The GCSE was intended as a better evaluation of pupils' abilities than pure examinations and would give prospective employers some idea of the candidate's ability. But, although standards continue to improve, a third of students did not achieve high passes and some 8 per cent did not pass a single subject in 1999.

The GCE A-level is associated with more academic children, who are aiming for entry to higher education or the professions and who spend two years on their studies in the sixth form or in sixth-form colleges. Good passes are now essential because the competition for popular courses in the universities and other colleges has become stiffer. This system was controversially changed in 2000 by the Labour government, which wanted to broaden the syllabus. Four AS level subjects are taken in the first year in addition to key skills tests, before a concentration on three A2 (A-level) subjects, and pupils may mix arts and science subjects. AS subjects may

PLATE 8.4 A science class in progress (© *Jacky Chapman/Format*)

serve as a lower-level alternative for students who do not wish to go on to A2 levels. The standards achieved continue to rise. But there is continuing discussion about the format and content of A-levels, and the new system has been criticized for over-examining students, reducing the time for other school activities and leading to teacher overwork. The Labour government is now reviewing the examination structure.

Alternative examinations are General National Vocational Qualifications (GNVQs) which are mainly taken by young people in full-time education between the ages of sixteen and nineteen and provide a broad-based preparation for a range of occupations and higher education; and National Vocational Qualifications (NVQs) which are job-specific examinations.

Scotland does not have a statutory national curriculum and pupils take the National Qualification at the age of sixteen. Those between sixteen and eighteen take the reformed Scottish Highers.

GCSE, AS, A-level and alternative examination results by pupils are the basis of school 'league tables', instituted by the previous Conservative government. Examination results and marks at individual schools are published so that parents and pupils can judge a school's performance. The exercise has been criticized for its methodology and creating a 'results mentality'. But it is now firmly established and influential.

Higher education

Should a pupil obtain the required examination results at A- or alternative levels, and be successful at interviews, he or she may go on to an institution of higher education, such as a university or college. The student, after a prescribed period of study and after passing examinations, will receive a degree and become a graduate of that institution. In the past only a small proportion of the age group in Britain proceeded to higher education, in contrast to the higher rates in many major nations. But, following a recent rapid increase in student numbers (with the ratio of female to male students being three to two), the numbers are now 33 per cent in England and Wales, 40 per cent in Scotland and 45 per cent in Northern Ireland. The Labour government wishes to raise these figures to one half of those aged between eighteen and thirty by 2010.

The universities

There were 23 British universities in 1960. After a period of expansion in the 1960s and reforms in 1992 when existing institutions such as polytechnics were given university status, there are now some 87 universities and 64 institutions of higher education, with 1.3 million full-time students in 1999. The Open University and the independent University of Buckingham are additional university-level institutions.

The universities can be broadly classified into four types. The ancient universities of Oxford and Cambridge (composed of their many colleges) date from the twelfth century. But until the nineteenth century they were virtually the only English universities and offered no places to women. However, other older universities were founded in Scotland, such as St Andrews (1411), Glasgow (1450), Aberdeen (1494) and Edinburgh (1583). A second group comprises the 'redbrick' or civic universities such as Leeds, Liverpool and Manchester, which were created between 1850 and 1930. The third group consists of universities founded after the Second World War and in the 1960s. Many of the latter, such as Sussex, York and East Anglia, are associated with towns rather than big cities. The fourth group comprises the 'new universities' created in 1992 when polytechnics and some other colleges attained university status.

The competition to enter universities is now very strong in popular subjects, and students who do not do well at A- or equivalent levels may be unable to find a place. Some 17 per cent of students now drop out of higher education because of work, financial or other problems. But the majority aim for a good degree in order to obtain a good job, or to continue in higher education by doing research (masters' degrees and doctorates).

PLATE 8.5   Students walking through the grounds of Hertford College, Oxford
(© *Chris Andrews; Chris Andrews Publications/CORBIS*)

The bachelor's degree (Bachelor of Arts or Bachelor of Science, BA or BSc) is usually taken in final examinations at the end of the third year of study, although some degree courses do vary in length in different parts of Britain (such as Scotland with a four-year MA degree). The degree is divided into first-, second- and third-class honours. Some degrees depend entirely upon the examination results, while others include continuing assessment over the period of study.

Universities are supposed to have uniform standards, although there are centres of excellence in particular subjects and there has been recent criticism about levels in some universities and some subjects. Students can choose from an impressive array of subject areas and teaching is mainly by the lecture system, supported by tutorials (small groups) and seminars. The student–lecturer ratio at British universities has increased because of expanded recruitment. Most students tend to live on campus in university accommodation, while others choose to live in rented property outside the university. Until recently few British students chose universities near their parents' homes and many seemed to prefer those in the south of England. But financial reasons now persuade many students to live at home or locally.

Universities are independent institutions created by royal charter, enjoy academic freedom, appoint their own staff, award their own degrees and decide which students to admit. But they are in practice dependent upon government money. This derives mainly from finance (dependent upon the number of students recruited) given by government to Universities Funding Councils for distribution to the universities through university Vice-Chancellors who are the chief executive officers of the universities.

Both Conservative and Labour governments have been concerned to make the universities more accountable in the national interest; have tightly controlled their budgets; and have encouraged them to seek alternative private sources of finance from business and industry. The universities have lost staff and research money; have been forced to adopt more effective management and accounting procedures; must market their resources more efficiently; must attract and recruit students in order to obtain government finance; must pay greater attention to teaching and research performance; and must justify their positions financially and educationally.

Government consequently intervenes more closely in the running of the universities than in the past. Such policies have provoked considerable opposition from the universities, which argue that the recent large expansion of student numbers has not seen an equivalent rise in funding or staff salaries. But they are being forced to adapt rather than continue to lose staff, finance and educational programmes. It is also argued that expansion has led to universities taking poorly qualified students to fill their places, who then drop out because of work pressure.

Other higher education colleges

The 1970s saw the creation of colleges (or institutes) of higher education, often by merging existing colleges with redundant teachers' training colleges or by establishing new institutions. They now offer a wide range of degree, diploma and certificate courses in both science and the arts, and in some cases have specifically taken over the role of training school-teachers. They used to be under the control of their local authorities, but the Conservative government granted them independence and some have achieved university status.

A variety of other institutions also offer higher education. Some, such as the Royal College of Art, the Cranfield Institute of Technology and various Business Schools, have university status, while others, such as agri-cultural, drama and art colleges such the Royal Academy of Dramatic Arts (RADA) and the Royal College of Music, provide comparable courses. All these institutions have a strong vocational aspect to their programmes which fills a specialized role in higher education.

Student finance

In the past, British students who gained a place at an institution of higher education were awarded a grant from their local education authorities. The grant was in two parts: one, it covered the tuition fees of a first degree course (paid directly to the institution); and, two, it covered, after means-testing of parents' income, maintenance expenses such as the cost of rent, food and course books during term time.

The Labour government radically changed this situation from 1998 by abolishing the student grant. Students now have to pay tuition fees of £1,075 in 2001–02 (except in Scotland) and provide for their maintenance expenses, usually through loans from the Student Loan Company. They start to pay back their loans when they reach certain salary levels. Students are means-tested on their parents' income and those from less affluent back-grounds (some 50 per cent) may not have to pay the full or any tuition fees. Other students now have to finance their own higher education; some are in financial difficulties; and most will finish their studies with an average debt of about £12,000. However, these changes in funding have not resulted (2001) in a reduction of students applying for university entry, except for mature students. But the Labour government is re-evaluating student finance because of its alleged detrimental effect on students from poor homes, with a possible return to a grant system.

The Open University

The Labour Party broached the idea of the Open University in the 1960s. It would be a non-residential service, which used television, radio, specially produced books, audio/video cassettes and correspondence courses to teach students of all ages. It was intended to give opportunities (or a 'second chance') to adults who had been unable to take conventional higher education. It was hoped that the courses might appeal to working-class students who had left school at the official school-leaving age and who wished to broaden their horizons.

The Open University opened in 1969 and its first courses started in 1971. It now caters for undergraduate, postgraduate and research students in a wide range of subjects. About 7,000 students of all ages and from very different walks of life receive degrees from the Open University each year. First (bachelors') degrees are awarded on a system of credits for each course completed and now include students from the European Union, Gibraltar, Slovenia and Switzerland.

Dedication, stamina and perseverence are necessary to complete the long, part-time courses of the Open University. Students, who are often employed, follow their lessons and lectures at home. Part-time tutors in local areas mark the students' written work and meet them regularly to discuss their progress. There are also special weekend and refresher courses throughout the year, which are held at universities and colleges, to enable students to take part in intensive study. The various television programmes and books associated with the Open University programmes are widely exported throughout the world. The Open University is generally considered to be a cost-effective success, has provided valuable alternative educational opportunities for many people and has served as a model for other countries.

Further, adult and lifelong education

An important aspect of British education is the provision of further and adult education, whether by voluntary bodies, trade unions or other institutions. The present organizations originated to some degree in the thirst for knowledge which was felt by working-class people in the nineteenth and early-twentieth centuries, particularly after the arrival of elementary state education and growing literacy. Today a wide range of educational opportunities are provided by self-governing state-funded colleges of further education and other institutions. These offer a considerable selection of subjects at basic levels for part- and full-time students. Some students may study in the evenings or on day-release from their employment. Such studies for students over sixteen are often work-related, include government training programmes and have close ties with local commerce and industry.

Adult education is provided by these colleges, the universities, the Workers' Educational Association (WEA), evening institutes, local societies and clubs. Adult courses may be vocational (for employment) or recreational (for pleasure), and cover a variety of activities and programmes.

Some 4 million students of very varying ages are taking further and adult education courses in one form or another. In the past a relatively low percentage of the sixteen to twenty-four age group in Britain were in further and higher education, compared to the much larger percentages in Japan, the USA and Germany. Although the figures have now improved considerably, it is still a matter of concern that too few people are being educated or trained further after the age of sixteen. This is particularly true at a time when there will be an increasing shortage of well-qualified people in the future workforce, especially in vocational technical fields.

Nevertheless, there has been a recent expansion of continuing-education projects and a range of programmes specifically designed for employment purposes and to provide people with access qualifications for further training. The Labour government sees further and adult education as part of a lifelong learning process, which it wants to prioritize. The aim is to encourage the continuous development of people's skills, knowledge and understanding. But further education is suffering at present from a lack of resources and funding, and inspectors found in 2001 that a third of further education colleges were inadequate and had low standards.

Attitudes to education

Concerns about the quality of British education and educational policy at all levels are consistently voiced by a majority of respondents to public opinion polls. They think that state schools are not run well and that more money should be spent on education generally. The Labour government has responded by giving more funding to the system and by tinkering with its structures. But serious dissatisfaction continued to be voiced in the polls in 2000–01, and education is likely to continue as a major problem in British life.

There have been continuous and vigorous debates about the performance and goals of British education at all levels since the 1970s. Traditionalist critics, who want disciplined learning programmes, feel that state comprehensive schools and 'creative/progressive' methods of child-centred teaching are not producing the kind of people needed for contemporary society. It is argued that pupils lack the basic skills of numeracy and literacy and are unprepared for the realities of the outside world. Employers frequently criticize both schools and higher education for the quality of their products.

The previous Conservative government's reforms from 1986 were based on centralized and consumer-choice policies. They were an attempt to rectify the educational situation and aimed at producing accountability, improved standards and skills in schools and higher education by more formal learning programmes. The government attempted to reform the teaching profession, improve pupils' performances, emphasize science and modern language studies and increase parental choice.

The Labour government is continuing this process by stressing compulsory homework, contracts with parents, concentration on the '3 Rs' (reading, writing and arithmetic) and grouping children by ability ('setting'). Progressive 'child-centred' practices are dismissed, funds are being provided for school fabric repairs and computers will be installed in every school. There is also a move away from having only one type of state secondary school (comprehensive) to embracing diversity and specialism through the creation of specialist and faith schools. The government also wants poorer and more working-class students to enter university.

Critics argue that an educational system should not be solely devoted either to elitist standards or to market considerations. It should try to provide a choice between the academic/liberal tradition, the technical and the vocational. The lack of adequate vocational or technical education and training is creating big problems for employers, who argue that they cannot find competently trained staff to fill vacancies. The future of British education will depend in large part on how government reforms work and how they are perceived by teachers, parents, students and employers.

On the other hand, a 1999 *MORI/British Council* poll found that 76 per cent of overseas respondents regarded the British as well-educated. Higher education was particularly well respected, with 88 per cent of respondents rating it as 'good'.

 Exercises

Explain and examine the following terms:

public schools	grammar schools	WEA
comprehensives	eleven-plus	tutorial
GCE A level	Open University	scholarships
LEAs	tuition fees	student finance
Eton	GCSE	'prep school'

the Butler Act	degree	vocational
streaming/setting	'3 Rs'	literacy
faith schools	AS levels	specialist schools

Write short essays on the following topics:

1   Critically examine state secondary education in Britain, analysing its structures, aims and achievements.
2   Describe the structure of British higher education and its roles.
3   Comment upon the desirability, or otherwise, of British education's division into state and independent sectors.

Further reading

Abercrombie, N. and Warde, A. (2000) *Contemporary British Society* Oxford: Polity Press, Chapter 14

Chitty, C. (1992) *The Education System Transformed* London: Baseline Books

Ryan, A. (1999) *Liberal Anxieties and Liberal Education* London: Profile Books

Walden, G. (1996) *We Should Know Better: Solving the Education Crisis* London: Fourth Estate

Websites

Department for Education and Skills: www.dfes.gov.uk

Independent education: www.isis.org.uk

The Times Higher Education Supplement: www.thes.co.uk

The Times Educational Supplement: www.tes.co.uk

Scottish Executive: www.scotland.gov.uk

National Assembly for Wales: www.wales.gov.uk

Northern Ireland Assembly: www.ni-assembly.gov.uk

Office for Standards in Education: www.ofsted.gov.uk

Chapter 9

The media

THE TERM 'MEDIA' MAY INCLUDE any communication system by which people are informed, educated or entertained. In Britain it generally refers to the print industries (the press or newspapers and magazines) and broadcasting (terrestrial or earth-based television, cable and satellite television, radio and video). These systems overlap to some extent with each other and with books, film and the Internet; are profitable businesses; and are tied to advertising, sponsorship, commerce and industry.

The media have evolved from simple methods of production, distribution and communication to their present sophisticated technologies. Their growth and variety have greatly improved information dispersal, news availability and entertainment opportunities. They cover homes, places of business and leisure activities and their influence is very powerful and an inevitable part of daily life. For example, surveys indicate that 69 per cent of Britons obtain their daily news from television, 20 per cent from newspapers and 11 per cent from radio. Electronic technology, such as the Internet, is an important part of media, business and education, while the British use of home-view videos is the highest in the world.

But the media provoke debates about what is socially and morally permissible in their content and methods. Questions are asked about the role of advertising and sponsorship, the quality of the services provided, the alleged danger of the concentrated ownership of media resources, influence on politics, restraints upon 'free expression' and the ethical responsibility of the media to individuals and society.

The print media

The print media (newspapers and magazines) began to develop in the eighteenth century. Initially, a wide circulation was hindered by transportation and distribution problems, illiteracy and government licensing or censorship restrictions. But, over the last two hundred years, an expanded educational system, abolition of government control, new print inventions and Britain's small area have eliminated these difficulties and created allegedly free print media.

The growth of literacy after 1870 provided the owners of the print media with an increased market. Newspapers and magazines, which had previously been limited to the middle and upper classes, were popularized. They were used for news and information, but also for profit and entertainment. Ownership, new types of print media and financially rewarding advertising increased in the competitive atmosphere of the late nineteenth and early twentieth centuries. Owners also realized that political and social influence could be achieved through control of the means of communication.

National newspapers

National newspapers are those which are mostly published from London (with some regional versions) and are available in all parts of Britain on the same day, including Sundays. Many are delivered direct to the home from local newsagents by newsboys and girls. The good internal distribution systems of a compact country enabled a national press to develop, and Internet online copies now offer updated and immediate availability.

The first British newspapers with a limited national circulation appeared in the early eighteenth century and were followed by others, such as *The Times* (1785), the *Observer* (1791) and the *Sunday Times* (1822). But most were so-called 'quality' papers, catering for a relatively small, educated market.

In the nineteenth century, the growth and composition of the population conditioned the types of newspaper which were produced. The first popular national papers were deliberately printed on Sundays, such as the *News of the World* (1843) and the *People* (1881). They were inexpensive and aimed at the expanding and increasingly literate working class. In 1896, Alfred Harmsworth produced the *Daily Mail*, which was targeted at the lower-middle class as an alternative to the 'quality' dailies. Harmsworth then published the *Daily Mirror* in 1903 for the working-class popular market. Both the *Mail* and the *Mirror* were soon selling more than a million copies a day.

The early twentieth century was the era of mass-circulation papers and of owners such as Harmsworth and Arthur Pearson. There was fierce competition between them as they fought for bigger shares of the market. Pearson's *Morning Herald* (later the *Daily Express*) was created in 1900 to compete with the *Daily Mail* for lower-middle-class readers.

The *Daily Mirror* was the largest-selling national daily in the early twentieth century. It supported the Labour Party and was designed for quick and easy reading by the industrial and increasingly politicized working class. The *Daily Herald* (1911) also supported the Labour Party, until it was sold in 1964, renamed the *Sun* and developed different political and news emphases. The competition between the *Sun* and *Mirror* continues today, with each aiming for a bigger share of the mass daily market. Battles are still fought between owners, since newspaper-ownership is concentrated in a few large publishing groups, such as Rupert Murdoch's News International (which has large media holdings in Britain, Australia and the USA) and Trinity Mirror (see table 9.1).

The success of the early popular press was due to growing literacy; a desire for knowledge and information by the working class; and political awareness among workers caused by the rise of the Labour Party. Newspaper owners profited by the huge market, but they also satisfied demand. The price and content of mass papers reflected lower-middle- and working-class readerships. This emphasis attracted large consumer advertising, and owners were able to produce cheaply by using modern printing methods and a nationwide distribution network.

The circulation of national papers rose rapidly, with 5.5 million daily sales by 1920. By 1973 these had increased to 17 million. But newspapers had to cope first with the competition of radio and films and later with television. Although they have survived, there has, since the 1970s, been a decline in sales and in the number of national and other newspapers.

Surveys find that Britons buy more papers than any other Europeans. Some 50 per cent of people over fifteen read a national daily paper and 70 per cent read a national Sunday newspaper. National newspapers have sales of 13.5 million on weekdays and 14.8 million on Sundays, but on average two people read each paper.

The national press in Britain today consists of ten daily morning papers and nine Sunday papers. It is in effect a London press, because most national newspapers have their bases and printing facilities in the capital, although editions of some nationals are now published outside London, in Europe and the USA. Most of them used to be located in Fleet Street in central London. But all have now left the street and moved to other parts of the capital. The reasons for these moves were high property rents, fierce competition and opposition from trade unions to the introduction of new printing technology. Newspapers and magazines have also had to face the expense of newsprint and rising production and labour costs.

Heavy labour costs were due to the overstaffing and restrictive practices of the trade unions. Owners were forced into new ways of increasing productivity while cutting costs. Regional owners outside London had in fact pioneered the movement of newspapers and magazines into new print technology and London newspapers had to follow in order to survive.

New technology meant that journalists' 'copy' could be printed directly through computers, without having to use the intermediate 'hot-metal' typesetting by printers. This gave owners flexibility in their printing and distribution methods and cheaper production costs. It allowed them to

PLATE 9.1   Daily Express's Newspaper building, Blackfriars, London
(© *Martin Jones/CORBIS*)

escape from trade-union dominance and the concentration of the industry in London. But it also resulted in job reductions, trade-union opposition and bitter industrial action such as picketing.

New technology, improved distribution methods and cuts in labour and production costs have increased the profitability of print industries. Despite the attraction of other media, they still have a considerable presence, although sales are declining. The business is very competitive and papers can suffer from a variety of problems. However, the high risks involved have not stopped the introduction of new newspapers. The 'quality' national daily *The Independent* was published in October 1986 and survives despite circulation losses. Sunday nationals, such as *The Independent on Sunday* (1990), have also appeared. But other dailies have been lost.

National papers are usually termed 'quality' or 'popular' depending on their differences in content and format (tabloid or broadsheet). Others are called 'mid-market', fall between these two extremes and are tabloids (see table 9.1). The 'qualities' (such as *The Times*) are broadsheets (large-sheet), report national and international news in depth and analyse current events and the arts in editorials and articles. The populars (such as the *Sun*) are mostly tabloid (small-sheet), deal with relatively few 'hard news' stories, tend to be superficial in their treatment of events and much of their

TABLE 9.1 National newspapers (average daily sales, 2000)

Name	Founded	Sales	Owned/controlled by
Popular dailies			
Daily Mirror	1903	2,263,000	Trinity Mirror
The Sun	1964	3,569,000	News International
Daily Star	1978	613,000	United News and Media
Mid-market dailies			
Daily Mail	1896	2,387,000	Daily Mail and General Trust
Daily Express	1900	1,062,000	United News and Media
'Quality' dailies			
The Times	1785	722,000	News International
The Guardian	1821	395,000	Guardian Media Group
Daily Telegraph	1855	1,031,000	Telegraph Group
Financial Times	1888	459,000	Pearson
The Independent	1986	224,000	Independent Newspapers
Popular Sundays			
News of the World	1843	4,023,000	News International
The People	1881	1,523,000	Trinity Mirror
Sunday Mirror	1963	1,927,000	Trinity Mirror
Mid-market Sundays			
Mail on Sunday	1982	2,298,000	Daily Mail and General Trust
Sunday Express	1918	974,000	United News and Media
'Quality' Sundays			
Observer	1791	417,000	Guardian Media Group
Sunday Times	1822	1,360,000	News International
Sunday Telegraph	1961	808,000	Telegraph Group
Independent on Sunday	1990	247,000	Independent Newspapers

Source: Newspaper Publishers Association, 2000

material is sensationalized and trivialized. It cannot be said that the down-market populars are instructive, or concerned with raising the critical consciousness of readers. But owners and editors argue that their readership demands particular styles, interests and attitudes. 'Mid-market' papers, such as the *Mail* and *Express*, cater for intermediate groups.

PLATE 9.2 Newspaper headlines (© *Alistair Daniel*)

Sales of popular papers on weekdays and Sundays far exceed those of the 'qualities'. 'Qualities' are more expensive than populars and carry up-market advertising that generates essential finance. Populars carry less advertising and cater for more down-market material. However, the press takes much of the finance spent on total advertising in Britain.

There is no state control or censorship of the British press, although it is subject to laws of publication and expression and there are forms of self-censorship, by which it regulates its own conduct. The press is also financially independent of the political parties and receives no funding from government (except for Welsh-language community papers).

It is argued that most newspapers are politically right-of-centre and sympathize with the Conservative Party. But their positions are usually driven by readers' opinions and political slants in fact can vary considerably over time and under the influence of events. For example, the small-circulation *Morning Star* has varied between Stalinist, Euro-Communist and Democratic Left views. Papers may have a political bias and support a specific party, particularly at election times, although this can change. A few, such as those of the Trinity Mirror group, support the Labour Party, some such as *The Times* and *The Independent* consider themselves to be independent, while others, such as *The Guardian*, favour a left-of-centre position. It appears that the British public receive a reasonable variety of political views from their newspapers.

The press is dependent for its survival upon circulation figures; upon the advertising that it can attract; and upon financial help from its owners. A paper may face difficulties and fail if advertisers remove their business. In fact all the media are currently experiencing a downturn in advertising revenue. A high circulation does not necessarily guarantee the required advertising and consequent survival, because advertisers now tend to place their mass-appeal consumer products on television, where they will benefit from a larger audience. Most popular papers are in constant competition with their rivals to increase their sales. They attempt to do this by gimmicks such as bingo games and competitions, or by calculated editorial policies which are intended to catch the mass readership. Owners may refuse to rescue those papers which make continuous losses. A number of news-papers in the twentieth century ceased publication because of reduced circulation, loss of advertising revenue, refusals of further financial aid, or a combination of all three factors.

However, despite a fall in hard-copy circulation, most national news-papers now have online Internet publication. This provides an additional medium for information and communication, as well as continuously updated news.

Regional newspapers

Some 1,300 regional newspapers are published in towns and cities throughout Britain. They contain a mixture of local and national news; are supported financially by regional advertising; and may be daily morning or evening papers, Sundays or weekly. Some nine out of ten adults read a regional or local paper every week and 75 per cent of local and regional newspapers also operate an Internet website.

Excluding its national newspaper industry, London has one paper (the *Evening Standard*) with daily sales of 440,000. But there are also about a hundred local weeklies, dailies and evening papers which appear in the Greater London districts.

'Quality' daily regional (and national) papers, such as *The Scotsman* (Edinburgh) and the *Glasgow Herald*, the *Western Mail* (Cardiff), and the *Yorkshire Post* (Leeds), have good reputations and sales outside their regions. But the best-selling papers are in Scotland, such as the *Daily Record* and the *Sunday Mail* (Glasgow) and the *Sunday Post* (Dundee).

There has also been a growth of 'free newspapers' in the regions, such as the *London Metro* (now available throughout the country with a circulation of 1.2 million), which are often delivered direct to homes and for which the consumer does not pay. Some 800 are published weekly on a local basis and are financed by local advertising, to such an extent that news is outweighed by the advertisements. It is estimated that they have a weekly circulation of some 35 million.

Britain's ethnic communities also produce their own newspapers and magazines, which are increasing in numbers, are available nationally in the larger cities and are improving in quality. There is a wide range of publications for Jewish, Asian, Afro-Caribbean, Chinese and Arabic readers, published on a daily or (more commonly) periodic basis.

Periodicals and magazines

There are 9,000 different periodicals and magazines in Britain, which are of a weekly, monthly or quarterly nature and are dependent upon sales and advertising to survive. They are aimed at different markets and levels of sophistication and either cover trades, professions and business (read by 95 per cent of occupational groups) or are consumer titles dealing with sports, hobbies and interests (read by 80 per cent of adults).

Although the number of periodicals has expanded, it is still difficult to break into the established consumer market with a new product. Some attempts, which manage to find a gap in the market, succeed, but most usually fail.

The teenage and youth magazine market is fiercely fought for, but has suffered large sales losses recently. This is attributed to greater Internet and mobile phone usage. The men's general interest magazine market is similarly volatile. Women's periodicals, such as *Take a Break*, *Woman* and *Woman's Own*, have large and wide circulations. But the best-selling publications are the weekly *Radio Times* and *What's on TV*, which contain feature stories and scheduled programmes for BBC and independent television. Other magazines cover interests such as computers, rural pastimes, gardening, railways, cooking, architecture, do-it-yourself skills and sports.

Among the serious weekly journals are the *New Statesman and Society* (a left-wing political and social affairs magazine); the *Economist* (dealing with economic and political matters); the *Spectator* (a conservative journal); and *New Scientist*. *The Times* publishes influential weekly magazines, such as the *Educational Supplement*, the *Higher* (Education Supplement) and the *Literary Supplement*. The lighter side of the market is catered for by periodicals such as *Private Eye*, which satirizes the shortcomings of British society.

The broadcasting media

The broadcasting media are divided into public and commercial (independent) sectors and consist of radio, terrestrial television and cable/satellite television. Three authorities oversee these services: the British Broadcasting Corporation (BBC), the Independent Television Commission (ITC) and the Radio Authority.

Radio was the first broadcasting medium to appear in Britain. Experimental transmissions were made at the end of the nineteenth century and systems were developed in the early twentieth century. After a period of limited availability, national radio was established in 1922 when the British Broadcasting Company was formed under John Reith.

In 1927 Reith became the first Director-General of the British Broadcasting Corporation (BBC) and set the tone and style for the BBC's development. The BBC had a monopoly in broadcasting and a paternalistic image. Reith insisted that it should be independent of government and commercial interests; strive for quality; and be a public service broadcaster, with a duty to inform, educate and entertain. The BBC built a reputation for impartial news reporting and excellent programmes, both domestically and internationally.

The BBC's broadcasting monopoly in radio and television (which had started in 1936 for a limited audience) led to pressure from commercial and political interests to widen the scope of broadcasting. As a result, commercial (independent) television financed by advertising and under the supervision of the Independent Television Authority (ITA) was created in 1954 and the first programmes were shown in 1955. The BBC's monopoly on radio broadcasting was ended in 1972 and independent radio stations were established throughout the country, dependent on advertising for their financing.

A duopoly (two organizations) covered broadcasting: the public service of the BBC and the commercial (independent) service of the ITA. This division has been expanded as cable, satellite and other broadcasting services have developed in recent years. The ITA evolved first into the IBA (Independent Broadcasting Authority) and finally the ITC (Independent Television Commission) and the Radio Authority was also created. British broadcasting is thus conditioned by the competition between the BBC and independent organizations.

Substantial changes to British broadcasting were made in the 1980s and 1990s by Conservative governments which created more radio and television channels. Greater deregulation was supposed to create competition among broadcasters and more choice for consumers. Broadcasting services are now moving to digital transmission. This is proceeding slowly because of technical problems and few paying customers for commercial offerings. But it will potentially create many more radio and television channels as analogue systems are phased out.

These changes are controversial and are criticized for their emphasis on competition and commercialism, rather than quality. A larger number of television channels may not lead to greater choice, but rather inferior programmes as broadcasters chase bigger audiences. There is a finite number of people to watch television; advertisers' budgets cannot be stretched to cover all available independent television offerings; and advertisers gravitate towards those programmes which attract large audiences. Television in 1995 accounted for 28 per cent of total advertising spending but advertising revenue for broadcasters declined sharply in 2001.

The BBC

The BBC is based at Broadcasting House in London, but has stations throughout the country, which provide regional networks for radio and television. It was created by Royal Charter and has a board of governors who are responsible for supervising its programmes and their suitability. They are appointed by the Crown on the advice of government ministers and are supposed to constitute an independent element in the organization of the BBC. Daily operations are controlled by the Director-General, chosen by the board of governors.

The BBC is financed by a grant from Parliament, which comes from the sale of television licences (£1.6 billion per year). These are payable by anyone who owns a television set and are relatively cheap in international terms (£104 annually for a colour set). The BBC also generates considerable income from selling its programmes abroad and from the sale of a programme guide (*Radio Times*), books, magazines and videos.

The BBC in recent years has come under pressure from government to reform itself. It has struggled to maintain its position as a traditional public service broadcaster, funded by the licence fee, at a time of fierce competition with commercial broadcasters. Internal reorganization has led to a slimmer and more efficient organization. But it has had to develop alternative forms of funding, such as subscription and pay services and must include independent productions in 25 per cent of its television schedules.

The BBC's external services, which consist of radio broadcasts in English (the World Service) and 42 other languages abroad, were founded in 1932 and are funded by the Foreign Office. These have a reputation for objective news reporting and programmes. The BBC also began commercially funded television programmes in 1991 by cable to Europe and by satellite links to Africa and Asia; *BBC World* (news) – now merged with the World Service – and *BBC Prime* (entertainment).

The BBC is not a state organization, in the sense that it is controlled by the government. But it is not as independent of political pressures as many in Britain and overseas assume. Its charter has to be renewed by Parliament and by its terms government can, and does, intervene in the showing of programmes which are alleged to be controversial or against the public interest. The BBC governors, although supposedly independent, are in fact government appointees. Governments can also exert pressure upon the BBC when the licence fee comes up for renewal by Parliament. The BBC does try to be neutral in political matters, to such an extent that all political parties have periodically complained that it is prejudiced against them. The major parties have equal rights to broadcast on the BBC and independent television.

Historically, the BBC was affected by the invention of television, which changed British entertainment and news habits. The BBC now has two television channels (BBC1 and BBC2). BBC1 is a mass-appeal channel with an audience share of 28 per cent. Its programmes consist of news, plays and drama series, comedy, quiz shows, variety performances, sport and documentaries. BBC2, with an audience share of 11 per cent, tends to show more serious items such as news analysis and discussion, documentaries, adaptations of novels into plays and series, operas, concerts and some sport. It is also provides Open University courses. The Labour government has approved (2001) the expansion of BBC television (digital) services by the creation of a BBC4 channel (culture and the arts) and two channels for children under six and over.

BBC Radio performs an important service, although some of its audiences have declined recently. There are five national channels (to be increased by five new digital channels); 39 local stations serving many districts in England; and regional and community services in Scotland, Wales and Northern Ireland. They all have to compete for listeners with independent stations but offer an alternative in news, debate and local information to pop-based local and national commercial stations. The national channels specialize in different tastes. Radio 1 caters for pop music; Radio 2 has light music, news, and comedy; Radio 3 provides classical and modern serious music, talks, discussions and plays; Radio 4 concentrates on news reports, analysis, talks and plays; and Radio 5 Live (established 1990) has sport and news programmes.

The ITC

The ITC (Independent Television Commission) does not make or produce programmes itself. Its government-appointed board regulates the independent television companies (including cable and satellite services). It grants licences to the transmitting companies and independent producers who actually make many of the programmes shown on three advertising-financed television channels (ITV/Channel 3, Channel 4 and Channel 5).

There are 15 ITV production companies at present, such as Granada (north-west England), Central (the midland counties of England) and Anglia (East Anglia). London has two companies holding one licence, with one providing programmes during the week (Thames), the other at weekends (London Weekend). These companies make programmes for the 14 regions into which Britain is divided for ITV television purposes.

The licences granted to ITV companies are renewable every ten years and the companies have to compete with any other interested applicants. It is by no means certain that a further licence will be granted to an existing company, or a new one to a high-bidding company. Much depends on past performance, financial standing and commitment to provide quality and regional programmes. The programme companies receive nothing from the television licence fee, which applies only to the BBC. The companies are consequently dependent upon the finance they receive from advertising and the sales of programmes, videos, books, records and other publications.

ITV (with 30 per cent of audience share) is the oldest independent channel and once seemed only to provide popular programmes of a light-entertainment and sometimes trivial type. But its quality has improved and it now has a high standard of news reports, drama productions and documentaries. Under legislation, ITV must provide programmes made in and about the region represented by the production companies. Channel 4 (with 10 per cent of audience share) was established in 1982 to create a commercial alternative to BBC2. It is a public corporation, which is funded by selling its own advertising time. It was intended to offer something different and challenging in an appeal to minority tastes, and provides programmes in Welsh in Wales. Channel 4 initially had serious problems with advertising and the quality of its programmes, but has now developed a considerable reputation.

Channel 5 (with 6 per cent of audience share) became operative in 1997 after a ten-year licence was awarded to Channel 5 Broadcasting Limited. It is funded by advertising, subscription and sponsorship; covers 70 per cent of the population; but had a shaky start in terms of the attraction of its programmes. Its programmes still have a dubious reputation but it has increased its financial base.

It is argued that the ITC does not always keep a close watch on independent broadcasting developments and lacks clear regulatory powers and consistent policies. There has been controversy over its system of awarding ITV licences, which have often gone to the highest bidder with little apparent regard to quality and production efficiency.

The ITC also regulates cable and satellite television. Television and associated technological developments have become very attractive in

Britain and a rich source of entertainment profits. At one stage, it was thought that cable television by subscription would considerably expand these possibilities. Cable television is growing steadily through digital technology (with its increased number of channels) and serves 3.3 million homes. But it has been challenged first by video equipment sales and secondly by satellite programmes.

Television broadcasting by satellite through subscription was established in Britain in 1989. The biggest UK satellite programmer is BSkyB (British Sky Broadcasting) with 7.8 million (4 million domestic) subscribers. Its channels provide news, light entertainment, sport and feature films. The choice of satellite channels is expanding steadily through digital technology, with over 250 satellite servers providing programming in Britain, particularly to the ethnic minorities.

Cable and satellite have a 15 per cent share of television viewing. This suggests that, while they are increasing their market share, they still lag behind ITV (30 per cent) and BBC1 (28 per cent).

The Radio Authority

The Radio Authority controls independent radio (three national stations and 150 local and regional stations throughout the country). All are funded by advertising, and revenue figures suggest that radio is the fastest-growing medium in Britain.

The national stations were created by government to expand radio broadcasting. The first licence was awarded in 1991 to Classic FM (popular classical music and news bulletins); the second in 1992 to Virgin 1215 (rock music); and the third in 1995 to Talk Radio UK (speech-based service).

Local commercial radio once seemed to provide mainly pop music, news flashes and some programmes of local interest. But expansion has occurred at city, local and community levels because broadcasting has been deregulated by the government in an attempt to increase the variety of radio and include more tastes and interests.

The role and influence of television

Television is an influential and dominant force in modern Britain, as well as a popular entertainment activity. Over 98 per cent of the population have television sets in their homes; 95 per cent of these are colour sets; and over 50 per cent of homes have two sets or more. Some people prefer to rent their sets instead of owning them because rented sets are repaired and maintained free of charge. However, recent reports (2001) suggest that radio (commercial and BBC) is now more popular than television, indicating that some people are deserting the latter because of its alleged superficiality. Nevertheless, television has an average viewing time of 26 hours per week.

A large number of the programmes shown on television are made in Britain, although there are also many imported American series. A few programmes come from other English-speaking countries, such as Australia, New Zealand and Canada. But there are relatively few foreign-language productions on British television and these are either dubbed or subtitled.

The range of programmes shown is very considerable, but they also vary widely in quality. Although British television has a high reputation abroad, it does attract substantial criticism in Britain, either because of the standard of the programmes or because they are frequently repeated. News reports, documentaries and current-affairs analyses are generally of a high standard, as are dramatic, educational, sporting, natural history and cultural productions. But there is also a wide selection of series, soap operas, films, quizzes and variety shows which are of doubtful quality.

The recent addition of Reality-TV (such as *Big Brother* and *Survivor*) and similar genres has led to charges of a 'dumbing-down' of British television. Programmes are calculated to appeal to a mass audience and high ratings, which the television companies need to attract advertising and justify expenditure. However, a *MORI/Voks Pops* poll in August 2001 reported that 61 per cent of fifteen to twenty-four-year-olds believed that reality television helps to teach them about the ways in which people interact with each other. But rather than imitating shocking behaviour in the programmes they are grateful for the chance to learn important life lessons and skills. Television, in this view, is taking on a parenting and teaching role.

Competition between the BBC and independent television is strong, and the battle of the ratings (the number of people watching individual programmes) indicates the popularity (or otherwise) of offerings. But competition can mean that similar programmes are shown at the same time on the major channels, in order to appeal to specific markets and attract the biggest share of the audience. It is also argued that competition has reduced the quality of programmes overall and resulted in an appeal to the lowest common denominator in taste. The BBC in particular is criticized for its failure to provide high-quality arts, drama and news programmes, with a slide into commercialism in the battle for ratings. It is argued that the BBC must maintain its public service obligations to quality and creativity in order to justify its universal licence fee.

Voices have been raised about the alleged levels of sex, violence and bad language on British television, particularly before the 'watershed' of 9 p.m. when young children may be watching. Some individuals have attempted to reform and influence the kind of programmes that are shown. Research suggests that the public can be morally harmed by the content of

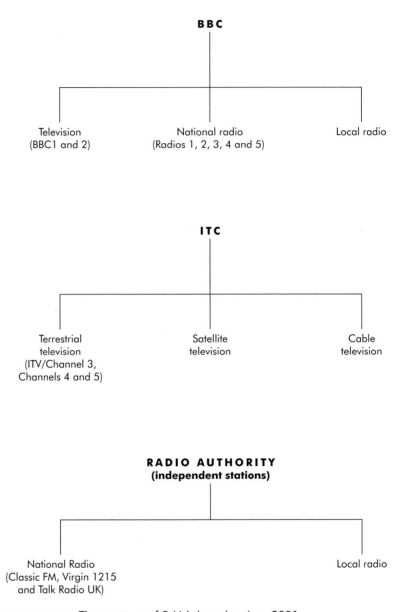

FIGURE 9.1   The structure of British broadcasting, 2001

some television programmes. The Conservative government considered that violence, sex and obscenity on television do affect viewers and was concerned to 'clean up' television. A Broadcasting Standards Complaints Commission monitors programmes, examines complaints, establishes codes of conduct for the broadcasting organizations and has tightened its rules concerning invasion of privacy by broadcasters. The sale and rent of 'video nasties' (videos which portray extreme forms of violence and brutality) have been banned and rules for the sale of videos have been tightened. Some 69 per cent of homes now own at least one video-cassette recorder. But *British Social Attitudes 2000–01* suggested that Britons are becoming more permissive about the portrayal of sex in the media if this is relevant to a plot, and more permissive if it occurs outside a family context on adult channels, video and cinema.

Today, there is fierce competition among broadcasters to attract viewers and advertising revenue. But it is questionable whether an 'entertainments' expansion means more genuine choice or declining quality. Digital broadcasting will increase television channels and may transform the medium into an interactive force which combines the Internet and personalized programming in one package. But broadcasters risk losing audiences and revenue as more people switch to the Internet itself as an alternative to television. In 2000, 25 per cent of British households had Internet access.

Media ownership and freedom of expression

The financial and ownership structures of the British media industry are complex and involve a range of media outlets, which include the press, radio and television. Sometimes an individual company will own a number of print products, such as newspapers and magazines, and will specialize in this area.

But this kind of ownership is declining. Today it is more common for newspapers to be owned and controlled by corporations which are concerned with wide media interests, such as films, radio, television, magazines, and satellite and cable companies. Other newspaper- and media-owning groups have diversified their interests even further, and may be involved in a variety of non-media activities. In Britain, only a few newspapers such as the *Guardian* and the *Morning Star* have avoided being controlled by multinational commercial concerns.

This involvment of large enterprises in the media, and the resulting concentration of ownership in a few hands, such as newspapers controlled by News International and Trinity Mirror, has caused concern. Although these concentrations do not amount to a monopoly situation, there have been frequent inquiries into the questions of ownership and control. Some critics argue that the state should provide public subsidies to the media industries in order to prevent them being taken over by big-business groups. But this suggestion has not been adopted, and it is felt that there are potential dangers in allowing the state to gain any direct or indirect financial influence over the media.

Today the law is supposed to guard against the risks inherent in greatly concentrated ownership of the means of communication. The purchase of further newspapers by an existing owner is controlled by law and newspaper owners' shareholdings in independent radio and television stations are restricted. Further restrictions, such as independent directors of newspapers; guarantees of editorial independence from owners' interference; and trustee arrangements to allow newpapers to maintain their character and traditions are usually imposed. These arrangements are intended to prevent monopolies and undue influence by owners. But such safeguards do not always work satisfactorily in practice, and takeovers of ITV television companies by rival companies and multimedia corporations are now permitted within limits.

The question of free expression in the media continues to be of concern. Critics argue that the media do not have sufficient freedom to comment on matters of public interest. But the freedom of the media, as of individuals, to express themselves, is not absolute. Regulations are placed upon the general freedom in order to safeguard the legitimate interests of other individuals, organizations and the state, so that a balance between competing interests may be achieved.

There are several legal restraints upon media freedom of expression. The *sub judice* rule means that the media may not comment on court proceedings and must restrict themselves to the court facts. The rule is intended to protect the individuals concerned, and if a media organization breaks the rule it may be found guilty of contempt of court and fined. Contempt of court proceedings may also be used by judges to obtain journalists' sources of information, or to prevent the media from publishing certain court details and documents.

The obtaining and publishing of state and official information is controlled tightly by the Official Secrets Act and by D-notices (directives to the media concerning information which should not be divulged). The media are also liable to court proceedings for libel and obscenity offences. Libel is the making of accusations which are proved to be false or harmful to a person's reputation. Obscenity covers any action that offends against public morality. In such cases, the media organization and all the individuals involved may be held responsible.

These restrictions prevent absolute media freedom of expression. It is argued that there is a need for reform if responsible investigative journalism is to do its job adequately. Britain is a secretive society, and the Labour government's proposed Freedom of Information Act may break down some of the secrecy and executive control. The Human Rights Act may also allow greater freedom of media expression.

On the other hand, the media can often act irresponsibly, invade individual privacy, behave in unethical ways and sensationalize events for their

PLATE 9.3 *Paparazzi at a royal event (Stephen Parker/Rex Features, London)*

own purposes. The media have won some libel cases brought against them and gained important victories for open information. But they have also lost other cases because of their methods. Some media practices do cause concern and the government may impose statutory restrictions on invasions of privacy unless the media reform themselves. The Human Rights Act may also allow individuals to complain about media abuse. But it is generally felt that freedom of expression could be less restricted than it is at present.

A restraining media institution, the Press Complaints Commission (PCC), was created in 1990. It is financed by newspaper owners and is supposed to guard the freedom and independence of the press; maintain standards of journalism; and judge complaints by the public against news-papers. Some critics argue that the PCC is not fighting as hard as it might for press freedom. Others maintain that it is not strict enough with news-papers when complaints against them are proved. A fear that the govern-ment might legislate against media abuses has led to a tightening of the PCC's rules about privacy invasion, harassment by photographers and protection of children. Newspaper owners have also created an ombuds-man system for each newspaper, through which public complaints can be made and investigated. It remains to be seen whether the PCC and the ombudsman system will be truly effective.

It is sometimes argued that the concentrated ownership patterns of the media might limit freedom of expression by allowing owners undue influence over what is included in their products. Ex-journalists have claimed that there is proprietorial interference in some of the media, which is not being curbed either by editorial guarantees or by legal and government restrictions. On the other hand, editors and journalists can be very independently minded people, who will usually strongly object to any attempts at interference. Owners, in practice, seem to be careful not to tread on too many toes, because there are always competing media sources which are only too willing to publish the facts.

A further concern about limitations on media freedom has been the extent to which advertisers might dictate policy when they place their products. The question of advertisers' influence is complex and might today be more applicable to the mass-consumer market of radio and television than the press. Advertisers dealing with the press are more concerned with the type or status of readers rather than their numbers. Arguably, the media have not succumbed in a substantial degree to the manipulations of the advertising agencies, in spite of the media's dependence upon advertising revenue.

Attitudes to the media

Apart from the issues discussed above, opinion polls suggest that the media are not a source of great concern to most British people. Respondents are reasonably, if not overly, satisfied with the BBC and independent broadcasters. However, most are generally very sceptical of the press and journalists, and mistrustful of the content of newspapers.

It is difficult to evaluate absolutely whether the media play a dominant part in influencing public opinion on a range of political and other matters. The left-wing view assumes that they do and consequently disapproves of the alleged right-wing bias in the British media. But, while some people may have their attitudes directly shaped in these ways, it is argued that a majority of readers and viewers have already made up their own minds and react against blatant attempts at indoctrination. On certain occasions and for specific events (such as general elections), the media may have an important effect on public opinion. But it is also likely that the media may merely follow popular trends.

Many people learn to read between the lines of newspapers and broadcasts and are conditioned early in life 'not to believe everything you read in the papers', or hear 'on the telly'. Since television in particular is often accused of being either right-wing or left-wing, depending on which government is in power, it would seem that the British people are receiving enough information from all sides of the political spectrum. In practice, most people object to having politics and other concerns 'thrust down their throats' and many take a sceptical attitude to such matters.

A *MORI/British Council* poll in 1999 found that only 28 per cent of overseas respondents (5 per cent for Germany) believe that the British media as a whole cannot be relied on to tell the truth. The British media were regarded as being more truthful than their counterparts in most of the overseas countries surveyed in the poll.

Exercises

Explain and examine the following terms:

media	circulation	'free newspapers'	Anglia
press	tabloid	*Private Eye*	'hot metal'
advertising	broadsheet	ownership	libel
The Times	*Sun*	Rupert Murdoch	*sub judice*
Fleet Street	John Reith	World Service	BBC
licence	ITC (IBA)	Channel 4	dubbing
PCC	mid-market	newsboys(girls)	duopoly

Write short essays on the following topics:

1   Describe and comment critically on the structure of British broadcasting.
2   Examine the problems of media freedom of expression.
3   Discuss the division of British national newspapers into 'populars' and 'qualities'.

Further reading

Bignell, J. *et al.* (2000) *British Television Drama: Past, Present and Future* London: Macmillan/Palgrave

Curran, J. and Seaton, J. (1997) *Power without Responsibility: The Press and Broadcasting in Britain* Routledge: London

Franklin, B. (2001) *British Television Policy: A Reader* London: Routledge

Stokes, J. and Reading, A. (eds) (1999) *The Media in Britain: Current Debates and Developments* London: Palgrave/Macmillan

Wedell, G. and Luckham, B. (2000) *Television at the Crossroads* London: Macmillan/Palgrave

Websites

Department of Culture, Media and Sport: www.culture.gov.uk

British Broadcasting Corporation (BBC): www.bbc.co.uk

Independent Television Commission: www.itc.org.uk

The Press Association: www.pad.press.net

The Times: www.the-times.co.uk

The Guardian: www.guardian.co.uk

The Daily Telegraph: www.telegraph.co.uk

Religion

BRITISH RELIGIOUS HISTORY HAS BEEN predominantly Christian. It has been characterized by conflict between Roman Catholics and Protestants and by division into separate Protestant churches and sects. But it has also included non-Christian faiths, such as Judaism, and groups with humanist and special beliefs. Today, Britain still possesses a diversity of religious denominations, which have been added to by recent immigrants.

However, despite these features, the country seems to be largely secular in terms of the low figures for all types (Christian and non-Christian) of regular religious observance. Secularization is affecting most faiths, particularly the Christian. But religion still arguably remains a factor in national life, whether for believers or as a background to national culture. It is reflected in active or nominal adherence to denominations and in general ethical and moral behaviour. Religiosity is greater in Wales, Scotland and (particularly) Northern Ireland than in England.

Religious history

There is little evidence of organized religion in very early British history, beyond archeological discoveries which suggest various forms of heathen belief. Some Christian influences had reached Britain before AD 400 and during the Roman occupation. But they were not widespread or permanent.

Ireland was converted to Christianity around AD 432 mainly by St Patrick, who brought the faith from Rome. His followers and others spread Christianity to Wales, Scotland and northern England, establishing religious centres, such as that of St Columba on the Scottish island of Iona. In 596–97 the Anglo-Saxons of southern England were converted to Christianity by St Augustine and other monks, who had been sent from Rome by Pope Gregory, and who also founded the ecclesiastical capital of Canterbury in 597. English conversion was encouraged by Anglo-Saxon kings, who thought that the hierarchical example of the Christian church would support their royal authority. The church also provided educated advisers and administrators, through whom the kings could control their kingdoms more efficiently. The connection between church and state was consequently established at an early stage in English history.

Southern English Christianity was based on the beliefs and practices of the Church of Rome. Although the faith of Ireland, Wales, Scotland and northern England was also founded on Roman doctrines, it had a more Celtic identification. Conflicts and divisions inevitably arose between the two branches of Christianity. But these were eventually resolved at the Synod (meeting) of Whitby in 663, where all the churches agreed to accept the Roman Catholic form of worship.

Christianity became a central and influential force in society. The church was based on a hierarchy of monks, priests, bishops and archbishops. It was a part not only of religious culture but also of administration, government and law. But it was increasingly accused of worldliness and materialism. It was thought to be corrupt and too concerned with politics at the expense of religion. However, monarchs maintained their allegiance to Rome and the Pope in spiritual matters, some with more conviction than others.

But the relationship between England and Rome became difficult and by the sixteenth century was at breaking point. English monarchs were jealous of the wealth and power of the church and resented the influence of Rome in national affairs. Henry VIII argued in 1529 that as King of England he, not the Pope, was the supreme legal authority in the country and that the church and its courts owed their allegiance only to him.

In 1534 Henry broke away from Rome and declared himself head of the church in England. The immediate reason for this breach was the Pope's refusal to accept Henry's divorce from his queen, Katharine of Aragon, who had not produced a male heir to the throne. But Henry also wanted to curb the church's power and wealth. In 1536 he dissolved many monasteries and confiscated a large part of the church's property.

Although Henry had established a national church, that church was still Roman Catholic in its faith and practices. Henry did not regard himself as a Protestant, nor did he consider the English church to be part of the Protestant Reformation, which was affecting religious life in continental Europe. Indeed, Henry had defended the papacy against Martin Luther in 1521. The Pope rewarded him with the title of Fidei Defensor (Defender of the Faith), which British monarchs still bear today, and which can be seen on most British coins.

Nevertheless, the influence of the European Reformation caused the English, Scottish and Welsh churches to move away from Rome's doctrines. This development in England increased under Edward VI (1547–53), when practices and beliefs became more Protestant. John Knox in Scotland also accelerated the process by founding the separate Protestant Church of Scotland in 1560. Meanwhile, Ireland remained mostly Roman Catholic.

Henry VIII's daughter, the Roman Catholic Mary Tudor, tried to restore the Roman Catholic faith during her reign (1553–58), but did not succeed. Her sister, the Protestant Elizabeth I (1558–1603), established the Protestant status of the now Church of England by the terms of her Church Settlement. The Church's doctrine was stated in the Thirty-Nine Articles of Faith (1562) and its forms of church worship were contained in the Book of Common Prayer (revised in later centuries). English replaced Latin in church documents and services and priests were later able to marry. The English church now occupied an intermediate position between Roman Catholicism and the Protestant churches of Europe.

However, the creation of the Protestant Church of England did not stop the religious arguments which were to affect Britain in later years. Many Protestants in the sixteenth and seventeenth centuries felt that the church had not distanced itself sufficiently from Rome. Some left to form their own religious organizations. Initially called Dissenters because they disagreed with the majority view, they were later known as Nonconformists and today are members of the Free Churches. Fierce religious conflicts between Protestants and Catholics, often resulting in martyrdom, continued during the seventeenth century. They culminated in the Civil War (1642–48) between the mainly Protestant Parliamentarians and the largely Catholic Royalists, which led to the protectorate of Oliver Cromwell.

The collapse of Cromwell's narrowly puritan regime after his death, and the restoration of the Stuart monarchy, did bring some religious moderation. But minority religions still suffered. The Roman Catholic Church underwent persecution and exclusion for three hundred years after the Reformation, and Jews and Nonconformists also experienced discrimination. These religious groups were excluded from the universities, the House of Commons and public positions. It was not until the early nineteenth century that most restrictions placed on them were removed. Meanwhile, the Church of England solidified its dominant position in 1688, when the Protestant William III succeeded James II, the last Catholic English king.

But further quarrels affected religious life in the eighteenth century, as groups reacted to rationalist developments in the Church of England. For example, the Methodists (founded 1739) stressed the emotional aspects of salvation and religion. They tried to work within the Church of England, but opposition to their views eventually forced them to separate. Nevertheless, an Evangelical wing within the Church was strongly affected by Methodism. The Evangelicals based their faith on a literal interpretation of the Bible and a humanitarian idealism. They accomplished many industrial and social reforms in nineteenth century Britain. Today, the 'Low Church' wing of the Church of England is influenced by Evangelicalism and Nonconformism.

Other groups reacted to the Church of England in the eighteenth and nineteenth centuries and founded a variety of Nonconformist sects, such as the Baptists. Nonconformists were (and are) particularly strong in Wales. On the other hand, the Oxford or Tracterian Movement, which developed in the 1830s, emphasized the Church of England's connections with Roman Catholicism. It followed Catholic doctrines and used elaborate ritual in its church services. It influenced succeeding generations and today is represented by the Anglo-Catholic and 'High Church' wings of the Church of England.

By the end of the nineteenth century the various Christian and non-Christian churches were spread throughout Britain. In the twentieth century, immigrants have added further religious diversity. Muslim mosques, Sikh and Hindu temples, and West Indian churches, such as the Pentecostalists, are common in areas with large ethnic communities.

In Britain today the growth of Christian and non-Christian religious observance and vitality is found outside the big traditional Christian churches. The Evangelical movement continues to grow as a branch of Christianity and is characterized by a close relationship among members and between them and God, Christ and the Holy Spirit. It breaks down the barriers of more traditional worship, places little reliance on church furniture and has many different meeting places. It has basic Christian beliefs, but expresses them in different ways. The growth of fundamentalist faiths, 'enthusiastic' Christian churches and some five hundred cults or religious movements have also increased the number of people active in religious life. Meanwhile non-Christian faiths, such as Islam in particular, have expanded significantly.

There is religious freedom in contemporary Britain; a person may belong to any religion or none; and religious discrimination is unlawful. There is no religious bar to the holding of public office, except that the monarch must be a member of the Church of England. None of the

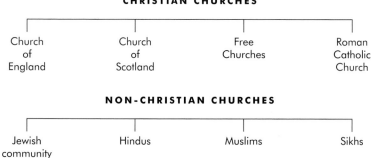

FIGURE 10.1 Main contemporary religious groups

churches is tied specifically to a political party and there are no religious parties as such in Parliament.

The Christian tradition

Christianity in Britain is represented mainly by the Church of England and the Roman Catholic Church (which are the largest), the Church of Scotland and the Free Churches. The Church of England attracts about a fifth of religiously active Britons and the Roman Catholic Church does only marginally better. It is argued that these two churches built too many buildings for too few people in the nineteenth century. They have since used resources to subsidize churches that should have been closed, and poorly attended services contribute to decline. A survey by *Churches Information for Mission* in 2001 suggested that traditional Christian churches have lost their ability to attract the young and need a more contemporary image: 42 per cent of members of existing congregations consist of retired people and the average age of churchgoers is over seventy. People under fifty-five tend to opt for more evangelical forms of worship.

The Church of England

The Church of England is the established or national church in England. This means that its legal position in the state is confirmed by the Elizabethan Church Settlement and Parliament. The monarch is the head of the church; its archbishops, bishops and deans are appointed by the monarch on the advice of the Prime Minister; and Parliament has a voice in its organization and rituals. But it is not a state church, since it receives no financial aid from the state, apart from salaries for non-clerical positions and help with church schools. The church therefore has a special relationship with the state, although there continue to be calls for its disestablishment (cutting the connections between church and state) so that it might have autonomy over its own affairs.

The church is based on an episcopal hierarchy, or rule by bishops. The two Archbishops of Canterbury and York, together with twenty-four senior bishops, sit in the House of Lords, take part in its proceedings and are the church's link to Parliament. Organizationally, the church is divided into the two provinces of Canterbury and York, each under the control of an archbishop. The Archbishop of Canterbury (called the Primate of All England) is the senior of the two and the professional head of the church. The two provinces are subdivided into 44 dioceses, each under the control of a bishop. Many of the bishops' seats are very old and situated in ancient cathedral towns, such as Chichester, Lincoln, Durham and Salisbury.

PLATE 10.1   Anglican village church, Northamptonshire (*Maggie Murray/Format*)

The dioceses are divided into some 13,000 parishes and each is centred on a parish church. Most parishes, except for those in rural areas, have a priest (called either a vicar or a rector) in charge and a large parish may have additional assistant priests (curates). The priest occupies rent-free accommodation in a vicarage, but does not have a large salary, which in most cases today is paid out of central church funds.

The main financial resources of the church come from its substantial property and investment holdings, and it is the third largest landowner in Britain (after the Crown and the Forestry Commission). The assets of the church, which have been estimated at over £400 million, are administered by the Church Commissioners. This wealth has to finance many very expensive demands, such as salaries for the clergy and administrators, maintenance of churches and cathedrals and activities in Britain and abroad. In recent years the finances of the church have been seriously depleted because of investment failures, and there are growing demands upon its capital finance.

The Church of England is considered to be a 'broad church' in which a variety of beliefs and practices coexist. Priests have freedom as to how they conduct their church services. These can vary from the elaborate ritual of High Church worship to the simple, functional presentation of Low Church services. The High Church or Anglo-Catholic wing (some 20 per cent of church membership) lays stress on church tradition and the historical influence of Roman Catholic practices and teaching. The Low Church or Evangelical wing (some 80 per cent of church membership) bases faith and practice on simplicity and often a literal interpretation of the Bible and is suspicious of Roman Catholic influences.

The two wings of the church do not always co-operate happily and between them there is a considerable variety of fashions. Some priests have introduced contemporary music and theatre into their services, in order to appeal to younger congregations and more modern concerns. Today priests have to deal with a wide variety of problems and pressures in their work, particularly in deprived and inner-city areas, and cannot easily be restricted to a purely religious role.

The membership of the Church of England is difficult to determine, because the church does not have adequate registers of members. Membership is assumed when a person (usually a baby) is baptized into the church. But only 40 per cent of the English population have been baptized. This membership may be confirmed at 'confirmation' at the age of fourteen or fifteen. It is estimated that only a fifth of those baptized are confirmed and that 1.8 million people are members of the church. In terms of regular weekly observance at under 1 million, the Church is the second-largest Christian faith (after Roman Catholicism). But numbers continue to decline slowly as does the number of priests (owing to retirement). However, many other Britons may nominally identify themselves with the Church of England, even though they are not members.

Lay members of the parish are associated with church organization at the local level through parochial church councils. These send representatives to the local diocesan councils (or synods), where matters of common concern are discussed. Cases may then be sent to the General Synod, which is the national governing body of the Church. It has spiritual, legislative and administrative functions and makes decisions on subjects such as the ordination of women priests.

Women in the past served as deacons (an office below the priest) and in women's religious orders, but could not be ordained as priests in the Church. Debate and conflict still surround this question, although the General Synod approved the ordination of women and the first women were ordained in 1994. There are now over two thousand and a small number have reached senior positions. The debate has split the church into factions, and driven some members and clergy into the Roman Catholic Church; there is significant hostility to women priests in many parishes and from some male priests.

The Church of England is sometimes referred to as the 'Anglican Church', in the sense that it is part of a worldwide communion of churches whose practices and beliefs are very similar, and many of which descend

PLATE 10.2 Westminster Abbey, coronation church for English monarchs and focus of English national religious life (*John Oakland*)

from the Church of England. This Anglican Communion comprises some 90 million people in the British-Irish Isles (with Anglican churches in Wales, Scotland and Ireland) and abroad, such as the Protestant Episcopal Church in the USA. Most of these churches have women priests and bishops. The Lambeth Conference (a meeting of Anglican bishops from all over the world) is held every ten years in London and is presided over by the Archbishop of Canterbury. It has great prestige, and its deliberations on doctrine, relations with other churches and attitudes to political and social questions can be influential.

Today, most Church of England membership is middle- and upper-class, rural-based and ageing and it is has been identified with the ruling establishment and authority. There is conflict within the church between traditionalists, who wish to maintain old forms and beliefs, and modernists, who want a more engaged and adventurous church to attract a contemporary congregation.

In recent years, the Church of England has been more willing to enter into controversial arguments about social and political problems in contemporary Britain, such as the condition of people living in the inner cities, and has been critical of government policies. This led it into conflict with the Conservative government, and its popularity among politicians at present is not high. It has tended to avoid such issues in the past and has been described as 'the Conservative Party at prayer' because of its safe, establishment image. It is still widely felt that the Church, like the monarchy, should not involve itself in such questions, and historically it has favoured compromise. However, some critics argue that the Church is mediocre, riven with squabbles, uncertain of its future and lacks both authority and charm. In this view, it must modernize its attitudes, organization and values if it is to continue as a vital force in British life.

The Church of Scotland

The Church of Scotland (commonly known as the Kirk) is the second established church in Britain. Its position as the official national church in Scotland has been confirmed by successive legislation from 1707, which has asserted its freedom in spiritual matters and independence from all parliamentary supervision. The church is completely separate from the Church of England, has its own organizational structures and decides its own doctrines and practices.

It was created in 1560 by John Knox. He was opposed to episcopal rule and considered that the English church had not moved sufficiently far from Roman Catholicism. The Scottish church followed the teachings of Calvin, a leading exponent of the European Reformation, and developed a rather severe form of Presbyterian Protestantism. Presbyterianism means government by ordained ministers and elected elders (who are lay members of the church).

The church has a democratic structure. Individual churches are governed locally by a Kirk Session, which consists of the minister and elders. Ministers (who include women) have equality with each other. The General Assembly is the supreme organizational body of the church and comprises elected ministers and elders. It meets every year under the presidency of an elected Moderator, who serves for one year and is the leader of the church during the period of office. There are some 600,000 adult members of the church.

The Roman Catholic Church

The Roman Catholic Church in Britain experienced much persecution and discrimination after the Reformation and had difficulties in surviving. Although its organization was restored and the worst suspicions abated by 1850, reservations about it still continued in some quarters.

Today Catholicism is widely practised throughout Britain and enjoys complete religious freedom, except for the fact that no Catholic can become monarch. There are 7 Roman Catholic provinces in Great Britain (4 in England, 2 in Scotland and one in Wales), each under the supervision of

PLATE 10.3 At prayer: Roman Catholic mass (*Judy Harrison/Format*)

an archbishop; 29 dioceses each under the control of a bishop; and over 3,000 parishes. The head of the church in England is the Cardinal Archbishop of Westminster and the senior lay Catholic is the Duke of Norfolk. In Northern Ireland, there is one province with 6 dioceses, some of which overlap with dioceses in the Irish Republic.

It is estimated that there are 5 million nominal members of the Roman Catholic faith in Britain, although the number of active participants is about 1.9 million. But regular weekly observance is just over a million, which makes it the largest Christian church in Britain. Its membership is centred on the urban working class, settlers of Irish descent, a few prominent upper-class families and some middle-class people.

The church continues to emphasize the important role of education for its children and requires its members to try to raise their children in the Catholic faith. There are many voluntary schools specifically for Catholic pupils, which are sometimes staffed by members of religious orders, such as the Jesuits and Marists. These and other orders also carry out social work, such as nursing, hospital duties, childcare and looking after the elderly.

The Free Churches

The Free Churches are composed of those Nonconformist Protestant sects which are not established like the Churches of England and Scotland. Some broke away from the Church of England after the Reformation and others departed later. In general, they refused to accept episcopal rule or hierarchical structures and have ordained women ministers. Their history has been one of schism and separation among themselves, which has resulted in the formation of many different sects.

Their egalitarian beliefs are reflected in the historical association between political and religious dissent, which were important in the formation of the Labour Party and the radical wing of the old Liberal Party. These churches have developed their own convictions and practices, which are often mirrored in their simple church services, worship and buildings. The Free Churches tend to be strongest in northern England, Wales, Northern Ireland and Scotland, and most of their membership has historically derived from the working class. The main Free Churches today are the Methodists, the Baptists, the United Reformed Church and the Salvation Army.

The *Methodist Church* is the largest of the Free Churches, with 353,000 adult members and a community of 1.3 million. It was established in 1784 by John Wesley after Church of England opposition to his evangelical views obliged him to separate and form his own organization. Further arguments and division occurred within the Methodist Church in the nineteenth century, but most of the doctrinal and administrative disputes were settled in 1932. Today the Methodist Church in Britain is based on the 1932 union of most of the separate Methodist sects. But independent Methodist churches still exist in Britain and abroad, with a worldwide membership of several million. Attempts were made in the 1960s and 1970s to unify the Methodists and the Church of England, but the proposals failed. In practice, however, some ministers of these denominations share their churches and services.

The *Baptists* (formed in the seventeenth century) are today grouped in associations of churches. Most of these belong to the Baptist Union of Great Britain and Ireland, which was formed in 1812 and has a total membership of some 145,000 people. There are also independent Baptist unions in Scotland, Wales and Ireland (bringing the total Baptists to some 240,000), in addition to a worldwide Baptist fellowship.

The ancient Congregational Church in England and Wales had its roots in sixteenth-century Puritanism. It merged with the Presbyterian Church in England (which was associated with Scottish Presbyterians) in 1972 to form the *United Reformed Church*, which now has some 96,500 members.

The Salvation Army emphasises saving souls through a practical Christianity and social concern. It was founded in Britain by William Booth in 1865; now has some 55,000 active members; has spread to 89 other countries and has a worldwide strength of 2.5 million. The Salvation Army is an efficient organization and has centres nationwide to help the homeless, the abused, the poor, the sick and the needy. Its uniformed members may be frequently seen on the streets of British towns and cities, playing and singing religious music, collecting money, preaching and selling their magazine *War Cry*.

Other Christian churches

Although active membership of the large Christian churches is declining, there are a considerable number of smaller Free Churches and Nonconformist Christian denominations throughout Britain. The dissenting tradition has led groups in very varied directions and they all value their independence and origins. For example, the *Religious Society of Friends* (Quakers) was founded in the seventeenth century. The role of its ministers and its meetings for worship are somewhat unconventional. But the Quakers' pacifism and social work are influential and their membership has increased since the early twentieth century to about 17,000 people.

There has been a significant recent increase in 'enthusiastic' Christian churches. These are defined as independent Christian groups, which number half a million members and are characterized by their Pentacostalist or charismatic nature. They emphasize the miraculous and spiritual side of the New Testament rather than dogma, sin and salvation. Among them are churches, such as the Assemblies of God and the Elim Pentacostal Church, which have many members of West Indian (Afro-Caribbean) descent. Fundamentalist evangelical groups have also been increasing. There are many other religious sects in Britain, such as the *Seventh Day Adventists* with a defined Christian ambience, and others such as the *Jehovah's Witnesses*, the *Mormon Church*, the *Christian Scientists* and the *Spiritualists* which are Christian variants.

This diversity of groups produces a very varied religious life in Britain today, but one which is an important reality for significant numbers of people. Some of it illustrates a growth area in religious observance, marked by frustration or disenchantment with the heavy, formal and traditional style of the larger churches and a desire to embrace a more vital, less orthodox and and more spontaneous form of Christianity.

The non-Christian tradition

The non-Christian tradition in Britain is mainly associated with immigrants into the country over the centuries, such as the Jews and, more recently, Muslims, Sikhs and Hindus.

The Jewish community

The first Jews immigrated with the Norman Conquest and were involved in finance and commerce. The present community dates from the mid-seventeenth century, following the expulsion of Jews in the thirteenth century. It now has 283,000 members and is estimated to be the second largest Jewish population in Europe. The community is composed of the Sephardim (originally from Spain, Portugal and north Africa) and the majority Ashkenazim (from Germany and central Europe).

In religious terms, the community is divided into the majority Orthodox faith (of which the main spokesman is the Chief Rabbi) and minority Reform and Liberal groups. The focus of religious life is the 250 local synagogues, and Jewish schools are attended by one in three Jewish schoolchildren. The majority of Jews live in North London, but the East End of London has traditionally been a place of initial Jewish settlement, while others live mainly in urban areas outside London.

The community has declined in the past twenty years. This is due to a disenchantment with religion; an increase in civil and mixed marriages; considerable emigration by young Jews; a relatively low birth rate; and a rapidly ageing population of active practitioners. For some British Jews,

PLATE 10.4   Jewish bar mitzvah boy reading out of the Torah
(© *Miriam Reik/Format*)

their Jewishness is simply a matter of birth and they are tending to assimilate more with the wider society. For others, it is a matter of deep religious beliefs and practice and this fundamentalism seems to be increasing. But the majority still have a larger global identity with Jewish history.

Other non-Christian religions

Immigration into Britain during the last fifty years has resulted in a substantial growth of other non-Christian religions, such as Islam, Sikhism and Hinduism. The number of practitioners is growing because of relatively high birth rates in these groups and because of conversion to such faiths by young working-class non-whites and middle-class whites.

There are now two million Muslims, of whom some 665,000 regularly attend mosque. Most are associated with Pakistan and Bangladesh, but there are other groups from India, Arab countries and Cyprus. The Islamic Cultural Centre and its Central Mosque in London are the largest Muslim institutions in the West, and there are mosques in virtually every British town with a concentration of Muslim people.

There are also active Sikh (400,000) and Hindu (165,000) religious adherents in Britain. Most of these come from India and have many temples

PLATE 10.5 Regent's Park Mosque, Central London (*Duncan Wheret/Barna by*)

located around the country in areas of Asian settlement. Various forms of Buddhism are also represented in the population, with about 50,000 active participants.

Non-Christian religions amount to some 1.4 million active or practising members and represent a significant growth area when compared to the Christian churches. But these communities constitute a relatively small proportion of the total British population, 46 per cent of which remains nominally Christian despite the growth of agnostics, atheists and those who claim no denominational identity. They have altered the religious face of British society and influenced employment conditions, since allowances have to be made for non-Christians to follow their religious observances and customs.

They have also become vocal in expressing their opinions on a range of matters, such as the Muslim demand for their own schools supported by state funds; Muslim outrage against the British author Salman Rushdie's novel *The Satanic Verses*, parts of which are considered to be blasphemous; and Muslim claims that British law and politicians discriminate against their religion.

PLATE 10.6   A Hindu wedding in Leicester (© *Roshini Kempadoo/Format*)

Co-operation among the churches

The intolerance and bigotry of Christian denominations in Britain have gradually mellowed after centuries of hostility, restrictions and repression. There is now considerable co-operation between the churches, although this stops short of ecumenism (full unity). Discussions continue between the Roman Catholic Church and other Christian churches about closer ties, and an Anglican-Roman Catholic Commission explores points of possible unity. The old enmity between Protestants and Catholics has been reduced. But animosity continues in parts of Scotland and most demonstrably in Northern Ireland.

On other levels of co-operation, Churches Together in Britain and Ireland has representatives from the main Christian churches, is presided over by the Archbishop of Canterbury and works towards common action and Christian unity. The Free Church Federal Council does a similar job for the Free Churches. The Anglican and the main Free Churches also participate in the World Council of Churches, which attempts to promote worldwide co-operation and studies common problems. The Council of Christians and Jews works for better understanding among its members and the Council for Churches of Britain and Ireland has established a Committee for Relations with People of Other (non-Christian) Faiths.

Such attempts at possible co-operation are seen by some as positive actions, which might break down barriers and hostility. Others see them as signs of weakness since denominations are forced to co-operate because of declining memberships and their lack of real influence in the contemporary world. Any movement towards Christian unity may also be threatened by the ordination of women priests in the Church of England, since the worldwide Anglican Communion accepts them, but the Roman Catholic Church is opposed.

Many church people at the grassroots level argue that the churches must adapt more to the requirements of modern life, or else decline in membership and influence. Religious life in Britain has become more evangelical and co-operative in order to reflect a diverse contemporary society and values. But some traditionalists wish to preserve the historical elements of religious belief and practice, and the tension between them and modernists in all religious groups is likely to continue.

Religion in schools

Non-denominational Christian religious education is legally compulsory in state schools in England and Wales. The school day is supposed to start with an act of collective worship, and religious lessons should be provided which concentrate on Christianity but also include the other main faiths. However, if a pupil (or parent) has strong objections, the pupil need not take part in either the service or the lessons. Religious services and teaching are not compulsory in Scotland.

In practice, few secondary schools hold daily religious assemblies. Custom differs for the religious lessons, particularly in areas with large ethnic communities. The lessons can take many different forms and may not be tied to specific Christian themes. Frequent proposals are made that the legal compulsion in religious education should be removed, but it is still enshrined in the latest Education Acts. Some people see religious education and collective worship as a way to raise moral standards and encourage social values. Others disagree. Many schools cannot meet their religious legal obligations and question the point of doing so.

Voluntary (religion-based) schools at primary and secondary levels have long existed in Britain and are now largely funded by the state but controlled by church authorities, such as the Church of England, the Roman Catholics, Judaism and Methodism. The Labour government wishes to increase the number of such faith schools because of their academic records and its wish to reflect diversity. The Church of England and the Methodists want to open more such schools, and the first state-funded Islamic secondary school for girls opened in 2001 (in addition to three existing Muslim schools).

These developments are controversial. It is argued that single-faith schools will institutionalize segregation, lead to a 'balkanization' of British society rather than an embrace of pluralism, increase intolerance from inside and outside the schools, and that children will grow up ignorant of other religions. Experience in Northern Ireland illustrates the potential dangers of segregated schooling.

Religious membership and observance

The decline in membership of the main Christian churches in the twentieth century has continued. But significant increases have occurred in some of the Free Churches, non-Christian denominations and new or independent religious movements.

It is difficult to obtain precise information about religious membership, observance and belief in Britain since denominations have their own methods of assessing membership figures. More accurate religious information will be available for the first time from the 2001 census. However, a survey in *British Social Attitudes 2000–01* found that 27 per cent of respondents considered themselves to be Church of England, 9 per cent

were Roman Catholic, 4 per cent were Church of Scotland, 6 per cent classified themselves as other Protestant, 10 per cent were other religion and
44 per cent had no religion. Over time, there has been a significant reduction in Church of England identification, a big increase in the number of
people without a religion and a rise in the 'other religion' category.
Secularization is increasing, but growth and pluralism is suggested by those
with 'other religions' (many of which are probably non-Christian).

The survey found that while church attendance outside special occasions, such as weddings, funerals and baptisms, was low, the degree of
decline, though continuing, had been (perhaps surprisingly) slight. But only
13 per cent of all faiths attended a service once a week; 54 per cent never
attended or practically never; 10 per cent attended at least twice a year;
and 6 per cent at least once a year. These figures had remained constant
over an eight-year period. They suggest a large overall decline in church
membership, but a smaller decline in actual church attendance.

It is now possible to be legally married in places other than churches
or register offices. It is estimated that only 25 per cent of British people are
now married in a religious building and about 80 per cent receive some
form of religious burial or cremation. The majority of British people therefore enter a religious building only for baptisms, weddings and funerals.

Attitudes to religion and morality

There are two opposed positions on religious life in modern Britain. The
first suggests falling levels of involvement with the main Christian churches
and a general decline of religious faith. Increasing secularization indicates
that religious institutions and consciousness are losing their social and
public significance. The second position indicates a religious renewal in
some churches and an actual growth in others because of religious
pluralism and a diversity of faiths.

While institutional observance may no longer be popular in Britain,
polls suggest that people still have religious beliefs on a personal level,
which include belief in a God, sin, a soul, heaven, life after death, the devil
and hell.

When respondents to a *British Social Attitudes 2000–01* survey were
asked about belief in a God, it was found that there had been little change
since 1991. The figures suggested that 52 per cent believed in a God, 22
per cent did not know and 25 per cent did not believe. Over time, this
meant that there had been only a small decline in belief in a God.

It is argued that such results mean that people in modern Britain are
becoming more individualistic and less dependent upon church authorities.
They consequently adopt a more personal approach towards religion and

no longer automatically follow the lead of organized religion. The statistics suggest that a distinction can be made between formal religious observance of an instititional or organized kind and the private individual sphere of religious or moral feeling. Despite the appearance of a secular state, religion in its various forms is still a factor in national life. Radio, television and the press concern themselves with religious and moral topics. Religious broadcasting on radio and television attracts large audience figures, and recent reports suggest further demand for this type of communication despite the attempts of some broadcasters to cut religious broadcasting.

On an institutional level, religion is also reflected in traditions and ceremonies, as well as being evident in national and individual morality. Religious denominations are relatively prominent in British life and are active in education, voluntary social work and community care. Religious leaders publicly debate doctrine, social matters, political concerns and the moral questions of the day, not always necessarily within narrow church limits.

But the large churches appear incapable of countering further secularization and, given increasingly aged congregations, this process seems likely to continue. At a more extreme level and according to a Leeds University survey in 1997, many Britons do not trust other people and see life as less predictable, more time-pressured, less secure, more materialistic and fast-moving, and their society as riddled with mistrust, cynicism and greed. Lacking traditional faith in conventional religion, people appear to put their trust in materialism, physical appearance and individualism.

Nevertheless, there also seems to be a longing for spirituality, otherworldly comfort and explanation, particularly among the eighteen to thirty age group. This search can lead in different directions. People believe increasingly in mysticism, alternative spiritual disciplines and New Age practices, the paranormal, telepathy, second sight and astrology. It is argued that this need for spirituality is not being provided by established churches.

Such religious concerns seem also to influence matters of personal morality and civic responsibilty. Although there are differences of emphasis between younger and older generations and between men and women, the British have strong views about right and wrong. But these are not necessarily tied to the teaching of any particular denomination. Polls suggest that a majority of people think, for example, that the following are morally wrong: hard drugs such as heroin, scenes of explicit violence on television, adultery, pornography on the Internet, scientific experiments on human beings and scientific experiments on animals.

But the British have become more tolerant, for example, of sex in films, homosexuality, cohabitation outside marriage, soft drugs such as cannabis, alternative lifestyles and euthanasia (allowing a doctor to end a patient's life) if the person has a painful incurable illness. A majority also feel that it is worse to convict an innocent person (miscarriage of justice) than to let a guilty individual go free.

In terms of civic responsibility, polls suggest that attitudes to authority remain relatively conventional in some areas. A majority of respondents feel that children should be taught in the home environment to respect honesty, good manners and other people. Feelings have hardened towards those individuals who reject society as presently constituted, who demonstrate and protest and who encourage disobedience in children. Most respondents agree that schools should teach children to obey authority. But the number of people who consider that the law should be obeyed without exception has fallen and more now believe that one should follow one's conscience, even if this means breaking the law.

These mixed views indicate that many British people now embrace an authoritarian posture in some questions of morals and social behaviour. 'Moral traditionalism', old values and civic responsibility are still supported. But there is often a greater adherence to concepts of personal and social morality than those dictated by official and legal restraints. This is reflected also in people's considerable concerns about drugs, law and order, crime, violence and vandalism, and their preference for strong action to be taken in these areas. In other matters, there seems to be a growing libertarianism.

 Exercises

Explain and examine the following terms:

Canterbury	Henry VIII	'Low Church'	confirmation
bigotry	Iona	Free Churches	General Synod
St Patrick	Episcopal	Church Settlement	John Knox
Whitby	Quakers	vicar	Salvation Army
baptism	ecumenism	denomination	evangelism

Write short essays on the following topics:

1 What does the term 'Christianity' mean in relation to British religious history?
2 Discuss religious membership and observance in contemporary British life.
3 Critically examine the role of the Church of England.

Further reading

Alderman, G. (1998) *Modern British Jewry* Oxford: Clarendon Press

Bebbington, D. (1988) *Evangelicalism in Modern Britain: A History from the 1730s to the 1980s* London: Routledge

Brown, C.G. (2000) *The Death of Christian Britain* London: Routledge

Bruce, S. (1995) *Religion in Modern Britain* Oxford: Oxford University Press

Sewell, D. (2001) *Catholics: Britain's Largest Minority* London: Viking

Websites

The Church of England: www.church-of-england.org

Church of Scotland: www.cofs.org.uk/3colcos.htm

Roman Catholic Church: www.tasc.ac.uk/cc and www.catholic.org.uk

United Synagogue: www.brijnet.org.uk

Judaism: www.jewish.co.uk

Islam: www.muslimdirectory.co.uk

Q-News (Muslim): www.aapi.co.uk/q-news

Leisure, sports and the arts

THE DIVERSITY OF LIFE IN CONTEMPORARY BRITAIN is reflected in the ways the British organize their personal, sporting, leisure and artistic lives. These features reveal a series of different cultural habits, rather than a unified image, and are divided between participatory and spectator pastimes. Some are associated with national identities and, in many cases, are also connected to social class and minority participation.

According to the authors of *We British* (Jacobs and Worcester 1990: 124), the rich variety of leisure, arts and sporting activities disproves the notion of Britain as a country of philistines who prefer second-rate entertainment to the best. Yet there are frequent complaints from many quarters about a 'dumbing down' of British cultural life in television programmes, films, the arts, literature, popular music and education.

Certain findings about 'leisure pursuits' and their social implications have been formulated by academics. Since most leisure time in Britain is now spent within the home and/or family environment, this would seem to indicate a separation from the wider social context. Much leisure provision is commercialized or profit-oriented and is therefore part of the consumer society. But access to leisure activities is unevenly distributed in the population, because it is dependent upon purchasing power and opportunity.

Nevertheless, the creative and cultural industries which service the 'leisure market' are an important part of Britain's social and economic life. According to a *DCMS* survey in 2001, these industries generate £112.5 billion a year in revenue, contribute £10.2 billion in export earnings, employ 1.3 million people and account for over 5 per cent of the gross domestic product.

Leisure activities

Leisure activities in earlier centuries, apart from some cultural interests exclusive to the metropolitan elite, were largely conditioned by the rural and agricultural nature of British life. Village communities were isolated and transport was either poor or non-existent. People were consequently restricted to their villages and obliged to create their own entertainments.

PLATE 11.1 A working men's club (© *Popperfoto*)

Some of these participatory activities were home-based, while others were enjoyed by the whole village. They might be added to by itinerant players, who travelled the countryside and provided a range of alternative spectator entertainments, such as drama performances and musical events.

Improved transportation and road conditions from the eighteenth century onwards enabled the rural population to travel to neighbouring towns where they took advantage of a variety of amusements and wider social opportunities. Spectator activities increased with the industrialization of the nineteenth century, as theatre, the music halls and sports developed and became available to more people. The establishment of railway systems and the formation of bus companies initiated the pattern of cheap one-day trips around the country and to the seaside, which were to grow into the mass charter and package tours of contemporary Britain. The arrival of radio, films and television in the twentieth century resulted in a further huge professional entertainments industry. In all these changes, the mixture of participatory, spectator, home-based and wider social leisure activities has continued.

Many contemporary pursuits have their roots in the cultural and social behaviour of the past, such as boxing, wrestling, cricket, football and a wide range of athletic sports. Dancing, amateur theatre and musical events were essential parts of rural life for all classes and were often associated with the changing agricultural seasons. The traditions of hunting, shooting and fishing have long been widely practised in British country life (not only by the aristocracy), as well as blood sports, such as dog and cock fighting and bear baiting, which are now illegal.

A feature of contemporary Britain is the continuing attempt to stop many kinds of rural activities (such as fishing) and hunting (especially fox hunting). A *MORI* poll in 1997 showed that two-thirds of respondents favoured a complete ban on fox hunting with horses and dogs. The countryside lobby opposes such a ban, and animal activists have become more violent in their objections to and campaigns against what they see as the cruelty of many rural traditions.

In addition to cultural and sporting pastimes, the British enjoy a variety of other leisure activities since many opportunities are now available and, despite their long working hours, more people have more free time. Most workers have at least four weeks' paid holiday a year, in addition to public holidays such as Christmas, Easter and Bank Holidays, although Britain has fewer public holidays than most other European countries. The growing number of pensioners has created an economically rewarding leisure market, while unemployment (although reduced) means that such groups of people have more enforced spare time.

Consumer patterns associated with leisure activities are also changing in Britain. These coincide with part-time and shift working and greater disposable incomes, particularly among young people. There is a demand for pubs and leisure services as well as shops, companies, businesses, doctors and schools to remain open longer or to be available for longer periods.

The most common leisure pastimes are social or home-based, such as visiting or entertaining friends, trips to the pub (public house), watching television and videos, reading books and magazines and listening to the radio, tapes, records and cassettes. The most popular non-sporting leisure activity for all people aged four and over is watching television (for 26 hours a week), and for men television viewing is apparently the single most popular pastime throughout the year. But, according to the *Henley* research centre in 2001, the British public now spends more time reading each year and less time listening to radio and television. Although television still tops the list, the decrease in viewing hours may be due to a dissatisfaction with the quality of the programmes shown on British television.

In 1999, 14 per cent of total household expenditure was spent on leisure goods and services (more than on food). The British now occupy some two-thirds of their spare time using electronic equipment. An increasingly large amount of money is spent on items such as television sets (owned by over 98 per cent of households, with 13 per cent subscribing to satellite television and 9 per cent to cable television in 1999), radio (listened to for some ten hours a week), video recorders (owned by nine in ten households in 1999), computers (a third of households in 1999) and compact disc players (68 per cent of households in 1999). 25 per cent of households had access to the Internet in 2000 and 45 per cent of adults had accessed it at some time.

The home has become the chief place for family and individual entertainment, and poses serious competition to other activities outside the home, such as the cinema, sports and theatre. Leisure activities for both males and females exclusively within the home include listening to the radio or music; watching television; studying; reading books and newspapers; relaxing; conversations; entertaining; knitting and sewing; and hobbies.

Despite the competition from television, the cinema and other electronic media, reading is still an important leisure activity for over half of men and women in Britain. There is a large variety of books and magazines to cater for all tastes and interests. In 1999 123 million books were sold in the UK and the value of exported books amounted to £890 million. The best-selling books are romances, thrillers, modern popular novels, detective stories and works of adventure and history. Classic literature is not widely read, although its sales can benefit from adaptations on television. The tie-in of books (of all types) with videos and television series is now a very lucrative business.

There are 5,000 public libraries in the UK which provide books, CDs, records and audio/visual cassettes on loan to the public, together with information, computer and Internet facilities. Libraries are very well used, with 34 million people (58 per cent of the population) in 2001 being members of local libraries and 50 per cent borrowing at least once a month. Only readers in Finland, Denmark and the Netherlands borrow more library books per head of population.

Do-it-yourself hobbies (DIY), such as house painting, decorating and gardening, are very popular and home repairs and improvements amount to a large item in the total household budget. The number of restaurants has increased and the practice of eating out is much more popular. This is catered for by a variety of so-called 'ethnic' restaurants (particularly Indian, Chinese, Italian and French) in most British high streets and fast-food outlets serving pizza, hamburgers, kebabs, chicken and fish and chips.

But visiting the pub is still a very important part of British life, and more money is spent on drinking and other pub activities than on any other single form of leisure. Some seven out of ten adults visit pubs and one-third go once or more a week. Research from Leeds University in 2001 suggested that the pub was a psychological necessity for most men, and visits were good for their health. They used the pub to bond, to recharge their batteries and as an emotional outlet. Almost half of the research sample said that they would still go to the pub if there was no alcohol.

But the pub, as a social institution, has changed over the years, although it still caters for a wide range of different groups and tastes. The

PLATE 11.2 An English pub, Nottingham (*John Oakland*)

pub is said to be Britain's most envied and imperfectly imitated institution, where people can gather on neutral ground and socialize on their own terms. However, falling custom, rising property prices, takeovers by large breweries and entertainment chains, an obsession with trendiness, faddishness and quick profits have led to a decline in Britain's unique pub heritage. The UK's 56,000 pubs are being depleted by more than twenty a month and turned into gentrified eateries, clubs or American-style bars in an attempt to emulate 'café society'.

Pub licensing hours, which apply to opening times for the sale of alcohol, have been liberalized, and pubs may now open from 11 a.m. to 11 p.m. (varying hours on Sundays), but children under fourteen are not allowed in the bar. Most pubs provide food in addition to drinks, and some, in more prosperous urban and rural areas, have restaurants attached to them, where the quality is variable.

But in recent years, the mushrooming of wine bars, café bars, discos and nightclubs has meant a considerable amount of competition for traditional pubs. The growth and popularity of the club scene with its music, drink and appeal to the young offers further competition to the pub trade, although people may move between different venues during an evening.

British nightlife for most young people is varied and vibrant, with nightclubs, large-scale pop gigs at arenas and sports grounds, music festivals and controversial outdoor 'rave' parties. British bands and DJs are much admired throughout the world. Use of recreational drugs such as cannabis, Ecstasy and cocaine has become so widespread that there are increasing calls, even from the police, for decriminalization. There is also a thriving lesbian and gay scene, more developed than in some other European countries.

Holidays and where to spend them have also become an important part of British life and have been accompanied by more leisure time and money for the majority of the people. They represent the second major leisure cost (after pub drinking). While more Britons in recent years have been taking their holidays in Britain itself, where the south-west English coastal resorts and Scotland are very popular in summer, much larger numbers now also go abroad in both winter or summer or both, and the great days of the British (particularly seaside) resorts have declined considerably. The number of holidays taken away from home by the British amounted to 56 million in 1998, with 33 million being taken in Britain itself. Some 26 million are taken abroad, with Spain, France and the USA being the main attractions for holidaymakers, who buy relatively cheap package tours. But the British seem to have become more adventurous and

PLATE 11.3   British holidaymakers in Gran Canaria in the Canary Islands
(© *Alan Copson*)

are now travelling widely outside Europe to Asia and Africa on a variety of holidays.

Many people prefer to organize their own holidays and make use of the good air and sea communications between Britain and the continent. In Britain itself, different forms of holiday exist, from the traditional 'bed and breakfast' at a seaside boarding house, to hotels, caravan sites and camping. Increased car ownership has allowed greater travel possibilities. Today, more than seven out of ten households have the use of at least one car and 27 per cent have two or more.

Leisure activities outside the home and their social implications consequently encompass travel; excursions; playing sport; watching sport; walks; church; civic duties; cinema and theatre; discos, dances, parties and bingo; social clubs; pubs; and visiting friends.

Sports

There is a wide variety of sports in Britain today, which cater for large numbers of spectators and participators. Some of these are minority or class-based sports (such as yachting and rugby league respectively), while others appeal to majority tastes (such as football). The number of people participating in sports has increased. This has coincided with a greater awareness of health needs and the importance of exercise. Spending on playing and watching sports, and buying sports equipment, amount to a considerable part of the household budget. But it is argued that Britain has inadequate sporting facilities and leisure centres in both the public and private sectors.

The 2001 *General Household Survey* reported that 71 per cent of men and 57 per cent of women (29 million people over sixteen) participate in outdoor and indoor sports or forms of exercise. The most popular participatory sporting activity for both men (49 per cent) and women (41) is walking (including rambling and hiking). Billiards, snooker or pool (20) are the next most popular for men, followed by cycling (15), indoor swimming (11) and football (10). Keep fit or yoga (17) is the next most popular sport for women, followed by indoor swimming (15), cycling (8) and snooker and pool (4). Fishing is the most popular country sport.

Amateur and professional football (soccer) is played throughout most of the year and also at international level. It is the most watched sport and today transcends its earlier working-class associations. The professional game has developed into a large, family-oriented organization, but has suffered from hooliganism, high ticket prices, declining attendances and financial crises. However, enforced changes in recent years such as all-seater stadiums, greater security, improved facilities and lucrative tie-ins with

PLATE 11.4 Manchester United fans at a football match between their team and Tottenham Hotspur (© *Popperfoto/Reuters*)

television coverage (such as Sky-Sport) have greatly improved this situation. Many of the top professional football clubs in the English Premier League have become public companies quoted on the Stock Exchange, and football is now big business.

But there is a widening gulf between these clubs and others in the lower divsions. Some 80 per cent of England's soccer clubs in 2001 were losing money despite television income, which goes largely to the twenty clubs in the Premiership. Most football clubs (even in the Premiership) are in a precarious financial position despite increased income, with only a few making a profit and many losing control over their costs. It is argued that this situation is due to poor club organization, bad business sense, huge salaries for players, inflated transfer fees and lack of success on the pitch.

Rugby football is a popular winter pastime and is widely watched and played. It is divided into two codes. Rugby Union was once confined to amateur clubs and was an exclusively middle-class and public-school-influenced game. But it became professional in 1995 (at least for the top clubs) and now covers a wider social spectrum. Rugby League is played by professional teams, mainly in the north of England, and still tends to be a working-class sport. Both types of rugby are also played internationally.

Cricket is a summer sport in Britain, but the England team also plays in the winter months in Commonwealth countries. It is both an amateur

PLATE 11.5   A football match: Liverpool versus Tottenham Hotspur
(© *Popperfoto/Reuters*)

and professional sport. The senior game is professional and is largely confined to the English and Welsh county sides which play in the county championships. Attendance at cricket matches continues to decline and the contemporary game has lost some of its attractiveness as it has moved in overly-professional and money-dominated directions. It has lost many spectators and is in danger of becoming a minority sport.

There are many other sports which reflect the diversity of interests in British life. Among these are golf, horse racing, hunting, riding, fishing, shooting, tennis, hockey, bowls, darts, snooker, athletics, swimming, sailing, mountaineering, walking, ice sports, motor-car and motor-cycle racing and rally driving. American football and basketball are increasingly popular owing to television exposure. These sports may be either amateur or professional, and spectator- or participator-based, with car and motor-cycle, greyhound racing and horse racing being the most watched.

The professional sporting industry is now very lucrative, and is closely associated with sponsorship schemes, television income, brand merchandizing and non-sport sales. Gambling or betting on sporting and other events has always been a popular, if somewhat disreputable, pastime in Britain, and is now much more in the open and acceptable. Most gambling (through betting shops or bookmakers) is associated with horse and greyhound racing, but can involve other sports. Weekly football pools (betting on match results) are very popular and can result in huge financial wins. The new-found acceptabilty of gambling in Britain was reflected in the establishment of a National Lottery in 1994. It is similar to lotteries in other European countries, and considerable amounts of money can be won. Some of its income has also funded artistic, community, leisure and sports activities which are in need of finance to survive. But falling ticket sales and profits in 2001 meant that the Lottery could no longer guarantee financial support for these 'good causes'.

A *National Centre for Social Research* survey in June 2000 found that 72 per cent of British adults gamble at least once a year. The National Lottery came top (65 per cent of adults) followed by scratchcards (22), fruit machines (14), horse racing (13), private bets with friends or workmates (11), football pools (9), bingo (7) and casino gambling (3).

It is interesting that many sports have contributed to institutionalized features of British life and provide a certain degree of national identity. For example, Wimbledon is tennis; the Football Association Cup Final is football in England (at Wembley Stadium before its closure in 2000); St Andrews is golf in Scotland; Twickenham in England, Murrayfield in Scotland, and Cardiff Arms Park in Wales are rugby union; Lord's Cricket

PLATE 11.6 Cricket in the city, Kennington estate, London (*Cleland Brims/Barnaby*)

PLATE 11.7   Cricket in the country, Kent *(Alexander Brima/Barnaby)*

Ground in London is cricket; the Derby is flat horse racing; the Grand National in Liverpool is steeplechasing; Henley Regatta is rowing; Cowes Week off the Isle of Wight is yachting; Ascot is horse racing; and the British Grand Prix is Formula One motor racing. Some of these sports may appeal only to certain sections of the population, while others may still be equated more with wealth and social position.

Some people feel that the professionalization and commercialization of sport in Britain has tended to weaken the traditional sporting image of the amateur and the old emphasis upon playing the game for its own sake. But these values still exist to some degree, in spite of greater financial rewards for professional sport, the influences of sponsorship and advertising and increasing cases of unethical behaviour in all sports. But tobacco sponsorship of most sporting events has now been banned by the Labour government.

British governments have only recently taken an active political interest in sport. They are now more concerned to promote sport at all levels and there are Ministers for Sport in England, Scotland, Wales and Northern Ireland, who are supposed to co-ordinate sporting activities throughout the country. The Labour government is concerned to improve sporting facilities in Britain by setting up sports councils, colleges, funds and action zones, operating on a regional basis. However, the national provisions for sport in Britain are allegedly inadeqate and there is a lack of professional coaches, capital investment and sporting facilities compared with other countries. Local authority sports and leisure centres, particularly in inner city areas, continue to be sold off, despite the Labour government's attempt to focus more money on playing fields and open spaces in deprived areas.

The sporting notion of 'a healthy mind in a healthy body' has long been a principle of British education. All schools are supposed to provide physical recreation and a reasonable range of sports is usually available for schoolchildren. Schools may offer soccer, rugby, hockey or netball during the winter months, and cricket, tennis, swimming and athletics during the summer. Some schools are better provided with sporting facilities than others and offer a wider range of activities.

However, there are frequent complaints from parents that team games and competitive sports are declining in state schools. School reorganization and the creation of large comprehensives have reduced the amount of inter-school competition, which used to be a feature of education; some left-wing councils are opposed to competitive activities; there is a shortage of playing fields; and a lack of adequate equipment and coaching facilities. The position is particularly acute in the inner city areas, and is of concern to those parents who feel that their children are being prevented from expressing their normal physical natures. They maintain that the state school system is failing to provide sporting provision for children and some parents turn to the independent sector, which is usually well provided with sports facilities. But government aid may improve the availability and standard of state school sports.

The Labour government (in a reversal of previous ideology) tried in 2001 to address the lack of sporting facilities and recent achievement in Britain by embracing the notion of competition between schoolchildren and creating databases of sporting facilities, since none were avaliable at school or local government level. Nevertheless, 70 per cent of the most talented youngsters drop out of sport between the ages of fourteen and seventeen, as opposed to 20 per cent in countries such as France. But better facilities in themselves may not be enough and some critics maintain that schools and local areas are in fact reasonably good in terms of provision. It is argued that more people of all ages should be encouraged to take up sport and that there should be greater co-operation between schools and local communities in the use of facilities and coaching.

The arts

The 'arts' once had a somewhat precious and exclusive image associated with notions of high culture, which were usually the province of the urban and metropolitan middle and upper classes. This attitude has lessened to some degree since the Second World War under the impetus of increased educational opportunities and the gradual relaxation of social barriers.

The growth of mass and popular culture has increased the potential audience for a wider range of cultural activities, and the availability and scope of the arts has spread to greater numbers of people. These activities may be amateur or professional and continue the mixture of participatory, spectator and home-based entertainment.

It is argued that the genuine vitality and innovation of the British arts are to be found in the millions of people across the country who are engaged in amateur music, art and theatre, rather than in the professional and commercial world. Virtually every town, suburb and village has an amateur group, whether it be a choir, music group, orchestra, string quartet, pipe band, brass band, choral group, opera group or dramatic club. In addition, there are 500 professional arts and cultural festivals held each year throughout Britain, many of which are of a very high standard.

The funding of the mainstream arts in Britain is precarious and involves the private and public sectors. The public sector is divided between local authorities and the regional Arts Councils. Local authorities raise money from the council (property) tax to fund artistic activities in their areas, but the amounts spent vary considerably between different areas of the country and local authorities are attacked for spending either too much or too little on cultural activities.

Members of the regional Arts Councils in England, Scotland, Wales and Northern Ireland are appointed by the Secretary of State for Culture, Media and Sport. They are responsible for dividing up an annual government grant to the arts and the finance has to be shared among theatres, orchestras, opera and ballet companies, art galleries, museums and a variety of other cultural organizations. The division of limited funds has inevitably attracted much criticism. It means that many artistic institutions are often dependent upon the private sector to supply donations and funding, in addition to their state and local government money, in order to survive and provide a service. But some cultural organizations, such as the Royal Opera and museums, have received much-needed finance from the National Lottery.

British theatre can be lively and innovative and has a deserved international reputation. There are some 300 commercial or professional theatres, in addition to a large number of amateur dramatic clubs, fringe and pub theatres throughout the country. London and its suburbs have about a hundred theatres, but the dominant influence is the London 'West End'. The majority of the West End theatres are commercial, in that they are organized for profit and receive no public funds. They provide a range of light entertainment offerings from musicals to plays and comedies.

However, some of the other London theatres are subsidized from grants supplied by the Arts Council, such as the National Theatre, the Royal Shakespeare Company (as well as at Stratford-upon-Avon) and the

English Stage Company. These cater for a variety of plays from the classics to modern drama. The subsidized theatres in both London and the regions constantly plead for more state financial aid, which the government is loath to give. The government subsidy is considerably less than that given to most comparable theatres in continental Europe. But there is a feeling in some quarters that these theatres should be more competitive and commercially minded like the West End, although Arts Council grants have been recently increased.

Many of the theatres in the regions outside London are repertory theatres, which means that they provide a number of plays in a season and have a resident theatre company and organization. The repertory companies have traditionally been the training ground for British actors and actresses. They present a specific number of classical and innovative plays and a variety of other artistic offerings in a season.

Most theatres in London and elswhere have had difficult times in recent years in attracting audiences and in remaining solvent, although the West End theatres brought £1 billion into the British economy in 2000. They have had to cope with increased competition from alternative and new entertainment activities. New commercial theatres in some cities are proving popular and are taking audiences away from the established repertory companies. These commercial theatres provide a wide range of popular entertainment, shows and drama, as well as plays prior to a London run. There are now signs that audience figures for all types of theatres are picking up again.

Opera in Britain occupies a similar position to that of the theatres and is divided into subsidized, commercial and amateur companies. The Royal Opera in London provides London seasons and occasional regional tours while the English National Opera Company supplies a similar midmarket service. It and the Royal Opera now share the reburbished facilities of the Covent Garden Theatre. There is a range of other opera companies, both in London and the regions, such as the English Opera Group, the Welsh National Opera and the Scottish Opera Company. There are also several light opera groups, and ballet companies such as the Ballet Rambert, the London Festival Ballet, the Scottish Theatre Ballet and the Royal Ballet, which operates in London and Birmingham. A number of contemporary dance companies have also been formed in recent years.

Britain has many high-quality orchestras, although most of them are based in London, such as the London Symphony Orchestra, the London Philharmonic and the BBC Symphony Orchestra. There are regional symphony orchestras of high quality, such as the Hallé in Manchester, the City of Birmingham Symphony Orchestra, the Ulster Orchestra, the BBC National Orchestra of Wales and the Royal Scottish National Orchestra and a number of chamber groups in London and the regions. Most of the

PLATE 11.8   People leaving an Odeon cinema (© *Paula Glassman/Format*)

opera, ballet and orchestra activities have their greatest appeal in London and still cater only for a minority of the people. But more popular forms, such as brass bands, choral singing and light music have a large following. The more exclusive entertainments are heavily dependent upon Arts Council subsidies, local government grants and private donations. The country's operatic, dance and classical music offerings can compete against international rivals.

The history of the cinema in Britain has shown a big decline since its early days as a very popular form of mass entertainment and from 1946 when annual visits reached a total of 1.6 billion. The domestic film industry had virtually ceased to exist, because of lack of investment and government help, although British films with British actors continued to be made abroad and in Britain with foreign finnacial backing. Although some government and National Lottery finance has been provided to support British film making, only 52 British films were made in Britain in 2000 compared with 70 in 1999, and the film industry has been criticized for making too many indifferent films.

In 1960 there were over 3,000 cinemas in Britain. But many have now either gone out of business, or changed to other activities such as dancing and bingo. But new screens have been built since 1996 and today there are 2,954 cinema screens situated either in single buildings or in multiplexes with five or more screens. Annual audience figures dropped from some 501 million in 1960 to 193 million in 1970. This decline was hastened by the arrival of television and continued as new forms of home entertainment, such as videos, have increased. However, although annual admissions sank to 55 million by 1984, there was an increase to 142 million in 2000. This improvement in audience figures has been encouraged by cheaper tickets, a wider range of films, responses to competition, appeal to younger people and the provision of an alternative leisure activity within more modern surroundings. But more than 30 per cent of the population never go to the cinema and 47 per cent of those aged over thirty-five never go.

A *Target Group Index (BRMB International) poll* in 2000 found that attendances at 'cultural events' of the population over fifteen in Britain are increasing and were 56 per cent for cinema, followed by theatre (23), art galleries and exhibitions (22), classical music (12), ballet (6), opera (6) and contemporary dance (4).

British popular music led the world from the 1960s and was both an economic and cultural phenomenon. Since the Beatles and early Rolling Stones, the domestic market for music sales has multiplied more than sixfold. However, in recent years, there has been a staleness in the popular field which has affected mainstream, avant-garde and 'ethnic' music alike. Some critics attribute this to commercial manipulation, overly packaged offerings and standardized bands, and others to a lack of substantial and consistent talent. Old-guard pop stars complain about the inadequacy of contemporary British pop music with its bland, vacuous material and ephemeral boy and girl bands, which have difficulty breaking into the global (and particularly the American) market.

But British popular and rock music today still has a domestic and international following, is attractive to the overseas youth market and constitutes a considerable and growing industry. Music was worth over £4 billion a year in 2000 with exports of £1.3 billion. The value of UK record sales rose by 3.3 per cent in 2000, with 200 million pop albums and 66 million pop singles. Sales of classical albums increased by 13 per cent in 2000 to a value of £66.5 million. The music business has expanded and constitutes a sizeable amount of British exports in the form of recordings, concert tours, clothing and books. Polls suggest that 81 per cent of Britons between sixteen and twenty-four spend their leisure time listening to CDs, tapes or records at least once a week, and more people attend live music performances than football matches.

There is a wide range of museums and art galleries in Britain, which provide for a variety of tastes. Most of them are financed and controlled by local authorities, although some are commercial ventures and others, including national institutions such as the British Museum and the National Gallery in London, are the province of the Secretary of State for Culture. In the past, entry to most of the public museums and art galleries was free of charge, but in recent years entrance fees have been charged for some institutions. This development has led to protests from those people who regard such facilities as part of the national educational and cultural heritage, which should be available to all without charge. But museums and art galleries are also finding it difficult to operate on limited funds and are dependent upon local government grants, Arts Council subsidies and National Lottery donations. The Labour government has now persuaded thirteen national galleries and museums to drop their entry charges. Museum and art gallery attendance in England rose from 25 million in 2000 to 27 million in 2001.

As in sport, certain arts activities and their associated buildings have become virtual institutions, such as the West End, repertory companies, the Last Night of the Proms, the Albert Hall, the Royal Festival Hall, the National Theatre, the Tate (including Tate Modern) and National Galleries and the Shakespeare Memorial Theatre at Stratford-upon-Avon. These have been added to in recent years by buildings such as the Tate Modern, together with associated (often controversial) prizes such as the Turner Prize. They reflect Britain's lively (and internationally important) contemporary art scene.

Attitudes to leisure, sports and the arts

MORI/We British public opinion polls in 1990 produced findings that are still valid according to later polls, although there have been decreases in some activities. They showed that Britain's cultural life was thriving on both home and wider social levels. A large number of people participate in a considerable variety of available pastimes, sometimes with surprising priorities. One poll asked interviewees 'which, if any, of these have you been to in the past twelve months?', with the following results: library (49 per cent); cinema (32); museum (27); theatre (25); art exhibition (17); football match (14); pantomime (13); orchestral concert (10); pop concert (10); modern dance (8); opera (3) and classical ballet (2).

A second poll asked interviewees 'which of these things have you done in the past month?', with the following results: watched television or a video (89 per cent); read a book (64); had friends round to your home for a meal or a drink (51); been to a restaurant (49); been to pubs (46); general exercise and keep fit (42); gardening (40); Do-It-Yourself (39); been away for a weekend (23); been to a sports club (20); been to a cinema (16); competitive sport (16); been to a nightclub or disco (15); been to the theatre (15); been to a social or working men's club (15); been away on holiday (13); and been to a wine bar (12). The interesting point in this list is the popularity and second place of reading, as well as the appeal of sporting and keep fit activities.

The authors of *We British* concluded that 'we can report that the nation is in no telly-induced trance. Its tastes mix watching and doing, 'high' and 'low' cultures, with a richness that contradicts the stereotypes of the British as divided between mindless lager louts and equally money-grubbing consumers. The mix we have found will not please everybody. Not enough football for some, not enough opera for others. But that is what we should expect in the culture of a whole nation' (*We British*, 1990: 133).

Exercises

Explain and examine the following terms:

Do-It-Yourself	the pub	rugby football
package tour	National Lottery	sponsorship
bear-baiting	scratchcards	'bed and breakfast'
high culture	cricket	the Arts Council
'West End'	brass bands	repertory theatres
football pools	ethnic restaurants	multiplexes

Write short essays on the following topics:

1   What do the above opinion polls reveal about the British people? Should one trust the polls?
2   What is your impression of the British people, in terms of their leisure, sporting and artistic activities?

Further reading

Bennett, A. (2000) *Popular Music and Youth Culture: Music, Identity and Place* London: Palgrave/Macmillan

Christopher, D. (1999) *British Culture: An Introduction* London: Routledge

Hill, J. (2001) *Sport, Leisure and Culture in Twentieth-Century Britain* London: Palgrave/Macmillan

Holt, R. and Mason, T. (2000) *Sport in Britain 1945–2000* Oxford: Blackwell

Jacobs, E. and Worcester, R. (1990) *We British: Britain under the Moriscope* London: Weidenfeld and Nicolson

Monk, C. and Sargeant, A. (2002) *British Historical Cinema* London: Routledge

Polley, M. (1998) *Moving the Goalposts: A History of Sport and Society Since 1945* London: Routledge

Websites

Department for Culture, Media and Sport: www.culture.gov.uk

UK Sport: www.uksport.gov.uk

Sport England: www.english.sports.gov.uk

The FA Premiership: www.fa-premier.com

Rugby Football Union: www.rfu.com

Artsonline: www.artsonline.com

The Arts Council (England): www.artscouncil.org.uk

Arts Council of Wales: www.ccc-acw.org.uk

Scottish Arts Council: www.sac.or.uk

Arts Council of Northern Ireland: www.artscouncil-ni.org

National Lottery Commission: www.natlotcomm.gov.uk

BBC: www.bbc.co.uk

ITC: www.itc.org.uk

Index